W9-APA-665

# Living in London

## A practical guide

**JUNIOR LEAGUE OF LONDON**
*Women building better communities*

ELEVENTH EDITION
WRITTEN AND PUBLISHED BY
THE JUNIOR LEAGUE OF LONDON

REGISTERED CHARITY NO. 1103298

**The Junior League of London**
9 Fitzmaurice Place
London, W1J 5JD
020 7499 8159, www.jll.org.uk

Copyright © The Junior League of London 2010

First published in 1981 by the Junior League of London
This eleventh edition published in 2010 by the Junior League of London

All rights reserved
No part of this book may be reproduced, stored in a retrieval system or transmitted in
any form or by any means, electronic, mechanical, photocopying, recording or otherwise,
without prior permission from the copyright owners

**Photo credits**
Front and back cover photos © Ashley Roop
Page 394 © Michael Stafford
Shutterstock pages 2 © egd, 22 © Socrates, 44 © C, 56 © Douglas Freer,
68 © alessandro0770, 86 © Tupungato, 112 © Africa Studio, 132 © Jason L Price,
166 © AVAVA, 204 © BlueOrange Studio, 226 © Gualtiero Boffi, 262 © Denis Tabler,
280 © Lazar, 288 © Neil Roy Johnson, 314 © Keith Gentry, 326 © Jose AS Reyes,
350 © Stephen Mulcahey, 380 © Vojta Herout

A CIP catalogue record of this book is available from the British Library

ISBN 0-9525195-5-0

The authors and publishers have made ever effort to ensure the accuracy of the
information in this book at the time of going to press. However, they cannot accept any
responsibility for any loss, injury or inconvenience resulting from the use of information
contained in this guide. Please help us keep the guide up to date. We have done our best
to ensure that the information in this guide is correct at the time of going to press, but
places and facilities are constantly changing and standards and prices fluctuate. We would
be delighted to receive any comments concerning existing entries or omissions, please visit
us on our website at www.jll.org.uk for appropriate contact information.

Printed and bound in Great Britain by Cambrian Printers Ltd, Aberystwyth, Wales

Design by Stafford Tilley, www.staffordtilley.co.uk

This book is proudly printed on paper that
contains wood from well-managed forests,
certified in accordance with the rules of the
Forest Stewardship Council.

# EXPLORE OUR BACKYARD.

The Americas
are waiting for you.
Nonstop from the UK.
Then easy connections
to wherever you
want to go. See for
yourself at AA.com.

 We know why you fly  **AmericanAirlines**

*AA.com*

AmericanAirlines, AA.com and We know why you fly are marks of American Airlines, Inc.
**one**world is a mark of the **one**world Alliance, LLC. © 2010 American Airlines, Inc. All rights reserved.

# TASIS

# THE AMERICAN SCHOOL IN ENGLAND

International student body

Coeducational, day (3-18 yrs) & boarding (14-18 yrs)

International Baccalaureate Diploma

Advanced Placement Courses and American High School Diploma

English Language Program

Settling-in programs for the whole family

Located on a spacious campus, close to London & Heathrow

Extensive summer programs in the UK & Europe

Coldharbour Lane, Thorpe, Surrey TW20 8TE
Tel: 01932 565252 • Fax: 01932 564644 • E-mail: ukadmissions@tasisengland.org
www.tasis.com

## The Junior League of London

The Junior League of London (**JLL**) is an organisation of women committed to promoting voluntary service, developing the potential of women and improving communities through the effective action and leadership of trained volunteers. Our vision is of a London where each person has the opportunity and the means to prosper. We provide volunteers and resources to support projects eliminating poverty and its effects in London. The organisation has been operating in London since 1979.

## Editor's Notes

British (not American) English spelling and terminology are used throughout the guide, although certain American terminology may be shown in brackets or listed within chapters and/or in the *Glossary* at the end of the book. As it is frequently used in the UK and Europe, all times are given in 24-hour time, i.e., 2:00am is written 02:00 and 2:00pm is 14:00. For all London addresses the word 'London' has been omitted and a shortened version of the postcode is given for most addresses. Details of facilities, services, prices and events were all checked and correct as we went to press. Before you go out of your way or make any major decisions, however, you're advised to check with an official source. Please note that no establishment has been included in this guide because it has advertised in any of the JLL publications and no payment of any kind has influenced any review.

## Acknowledgements

First and foremost, thank you to all of our corporate and individual sponsors, in particular American Airlines and TASIS The American School in England, whose financial assistance allows the proceeds of this 11th edition of *Living in London* to go directly to charity. Updating and editing this guide would not have been possible without the hard work and thoughtfulness of our volunteer members, in particular the Living in London committees for 2009/10 and 2010/11. Finally, a special thank you to Mike Stafford of Stafford Tilley for all of his invaluable input.

Sincerely,
Britta Jacobson
Editor, *Living in London* 11th edition

# Sponsors

## Corporate Sponsors
American Airlines
Latham & Watkins LLP*
TASIS The American School in England

## Benefactors
Hallie and Bruce Ambler
Jack and Jennifer Clarke
Amy and Mike Corcell
Debbi Del Favero
Susan Fisher
Kathleen and David Glaymon
Britta Jacobson
Patricia Lewis

George and Sara Niedringhaus
Meredith and Brian Niles
Anne Bahr Thompson
Sandra Ulrich
Carla Vaccaro
Patricia White
Caron Young

## Patrons
Lisa Bajardi
Mrs David Bruckmann
Anne Ettinger
Amity and Derik Farrar
Melissa Gabrielian
Karianne Gaede

Anna Mazzone
Eileen Meidar
Jennifer Noe-Nordberg
Ann Riker
Karen Young

## Friends
Selma Audi
Meleesia Avant
Alyce Faye Cleese
Ashley Klaasmeyer
Susan Lenora
Jennifer Mahoney
Carol Martin

Liz and Tom Murley
Shalena Poffenberger
Maria Sebastian and Bob Severson
Marla and Fred Simkin
Kelly Welch
Joanne B. Horton Wilber
Lady Susan Willis-Reickert

*In-kind. The Junior League of London is grateful to Latham
& Watkins for the pro bono legal support they provide.

# Contents

# Contents (continued)

London is an amazingly cosmopolitan city with a thriving economic heart. It is a place where history and cutting-edge art and fashion sit next to gleaming towers of modernity and world-class education and research facilities. For centuries, London has been a magnet for those wishing to fulfil their dreams and ambitions, something I'm glad to say continues to this day.

It is a truly exciting place to live, but, for the newly arrived, London can be somewhat overwhelming. For those, *Living in London* will undoubtedly become a well-thumbed companion as they wander around their new home, immersing themselves in each newly discovered neighbourhood, making friends and enjoying all that this great city has to offer.

Boris Johnson
MAYOR OF LONDON

# Introduction

You can count yourself lucky if you are moving to or living in London! This ancient city that dates back to the 2nd century is one of the most exciting places to be living in the 21st century. London is a diverse global centre for industry, education and culture and has something to offer everyone, no matter where you've come from.

As a large, cosmopolitan city, London can take some time to navigate. For, even if you speak the language, it can quickly become clear that things are done a bit differently here: Londoners drive on the left-hand side, flip light switches down to turn them on and politely queue for just about everything. However, a few tips from others who have also relocated to this great metropolis and have been in your shoes should make your life a bit easier.

The wide range of information and guidance in this, the 11th edition of *Living in London*, is meant to help new Londoners settle into the city and navigate their way through it, not only with information about transportation and how to get around, but also information about how to find childcare, schools or someone to hang your paintings and make your flat feel like your home.

*Living in London* is designed to help you make the most of your time in this captivating city from the moment you find out you're moving until it may be time for you to move on.

The authors of this book are all volunteers with the Junior League of London, a UK-registered charity. All profits from the sale of *Living in London* are used to support our projects working towards eliminating poverty and its effects in London. Thank you for your support, we hope that you enjoy living in London as much as we do!

# Moving

Moving to London from abroad can be a daunting and often confusing task. While the language might be familiar, the culture can seem quite foreign and navigating the move can easily prove overwhelming. Many of the systems and processes we are accustomed to at home are different in the UK and it's important to do your homework and start planning well in advance of your move. In particular, it is essential that you have the appropriate visas, work permits and/or other documentation you may need to allow you to enter the UK. The following pages highlight some of those items that should be considered prior to moving to the UK, as well as helpful tips for making the move much easier.

## IN THIS CHAPTER...

- Immigration
- Moving your belongings
- Climate and weather
- Electrical appliances
- Bringing your pet to the UK
- Arrival at the airport
- Moving within London

# Immigration

Before moving to the UK, you must ensure that you have permission from the British government. Depending on your nationality and the purpose and length of your stay in the UK, you may need to obtain a visa before entering the country. Please note that most people travelling to the UK for more than six months must now obtain entry clearance before travelling. Immigration into the UK is under the jurisdiction of the Home Office's Border Agency (**UKBA**). Details, application forms and instructions for applying to live and/or work in the UK can be found at **www.ukba.homeoffice.gov.uk**. If you do not arrive in the UK under the correct category, you may not be allowed to enter or you may be deported. It is imperative to organise the process correctly before moving.

Information about immigration is often the subject of rumour so be sure that you get advice from a reliable source. If you are moving in connection with a job, your company's human resources department often organises the process for you. If you need independent advice, be wary. If your adviser is not a lawyer, solicitor, barrister or legal executive, you should make sure they are authorised by the Office of the Immigration Services Commissioner (**OISC**). A list of OISC-authorised advisers is available from at the OISC on © 0845 000 0046 or visit **www.oisc.gov.uk**. In addition, you may wish to contact the British consulate or diplomatic post closest to where you live for advice. The Foreign and Commonwealth Office (**www.fco.gov.uk**) lists all diplomatic missions. Embassies also often have lists of attorneys practising in the UK who can assist with immigration matters.

## Entry clearance (visas and work permits)

You will not need a visa (entry clearance) if you hold a UK, Swiss or other European Economic Area (**EEA**) passport. For all others, the UKBA considers applications for permission to enter or stay in the UK through its visa services around the world. The UKBA's agency responsible for visas is UK Visa Services (**www.ukvisas.gov.uk**). Contact the British consulate or diplomatic post closest to where you live or visit the UK Visa Services website to find out if you need a UK visa or other type of entry clearance, which is generally dependent on the purpose of your visit (e.g., work, study, visit) and your nationality. Depending on your nationality, you will be considered either a visa national (who always requires a visa to come to the UK no matter the purpose) or a non-visa national. If you are a non-visa national, you will need entry clearance (and an entry certificate) to come to the UK for more than six months. To apply for entry clearance, you must be outside the UK. Visit **www.ukba.homeoffice.gov.uk/travellingtotheuk** for more information.

Many foreigners moving to the UK, who are not Swiss or EEA nationals, are sponsored by their UK-based employers. Under the sponsored skilled workers (Tier 2) work permit system, the employing company must need to fill a vacant position with a specific person. The employer applies for an employer sponsor licence prior to your arrival. Allow at least two to three months before the date you need to begin work in the UK for the application process. The sponsor licence granted to the employer applies specifically to the job and to the individual. You must also pass the points-based assessment. Upon entry into the UK, the work permit along with your passport and any other pertinent documentation must be presented to the immigration authorities. Check with your employer or adviser regarding your individual circumstances and visit **www.ukba.homeoffice.gov.uk/workingintheuk** for more information about working in the UK. Generally, the work permit is granted for up to three years to live and work in the UK for that employer, although this period can later be extended.

Spouses, partners and dependent children of overseas nationals who hold a work permit can apply for entry clearance at a British consulate or diplomatic post before moving to the UK. A same-sex partner who can demonstrate that he or she has been in a relationship akin to marriage for at least two years can also obtain entry clearance. For specific advice about immigration to the UK as a same-sex partner, visit the website of the UK Lesbian & Gay Immigration Group at **www.uklgig.org.uk**. The application should be done after the spouse or partner's sponsorship licence is granted and you should allow at least one month to apply. The partners of work permit holders will have the same conditions as their partner's placed on their visa. For more information on working in the UK see *Chapter 4: Working*.

### EEA nationals and their families

A national of a member state of the EEA or Switzerland is free to enter the UK to work and live. No prior permission is required and no work permit is needed for employment, but nationals of the Czech Republic, Estonia, Hungary, Latvia, Lithuania, Poland, Slovakia and Slovenia must register under the Worker Registration Scheme. Visit **www.ukba.homeoffice.gov. uk/workingintheuk** for more information.

EEA nationals exercising their rights of free movement are entitled to bring their dependents with them to the UK, even if they are non-EEA nationals. Non-EEA family members require entry clearance in the form of a family permit, which must be obtained before entering the country. The non-EEA dependents of an EEA national may stay in the UK so long as the EEA national spouse is exercising his or her treaty rights by working in the UK.

## Other immigration categories

There are many other categories under which people can move to the UK, including: British ancestry, domestic workers, sole representatives of overseas firms, students and highly skilled workers, investors and entrepreneurs (Tier 1). For details about any of these schemes, go to the Home Office website at **www.ukba.homeoffice.gov.uk/workingintheuk**. Please note that most of these categories are paper intensive and require you to apply at a British Consulate or Diplomatic Post before arriving in the UK. Be sure to reserve plenty of time to gather all supporting evidence and documents and have your application reviewed. Again, your local British consulate or diplomatic post will be able to advise you on these schemes.

## Registration with the police

A limited number of non-EEA nationals are required to register with the police. The immigration officer will put a stamp in your passport when you arrive in the UK if you are required to register. You and members of your family residing with you in the UK must then register with the Overseas Visitors Records Office (**OVRO**) within seven days of your arrival in the country. Children under the age of 16 do not need to register. You should contact your local police station for information about where you need to register. You will have to pay a registration fee.

You will be given a green booklet (certificate) called a Police Registration Certificate that you must produce within 24 hours, if asked to do so by the police or immigration officers. It is best to always carry this certificate with you while in the UK. The certificate will also make re-entry into the UK easier when you travel abroad on trips lasting less than two months. The certificate should be submitted to an immigration officer on departure if travelling abroad for more than two months. Any change of address or name change must be given to the OVRO within seven days.

# Moving your belongings

When selecting an overseas moving company, choose a reputable one. Investigate the company's performance record and check references. Go over all items in detail with the moving company's representative and have everything in writing. Get more than one estimate. Do not choose a firm simply because it is the cheapest, it may turn out to be a 'penny wise, pound foolish' decision. If you are moving abroad for work, your company may have a list of preferred carriers. Do not be afraid to ask questions about the process and make sure that you receive copies of all important documents.

You may have the option of shipping your goods via air and/or sea. Air shipments normally take one to two weeks and are usually the most expensive. Sea shipments will likely be in a container and normally arrive within four to six weeks. If you are moving abroad for work, your company may specify a certain size container. Be sure that you ask about the specifics before scheduling the estimates.

If you are shipping via sea, you should know which ship is going to carry your container and when it is scheduled to depart for and arrive in the UK. Upon arrival, your moving company should make arrangements with HM Revenue & Customs and the UK removal company that will transfer your shipment from the port to your home. It can take a few days or a couple of weeks to clear customs. Be sure that you have the appropriate contact information for all steps of the journey.

You should be knowledgeable about the moving and removal companies' loss and damage protection policies – read all of the small print on any contract. It is essential to have insurance. Your local homeowners' policy stops covering your belongings when they leave port, so be sure to know the scope and coverage of the insurance for the shipment. It might be wise to check with one or more private insurance companies instead of relying on the moving company's insurance programme.

For insurance purposes, it is necessary to have an itemised inventory. This list might be done by categories, such as furniture, silver, paintings and accessories, or room by room. Pick the system that best suits your needs and remember to value all items at replacement value. It is a good idea to have everything appraised and to record everything with photographs.

Make several copies of the inventory. One copy has to go to the insuring company, which may be the moving company or an insurance agent.

Take more than one copy with you when the shipment arrives in England. This inventory list makes it easy to record any possible damage which might require repair and an insurance claim. If possible, be present when your goods are unpacked at your home. Bring up any insurance claims quickly since most policies do not permit claims after a certain amount of time has passed.

### Shipping household effects

Deciding which household effects to take with you depends on many factors, including the anticipated length of your stay and the type of accommodation to be maintained. A total move can take several months to arrange while a temporary or short-term move can happen almost immediately. If possible, try to schedule a house-hunting trip to view different types of properties before you move (see *Chapter 2: Housing* for information about London neighbourhoods and looking for properties). UK housing typically has little storage space both inside (e.g., wardrobes) and outside (e.g., garages). Also keep in mind that if you're planning to rent accommodation in London, many rental flats and houses are fully furnished (including dishes, sheets, towels, etc.). Storage centres are often expensive so you should think about how your household effects will fit into your new home.

Start by making lists:

- What is going with you on the airplane?
- What is needed soon after you arrive (if you are going into temporary housing, it may be necessary to bring these items with you as excess baggage or via an air shipment)?
- What is being shipped in a container via sea/air?
- What is going into storage?
- Things to give away?
- Things to sell?
- Things to discard?

It is important to remember when choosing items to bring that many flats are converted 19th century houses. They are very beautiful, however, the hallways, doors and staircases can be very narrow and may not accommodate large pieces of furniture. Make sure your removals company is aware of any large items as they can arrange to hire a lift to fit furniture through windows or rooftop patio doors.

Once you have finally made all of these decisions, it is a good idea to have the lists duplicated. There is nothing more frustrating than misplacing your only copy of one of these important lists.

## Packing your household

Make sure your specifications and instructions are being carried out to your satisfaction. Ensure that each and every box is labelled with its contents and destination (even the room).

If you are doing any of the packing or unpacking, check for insurance coverage. Usually breakables are covered only when packed and unpacked by the moving company. The shipping charges normally include all packing and unpacking.

## What to bring

What to bring when you move to London is an individual decision. Obviously, your decisions will be based on the anticipated length of time you will reside in the UK. It will also depend upon your housing – whether furnished or unfurnished, house or flat.

The following items may not be readily available or easily replaced in the UK. If they are available in the UK, they may be considerably more expensive than they are abroad.

### Personal items

• Medical prescriptions may be branded differently. Ask your doctor or pharmacist for the name of the underlying compound to ensure that you receive the same medicine when you fill your prescriptions in the UK.

• Any over-the-counter medicine that you particularly like. See *Chapter 8: Children – Medical needs* for a listing of equivalent children's medicines and products available in the UK.

- Eyeglasses, contact lenses and related products.
- Special cosmetics and beauty products, particularly dermatologist-recommended ones.

### For the home
- European and UK beds and bedding vary greatly in size from those sold elsewhere, particularly the United States, and are relatively expensive. If you bring your beds, bring the appropriate bedding.

British recipes use imperial and metric measurements, and some UK measuring utensils differ in size from those sold elsewhere. To ensure that you can make your recipes in the UK, you may wish to bring a set of measuring cups and spoons along with your favourite cookbooks. For cooking tips and measurement conversion tables, see *Chapter 10: Cooking, food and drink*.

### Miscellaneous
- Children's games, sports equipment (baseballs, softballs, bats, footballs, basketballs and bicycles).
- Special decorations for various holidays you celebrate throughout the year.

### On the plane
- Copies of any important legal documents with you (make a full copy of your passport and any visa or work permit information).
- Copies of any wills, insurance policies, rental contracts on properties and investments, and a list of current charge accounts with their account numbers (make sure a trusted friend or attorney knows the whereabouts of the originals).
- Copies of family medical records.
- Sewing kit, small first-aid kit, extra pair of glasses, extra prescriptions, small toolkit, some old clothes for cleaning or painting, and a set of linens.
- Jewellery.

### What not to bring
- Cordless telephones.
- Light bulbs (except appliance bulbs – see the section Electrical appliances below for an explanation of electrical differences).
- Christmas tree lights.

- Electric clocks (if moving from the Americas or Japan).

- Liquor/spirits (excluding wine), except duty-free allowances.

- Cigarettes, except duty-free allowances.

- Perfumes, except duty-free allowances.

- Paints, cleaning agents or other combustible or flammable items.

- Plants and bulbs.

- Meat, fruits and vegetables.

- Certain fish and eggs.

- Most animals and all birds (except pets, see *Bringing your pet to the UK* below).

- Items made from protected species, including reptile leather, ivory and fur skins.

HM Revenue and Customs has information regarding what not to bring and frequently asked questions on their website at **www.hmrc.gov.uk**.

**DID YOU KNOW?**

The laws regarding firearms being brought into the UK for sports purposes and/or decorative sports equipment are extremely restrictive. You are advised to check the current law when you move. Applications and more information are available from the Metropolitan Police at **www.met.police.uk/firearms_licensing**.

## Customs and VAT

The British government allows importing of all household or personal effects duty free if they have been owned six months prior to the date of entry into the UK. Proof of purchase must be available on items less than six months old. Certain other household items may be dutiable. There are also special regulations regarding the importing of inherited goods and antiques into the UK. In addition, excise taxes are payable on certain items, such as liquor and cigarettes.

If possible, have a file with a copy of the bill of sale for every valuable item, such as cameras, watches, jewellery, silver, major appliances, etc. If you do not have these bills of sale, an alternative is a copy of an old insurance policy that itemises these articles. Carry these documents with you; do not ship them.

All items that are not at least six months old are subject to duty charges and

VAT (Value Added Tax, which is currently 17.5 per cent on most goods and due to rise to 20 per cent in 2011). Check with your moving company regarding which items may be subject to duty and excise tax plus VAT, as the customs and duty charges can vary depending on the item in question. For additional information visit HM Revenue & Customs at **www.hmrc.gov.uk**.

# Climate and weather

Weather in London is unpredictable, however, extreme conditions are rare. The average temperature varies from a low of 0°C (32°F) to a high of 24°C (about 75°F). July is the warmest month and January is the coldest month. One common climate condition is a very soft drizzle, so carrying a brolly (umbrella) or rain hat is almost always a good idea. And don't forget to pack your wellies (Wellington boots/rain boots)! You will find that it can get quite cool at night, even in summer, and carrying a sweater or light jacket is advisable.

Temperatures are usually reported in Celsius. An approximate conversion from Celsius to Fahrenheit is to double the Celsius and add 30.

Celsius (Centigrade) to Fahrenheit

-5°C  =  23.0°F
-1    =  30.2
0     =  32.0 (freezing point)
1     =  33.8
5     =  41.0
10    =  50.0
15    =  59.0
20    =  68.0
25    =  77.0
30    =  86.0
37    =  98.6 (average human body temperature)
100   =  212.0 (boiling point)

# Electrical appliances

Deciding on which electrical appliances and equipment to bring to the UK or leave home can be confusing, especially if you are relocating from North America. British (and most of Europe's) electrical current is 220/240 volts and 50 Hz (frequency or cycles per second) while the North American current is 110 volts and 60 Hz (frequency or cycles per second). Understanding which voltage and frequency is compatible with your electrical devices will facilitate your decision-making. Some devices, if designed for several voltages, can be used directly in the UK with a plug adaptor. Others can be used with a voltage transformer, and some cannot be used at all. Given the expense of adaptors and transformers (and the shortage of space in most London flats) you may find it easier to purchase smaller appliances after settling into your new home.

### Adaptors

Most UK plugs have three square prongs. Electrical devices that do not need voltage transformers can be used with a plug adaptor or the non-UK plug can be replaced with a UK plug. While the latter option is cheaper, be sure to ask an electrician or local hardware store if you are unsure of how to replace the plugs.

### Transformers

In general, most non-European electrical goods are incompatible with UK electrical supply because of the voltage difference (220/240V for UK versus 110V for North America, for example). This means that if you try to use them in the UK they will burn out. You can get them to work if you use a transformer, which is a plug-in device that will convert 110V to 220/240V. Transformers are available in shops in London and the surrounding area. Transformers are sized from 30 watts to 1,500 watts and are priced according to their wattage. A hair dryer or electric curler will require up to a 250-watt transformer. A blender or food processor will require up to a 500-watt transformer, while a refrigerator will require up to a 1,500-watt transformer.

Transformers, depending on the size, can be used to power several appliances so you do not necessarily need one transformer for each device. However, they are bulky and heavy and therefore not very portable.

### Dual-voltage appliances

Some appliances, such as cameras, home computers, printers, video recorders, televisions and stereos, are dual voltage and can function on 120V or 240V. The appliance may automatically adjust to the correct voltage or a switch on the appliance may need to be adjusted. Check your appliances for this feature because it will allow you to use it in the UK without a transformer.

**DID YOU KNOW?**

Most laptops and mobile device chargers can be used in the UK with an adaptor. However, it is always wise to check the label on your cord to verify that the device is rated for the higher voltage.

### Appliances incompatible with the frequency

The electrical supply in most of the world, including the UK, is 50 Hz, while it is 60 Hz in North America and parts of South America and Japan. This frequency difference comes into play in motorised appliances, where the speed of the motor is important. There is no simple device that will convert 60 Hz to 50 Hz, so any device with a motor will run at a bit more than 80 per cent of its normal speed when it is run on a transformer. For hair dryers, fans, washers, blenders, refrigerators and dryers that might not be a problem. For analogue clocks, it is a problem.

In using certain devices with motors, like video recorders, personal computers and audio equipment, the frequency difference is not an issue because the electrical current is automatically converted to Direct Current in the machine so the device will run at the right speed, independent of frequency.

### Specific appliances

#### Refrigerators

A refrigerator can be run on an appropriate-size transformer to convert to UK voltage. North American-sized refrigerators may be purchased in the UK. If you are renting and wish to have a large refrigerator, make sure that there is space in the kitchen to accommodate one since British refrigerators are often small.

#### Washing machines and electric dryers

A washer can be run on an appropriate-size transformer to convert to UK voltage. The dryer will probably be 240V and may work without a transformer, but the machine should only be installed by a qualified electrician. North American washers and dryers are larger than UK appliances and may not fit in your particular house or flat. If you wish to have larger appliances, be sure that you have adequate space for them.

Gas dryers can be used in the UK if your flat or house is serviced with gas, but they will need a transformer for the motor and may need a different pressure regulator for the gas.

**DID YOU KNOW?**

Most flats in London come with washing machines, which also have a drying function, fitted in the kitchen. In larger flats or houses, there may be room for a separate dryer.

If you are interested in buying American appliances during your stay in the UK, try Anderson Sinclair Appliances on ℂ 017 0844 3551 or visit **www. americanappliances.com**.

Televisions and DVD players

It may be wise to sell these appliances before moving and buy new or used ones when you arrive. While televisions and DVD players purchased abroad can be run in the UK with a transformer, they have limited use because of the differences in broadcasting standards. The television will not pick up UK stations by antenna or cable unless it is a multi-system TV equipped with a switch for the PAL system, which is the UK standard. Similarly, an American DVD player will not play UK videos unless it is a multi-system machine equipped with a switch for the PAL system.

**DID YOU KNOW?**

DVDs are coded differently for different regions of the world. For example, North America is coded as Zone 1, Europe and Japan are coded as Zone 2 and South America is coded as Zone 4. If you are bringing your DVDs, make sure the DVD player you purchase in the UK is multi-regional and can play DVDs from the appropriate zone. Likewise, do not buy DVDs in the UK and expect to be able to play them when you return home.

If you happen to be one of those people addicted to the television programming in their home country, think about getting a slingbox (**www.slingbox.com**). Slingbox is connected to your cable/satellite box in your home country and streams the television programming to your computer. It is easy to buy cables in the UK to connect your computer to your television.

### Telephones

North American telephones are not compatible with the UK system, although some telephones may be used in the UK after purchasing an adaptor. However, the price of an adaptor may be more expensive than the price of a new phone. Therefore, it is not advisable to bring these cordless telephones to the UK.

### Computers

Most computers are dual voltage and can function as either 120V or 240V. However, your computer accessories (e.g., speakers and printers) may not be. Contact customer service or review your user manuals for verification. If they are not dual voltage, your computer, monitor and printer will run on a transformer in the UK. Bring your surge protector or purchase one when you arrive in the UK.

### Lamps

All lamps (except those using halogen or fluorescent bulbs) can be used in the UK if they are used with an adaptor or are fitted with UK plugs. 110V light bulbs will explode if used in the UK because of the voltage difference, so you may need to leave your light bulbs at home. The ballast in halogen lamps must be changed and may be difficult to find.

### Miscellaneous electrical information

Some electrical appliances purchased in the UK do not come with socket outlet plugs, however attaching a plug is an easy procedure. Different appliances require different fuses, so be sure to have the correct fuse for each appliance. If your appliance fails to work, check the fuse and plug before calling the electrician. Obviously, all electrical appliances are potential fire hazards and should be used with caution. Always consult an electrician if you are not absolutely certain how an appliance should be correctly operated.

If you have electrical appliances that require appliance bulbs, such as sewing machines, refrigerators and freezers, bring the bulbs with you.

For your electrical questions and needs, contact Ryness Electrical Supplies on ✆ 020 7278 8993 or visit **www.ryness.co.uk**. They have branches located throughout London.

**DID YOU KNOW?**

If you plan to rent accommodation, keep in mind that most flats and houses come furnished with basic appliances.

# Bringing your pet to the UK

To guard against the importation of rabies and other animal diseases, the Department of Environment, Food and Rural Affairs (**DEFRA**) requires a six-month quarantine for cats, dogs and other rabies susceptible animals coming into the UK. It may possible to bring your pet into the country without quarantine under the Pet Travel Scheme (**PETS**). PETS applies only to certain types of domestic animals (dogs, cats and ferrets) arriving from certain countries if they meet certain other requirements. If you are planning to take your pets to the UK through the scheme, begin the process approximately eight months before you expect to move to ensure that your pet will not have to spend any time in quarantine. The scheme requires a substantial amount of paperwork and coordination with both your local veterinarian and the local agricultural authority in your home country. It is highly important that all procedures are adhered to exactly, including in the order instructed. Failure to do so may result in your pet not being admitted to the UK and potentially having to start the process from the beginning. DEFRA has extensive information about the PETS and the EU pet passport, including forms and checklists, on © 0870 241 1710 or visit **www.defra. gov.uk**.

A brief outline of the necessary steps are:

- You must microchip your pet and verify that the microchip can be read by standard scanners.
- After the microchip has been fitted, your pet must be vaccinated against rabies and a blood test must be sent to an EU-approved laboratory. If the test is successful, then your pet will be able to enter the UK at least six months after the date of the test result. If you enter the country before then, your pet must go into quarantine until the expiry of this six-month period.
- Immediately before entering the UK, your pet must receive a tick and

tapeworm treatment and all paperwork must be correctly completed.

- As well as complying with the PETS, you must arrange for your pet's transportation. The scheme requires that your pet enter the country using an approved transport company and route (a list of which can be found on DEFRA's website). You must purchase a carrier for your pet that meets the airline's kennel guidelines and labelling requirements (this information is usually available on each airline's website and kennels can be purchased from the airline or a pet supply store). Note that the guidelines are strictly enforced and the airline can and will refuse to ship the pet if the guidelines are not adhered to.

- Most airlines also require a certificate of acclimation from your veterinarian and a statement regarding food and water from the pet owner. The certificate of acclimation states that your pet can fly at certain temperatures. It can only be obtained 24 to 48 hours before departure. This certificate can be problematic if you are travelling during very high or very low temperatures. Check with your airline for any additional documentation they may require from the veterinarian, as some require the veterinarian to declare within 48 hours of the flight that the pet is in good health to fly. These forms can be completed by the veterinarian at the same time as the tapeworm process.

- You must complete a customs form for your pet and ensure that it will clear customs upon arrival in the UK. Most airlines require a broker to clear pets through customs and often can provide these services if asked. If they cannot, then call customs or DEFRA to get more information. Note that is essential to clarify your point of entry (e.g., Heathrow, Gatwick or other UK airport) to ensure the broker is at the airport where you will arrive. You must also have all the original documentation as copies are not accepted.

- If your pet is arriving in the UK by one of the approved airlines, the airline will transfer your pet to the Animal Reception Centre at the airport facilities. There, your pet's paperwork will be examined. You will need to collect your pet from here. Note that it is somewhat of a distance from the terminals and no public transportation is available, so having or hiring a care is recommended.

**DID YOU KNOW?**

There are several breeds of dogs not permitted in the UK, including pitt bulls. It is important to check the list of dog breeds permitted by DEFRA. If there is any question as to the dog's breed or it is unknown, a behaviour test will be performed or you can have a relatively inexpensive DNA test done by mail order.

For a more complete listing of the current quarantine requirements and procedures, including approved quarantine premises and carrying agents, visit the DEFRA website or call ℂ 01245 454 860. Kennel recommendations can also be found in *Chapter 11: Services – General*.

Travelling with a pet can be very expensive. The price of your pet's ticket varies by airline, but may be determined by size of carrier and combined weight of carrier and dog. Your approved carrier may require you to travel on the same flight as your pet. If this is the case, check with your airline to understand when a reservation can be made for your pet as your pet's flight usually needs to be booked by the airline's cargo division. It is recommended to pick your flight, but not book until you have confirmed with cargo that there is also space available for the pet. Most airlines' cargo space has a special environmentally controlled segment for pets that you may want to book well in advance.

While it is possible for you to navigate the Pet Travel Scheme on your own, several companies offer services that make it easier for you.

Passport for Pets
ℂ 0800 137 321, www.passportforpets.co.uk

Pet Relocation
ℂ +1 512-264-9800, www.petrelocation.com
For animals moving from the US.

If your employer is handling your moving arrangements, enquire about their resources and make sure that the costs of your pet's move will also be covered.

In the event that your pet must be quarantined in the UK, arrangements for boarding kennels must be made and confirmed by letter before you leave your home. Allow four to six weeks to complete all associated paperwork and keep in mind that the most accessible kennels may have waiting lists.

**DID YOU KNOW?**

Penalties for smuggling animals are severe. Such an offence will result in a heavy fine, a prison sentence for yourself or the destruction of the animal.

# Arrival at the airport

There are five airports in London, but you will most likely arrive at Heathrow or Gatwick. It is a long walk from the gates to Passport Control. Therefore, if you require a wheelchair, are travelling with a newborn infant or have medical problems, you should pre-arrange special assistance with your airline.

Once at Passport Control, you will have to join the correct queue: *EU/EEA Nationals* or *All Other Passports*. If you are a non-EU passport holder, you will submit a completed landing card given to you on the flight, or at Passport Control. The immigration officer may ask to see your travel documents or work permit so that he or she can stamp your passport accordingly. He or she may ask you a few questions regarding the reasons for your entrance into the country. After you are through Passport Control, check the electronic board to find out the area for your flight's baggage claim. In the UK, and in many other European international airports, luggage pushcarts are usually offered free of charge. If some, or all, of your luggage does not arrive, contact a representative of your airline before you leave the airport.

## Customs

Once you have collected your luggage, proceed through Customs. The belongings you are allowed to bring into the UK tax and duty free depend on where you've come from, your immigration status and how long you've owned them. For additional information visit HM Revenue & Customs at **www.hmrc.gov.uk**. If you have nothing to declare and are arriving from a non-EU country, proceed through the area marked with the *green* sign. If you are arriving from another EU country, proceed through the area marked with the *blue* sign.

If you have items to declare, you must go to the area marked with the *red* sign. The customs inspector will probably ask you a few questions and may ask to see these items. You are required to pay any duty or tax at the time the belongings are brought into the country so be sure to travel with UK currency.

Foreign currency or travellers cheques can be cashed at the airport banks. There are also cash points available in most airports that will automatically dispense UK currency, and can often be found in baggage claim. It is often cheaper, and easier, to use cash points. Check with your bank beforehand regarding your PIN number and whether you will incur any fees for using foreign cash points.

For details about options for travel from the airports to London, see *Chapter 6: Transportation – London airports.*

## Moving within London

Moving within London can sometimes be as big a production as moving to the UK. Some things to remember are:

- If you need to secure parking for unloading or loading a lorry or van, contact your local council at least two weeks ahead of time. Your local council will block parking spaces for you for free, or for a small fee. For more information regarding your local council, please refer to *Chapter 5: Utilities – Local councils.*

- Transfer your TV licence to your new home (visit **www.tvlicensing.co.uk**) and cancel all direct debits for services to your former home.

- Try to set up services (e.g., cable and telephone) before you move into your new home.

- Royal Mail offers a redirection service (visit **www.royalmail.com**). For a fee, they will forward all of your mail from any UK address – including magazines and packages – to your new address in the UK or abroad for up to two years. Any local post office will have the requisite forms for you to fill out.

When hiring a removals company, be sure to check references and inquire about insurance limits. Many removals companies will move boxes that you have packed yourself, which can be less expensive than purchasing a full moving service. Prices are sometimes lower if you move during the week rather than on a weekend. For recommendations for movers and self-storage, see *Chapter 11: Services – Home.*

# Housing

What makes London such a wonderfully liveable city is that it is made up of many small villages, each with its own particular charm. Deciding on the best location for you and your family is difficult only because the choices are so great. You must consider a number of factors: the high cost of certain areas, proximity to work and schools (or easy transportation to them), convenience of shopping facilities and atmosphere. If it is at all possible, any house-hunting trip should begin with a day spent driving around the city, taking in the flavour and overall feel of each area.

If you are new to the London area, find an experienced guide to take you around the city. Your relocation/estate agent, black cab or minicab companies are good sources. By the time your tour ends, your list of areas in which to search for housing may be considerably shorter than it was earlier. Once you have narrowed down your preferences, it is also wise to revisit the area after dark, as darkness falls very early in the winter and you should make sure you are comfortable in the area even after nightfall. Those few hours of touring can save you days of wasted time and energy, not to mention frayed nerves.

## IN THIS CHAPTER...

- London neighbourhoods
- Greater London
- Living in the country
- Letting property
- Council tax
- Buying property
- Online resources
- British terminology

The first decision to make is whether you want to live in Central London, in one of the suburban communities of Greater London or in the country. London stretches across some 30 miles and is divided into 32 areas, each with its own council providing local public services, such as street cleaning, social housing, libraries and parking. To pay for these services, each area sets its own level of local council tax (see *Council tax* section below), which can vary significantly even between neighbouring areas. For example, the boroughs of the City of Westminster and Wandsworth have very low council tax rates, while the boroughs of Islington, Camden and Kensington & Chelsea have much higher council tax rates. There are also differences in the quality of services, particularly in the state schools, which are mostly run by each council.

Parking within London can be challenging and violators will receive a fine or worse – have their vehicle clamped or towed. Certain London neighbour-hoods or boroughs (notably the City of Westminster and Kensington & Chelsea) only offer metered parking to visitors. Other boroughs offer visitor passes to residents that can be used on an hourly basis or for an entire day. If you own a car, you must purchase a residents' parking permit from your local council that allows you to park in designated residential areas.

## London neighbourhoods

The following brief descriptions of some popular areas in London may be of assistance.

### Central London (SW and W postcodes)

The communities of Central London are expensive, but convenient for shops, theatres, restaurants, clubs and public transportation and generally allow for a shorter commute to work in the City. These areas have a high proportion of international residents.

### Belgravia (SW1)

Near Buckingham Palace and Hyde Park, this area consists of magnificent Regency squares, late Georgian terraces and mews houses. Some of the larger houses are now used as embassies and consulates while others have been divided into flats. Belgravia is one of the more expensive and desirable areas of London and, like Mayfair, supermarkets are limited in size and therefore, provide a limited selection of goods. This area is served by Victoria and Sloane Square tube stations.

### Chelsea (SW3 and SW10)

South of Knightsbridge, South Kensington and bordering the Thames, Chelsea features a range of mostly low-rise period buildings, including Victorian cottages and mansion blocks. Sloane Square and the King's Road are convenient for shopping, although the latter's reputation as one of London's trendiest areas is now more tradition than fact. Chelsea also boasts many cosy local pubs and restaurants, as well as excellent antique shops and markets. The area is not well served by public transport as there is no tube station beyond Sloane Square.

### Kensington (W8)

South and west of Kensington Gardens, Kensington features tree-lined residential streets and squares – a mixture of Georgian and Victorian terraced houses, red-brick mansion blocks and elegant villas. Kensington High Street and Notting Hill Gate offer convenient shopping and access to public transport. There are also numerous cinemas, restaurants and pubs in the area.

### Knightsbridge (SW1, SW3 and SW7)

Bordering Hyde Park to the south, this expensive area features Victorian terraces and squares, cobbled mews, red-brick Victorian mansion blocks and new builds. Once part of a forest on the outskirts of London, Knightsbridge today is home to Harrods, Harvey Nichols and other fine stores, making it one of the world's most famous shopping destinations. The tube station is on the Piccadilly line, serving the West End and Heathrow.

### Marylebone (W1)

North of Oxford Street and south of Marylebone Road, this area has many 18th century streets and squares, mews houses and portered Edwardian mansion blocks. It is convenient for the West End shops, and has excellent public transport links to the City and to nearly all of London's mainline rail stations. Marylebone High Street has become a fashionable spot for shopping and has many excellent restaurants and pubs. Regent's Park is also nearby.

### Mayfair (W1)

Bordered by Hyde Park, Oxford Street, Regent Street and Piccadilly, Mayfair has been a fashionable central neighbourhood since the 1700s. Many of the large Georgian houses have been divided into flats or have been converted into luxury hotels and offices. There is a good supply of flats in large, well-maintained mansion blocks. The area is limited for grocery shopping (the local custom of daily shopping still prevails), however, it is well situated for many of the finest clubs, restaurants, antique shops and designer boutiques.

### Pimlico (SW1)

South of Victoria Station, bordering the Thames, this area has lovely white stucco squares and terraces. Its quietness owes much to the complicated one-way street system. Pimlico is a more affordable alternative to its neighbouring communities of Belgravia and Chelsea, and is popular with members of Parliament and other government workers based in Westminster.

### South Kensington (SW3, SW5 and SW7)

South Kensington's streets feature large terraced houses, many converted into flats, often with access to private garden squares. One of the most central residential areas in London, South Kensington benefits from plentiful tube and bus services providing easy access to the West End, the City and Heathrow Airport. The area is also home to four of the capital's major museums, as well as the Lycée Français, which attracts many French families to the area.

## West London (W postcodes)

In addition to the west/central neighbourhoods listed below, going westward from Knightsbridge are the residential areas of Brook Green, Chiswick, Hammersmith, Shepherd's Bush and West Kensington. These contain tree-lined streets with large houses, many of which have been converted into flats. These neighbourhoods are well served by public transport with the Central, Piccadilly and District lines. It is also on the right side of London for a quick journey on the M4 motorway to Heathrow Airport. With riverside walks, pubs and excellent facilities for shopping, leisure and health, this area is ideal for families planning to settle in London for a considerable amount of time.

### Bayswater and Paddington (W2)

West of Marble Arch and to the north of Hyde Park, this area has modern blocks of flats, as well as some squares mostly rebuilt after the war. It is convenient for Oxford Street shopping and Mayfair, and is considerably cheaper than neighbouring Notting Hill. Paddington is nearby, which has benefited from wide-scale development and urban regeneration of the Paddington Basin, as well as the Heathrow Express rail link. It also has some very pretty period cottages and magnificent stucco terraces.

### Holland Park (W11 and W14)

Surrounding Holland Park, this area features leafy streets and some of the largest detached and semi-detached houses in London. The area also offers a good supply of flats in large mansion blocks and converted Victorian houses. It is convenient to the shopping and entertainment facilities of Kensington High Street, Notting Hill Gate and the Westfield London shopping centre. There is easy access to the West End and the City by public transport.

### Maida Vale (W9)

Maida Vale has a rich supply of flats of various sizes and types. The area's wide streets are lined with large terraced houses and red-brick mansion blocks, often with access to large private gardens, including some with tennis courts. The area surrounding the Grand Union Canal, known as Little Venice, has many large stucco houses, some of which remain single-family homes while others have been converted into flats.

### Notting Hill (W11)

Just north of Kensington, Notting Hill has large houses, often with good-sized private or communal gardens, and easy access to the West End and the City by public transport. The area is close to both Holland Park and Kensington Gardens, and has a large variety of local restaurants, trendy shops, bars and antique shops. Notting Hill is home to the Portobello Market and hosts the largest annual street party and carnival in Europe, held over the August bank holiday weekend.

## North London (N and NW postcodes)

### Hampstead (NW3)

Hampstead offers the quaint ambiance of an English village while affording the convenience of being close to Central London. The High Street is dominated by exclusive boutiques, cafes and restaurants. Its winding, hilly streets feature brick townhouses and large detached houses, many of which have been converted into flats. It is adjacent to Hampstead Heath, which has many walking paths, large ponds for swimming and fishing, art shows and outdoor concerts in the summer at Kenwood House, one of the most glorious country houses in London.

### Hampstead Garden Suburb (NW11)

North of Hampstead, this area is definitely a suburban enclave. It features cottages and beautiful four-, five- and six-bedroom homes, many stately Georgian and ambassadorial types, with well-manicured gardens. It has two small but varied shopping areas. Many homes back onto Hampstead Heath, however, in some parts, it is necessary to have a car.

### Highgate (N6)

Northeast of Hampstead Heath, Highgate Village is quietly residential with a definite country atmosphere. It has a golf club and many homes, both old and new, with large gardens. Parking and driving are quite easy.

### Islington (N1)

North of the City, Islington is a friendly, lively place with modern terraced houses, Victorian villas and smartly restored Georgian squares. Camden Passage, noted for its antique shops and market, is there, and the area enjoys easy access to the City and the West End. While there is a lack of green open spaces, the restaurants and bars along Upper Street near Angel tube station are the centre of the area's vibrant nightlife.

### Regent's Park and Primrose Hill (NW1)

The elegant residential area around Regent's Park is most famous for its Nash terraces overlooking the park. Its impressive homes include Winfield House, the residence of the American Ambassador. Modern blocks of flats, the London Zoo and the Open Air Theatre all add to the diversity of Regent's Park. The more bohemian High Street of Primrose Hill offers a plethora of independent shops and restaurants and stunning views of London from the top of the hill.

### St. John's Wood (NW8)

Northwest of Regent's Park and suburban in feeling, St. John's Wood has many large detached and semi-detached houses as well as large blocks of flats with good views over the park. The American School in London is located here. The Jubilee line provides easy access to Canary Wharf and the West End and the High Street provides all the necessary amenities.

### Swiss Cottage (NW3)

North of St. John's Wood, Swiss Cottage offers leafy streets with large blocks of flats, low terraced houses and modern townhouses with a cosmopolitan flavour. A large public leisure centre attached to the main library dominates the heart of Swiss Cottage.

## The City of London and East London (EC and E postcodes)

Living in the City, London's financial centre, can provide easy access to work, but it is quite quiet outside working hours. Slightly north of the City, Clerkenwell offers good transport links and a more vibrant social aspect.

Relatively new developed areas are Shoreditch, Wapping and the Docklands. Housing is mainly either warehouses (which have been converted in the last 10 years to a very high standard) or new builds (which often have river views). Some residences have off-street parking, 24-hour porters, indoor swimming pools and other fitness facilities (these costs are included in service charges). Transport is improving and the Docklands Light Railway runs a service between Tower Gateway, Bank, Beckton, Stratford, Greenwich and Island Gardens stations. Canary Wharf, in the heart of the Docklands, is home to a number of banks and other financial institutions, which has made East London particularly appealing to young professional couples. In this up-and-coming area, new shops and restaurants continue to open regularly.

## South London (SE and SW postal codes)

### Battersea (SW8 and SW11)

On the south side of the Thames across from Chelsea Harbour, Battersea is dominated by Battersea Park and the now-derelict Battersea Power Station. Battersea is cheaper than living north of the river, with many brick Victorian mansion blocks and larger late Victorian properties. With excellent facilities for shopping, parking, education, health and sports, it is very popular with young Londoners. Battersea does not have a tube station, but is served by buses and mainline trains.

### Clapham (SW4 and SW9)

Always popular with families, this area surrounds Clapham Common and features large Victorian family properties on tree-lined streets with on-street parking. Clapham's three tube stations are served by the Northern line, making this a recommended location for young City professionals who are looking to buy rather than rent.

### Fulham (SW6)

Just west of Chelsea, Fulham has a number of large parks and is home to Chelsea Football Club. The area is popular with young English professionals and their families, as well as increasing numbers of expatriates who are attracted by the larger private gardens and better value for money. The typical Fulham street is lined with two- and three-storey Victorian terraced houses, many of which have been converted into flats. Several large mansion blocks are located near the river.

### Putney (SW15)

Along the south bank of the Thames, Putney has a chain of attractive open spaces with extensive sporting grounds, especially rowing clubs. It contains the oldest high-rise flats in London as well as many two-storey homes with gardens. There is a busy and convenient street for shopping as well as the Putney Exchange, an enclosed shopping mall. Putney has main line and bus links to Central London as well as a tube station (which is not particularly close to the area's residential neighbourhoods).

### Shad Thames (SE1)

This riverside neighbourhood stretches east from Tower Bridge. The area boasts a high concentration of warehouse conversions and newly constructed apartment complexes. It is also home to the Design Museum, and there is a Friday antiques in the nearby Bermondsey Market. There are numerous restaurants, speciality food shops, clothing stores and bookshops. Its location provides easy access to the City and the Docklands with London Bridge being the main tube stop.

# Greater London

More and more newcomers to London are moving to communities farther from the centre. These communities are often less expensive and are generally regarded as good places to bring up families. Typically, the homes have larger gardens, there is less crime and the schools are better. Most have every type of housing, from rows of brick terrace houses to tall stately Georgian terraces to large detached houses.

The disadvantages to these communities can be the longer commutes to Central London and the City, and the necessity for a car in most locations. However, express trains can make it faster to commute from towns in Greater London than from sections of Chelsea so it is worth checking out the transportation links.

### Barnes (SW13)

Located west of Putney on the Thames, this area features low terraced houses from the late Victorian and Edwardian eras. It has a wonderful Wetland Centre, sporting grounds and a swan pond. Barnes offers bus and train transportation, but not a tube station.

### Richmond (TW10)

Southwest of Barnes, Richmond is a lovely suburban village with large houses and beautiful gardens. Its many parks add a delightful country atmosphere and it is home to the botanical Kew Gardens. Richmond Park comprises 2,000 acres of parkland, and Richmond Green is often the setting for cricket matches.

### Wimbledon (SW19)

Wimbledon, famous for the tennis tournament held here every summer, is located eight miles southwest of Central London. Wimbledon has a suburban atmosphere, with Wimbledon Common comprising 1,200 acres of land for riders, walkers and picnickers. The village has a wide range of shopping, including the Centre Court shopping complex, and the train and tube station offers convenient transportation to London.

Other equally charming areas worth considering are Blackheath (SE3), Dulwich (SE21), Kew (TW9), Greenwich (SE10) and Wandsworth (SW18).

## Living in the country

Within commuting distance of London are some wonderful suburban communities with large houses and enormous gardens. There is no question that one can find almost palatial splendour in the rural areas for what one has to pay for a house in London. Yet, again, the commute into London must be considered, although trains can offer several options.

South of London, the county of Surrey encompasses many charming villages – including Cobham, Esher, Walton-on-Thames, Weybridge, West Byfleet – all with good public transport into Central London. TASIS The American School in England, the American Community Schools (ACS) and Marymount International School are also located in Surrey.

Northwest of Central London are the communities of Wembley, Harrow, Pinner and Ruislip. These areas are popular for their suburban atmosphere and more garden-for-the-money value. They primarily contain semi-detached and small detached houses.

Further northwest are the communities of Northwood, Chorleywood, Moor Park and Watford – all with large houses and gardens. These areas are convenient to the London Orbital (M25) and the many suburban superstores.

**DID YOU KNOW?**

The term **High Street** refers to the main street of a neighbourhood or town. There is usually a selection of shops, restaurants, pubs and banks located on the High Street.

# Letting property

Once you have narrowed down your list of areas, there are other crucial issues to consider depending on whether you are going to rent or buy a home in London. Indeed, once you are established in London, you may see what a unique and exciting investment opportunity London can offer.

## Letting property

Estate agencies located on a High Street will normally carry listings only for that particular neighbourhood. The decentralised nature of the rental market can make it difficult to look for property if you haven't narrowed your search. A good starting point is the website **www.primelocation.com**, which combines most estate agents' lists of properties to buy or rent in London and the rest of the UK (see also *Online resources* below).

The UK rental market can move quickly and properties frequently are not on the market more than one month before their availability date. As a result, it is not beneficial to house-hunt too far in advance. You may want to consider moving into temporary housing first and then taking time to find your permanent home.

**DID YOU KNOW?**

Larger estate agents can charge expensive administration fees. Sometimes it is better to use a smaller agency that specialises in a particular area.

Renters should be aware of the Housing Act 1988, which regulates your right to extend your tenancy and the landlord's right to repossess the property or increase the rent. Your solicitor or relocation agent can explain this in detail. You should not sign a tenancy agreement or lease without first having it approved by a solicitor familiar with such documents. Your company may have an in-house lawyer who can do this for you, or you can contact the Law Society (© 020 7242 1222, **www.lawsociety.org.uk**) for names of firms specialising in such work.

There are two important and potentially novel aspects of the housing market that you may encounter:

- Many rentals are fully furnished (including dishes, sheets, towels, etc.), which can make your move very straightforward. You only need to bring your clothes, the childrens' toys and other personal items. But sometimes the furnishings may not be of a very high quality. It may be possible to negotiate with the owner to remove the furnishings and move in your own, though the owner may ask you to pay for the storage costs. If you find you need additional storage for furniture that will not fit into your house or flat, see *Chapter 11: Services* for self-storage locations.

- Some rentals are only available as a 'company let', which means that the lease is made out to your corporation and must be signed by the Managing Director or his or her appointee. The company therefore guarantees the tenancy.

## Defining your rental checklist

For happy renting, it is important to get the legal and practical aspects right. Negotiation is all about striking a balance between your needs and requirements and those of the landlord. Here are a few tips.

### Read the small print

There are three main types of tenancy agreements: an Assured Shorthold Tenancy (AST) for rents up to £25,000 per annum; a Standard Tenancy Agreement for rents above £25,000 per annum; and a Company Tenancy Agreement, where the company is the tenant and you are the 'permitted occupier'. Although the wording is very similar, you should watch out for the following:

- Do you have a break clause? Job mobility makes it sensible to be able to terminate early and this is usually granted subject to a minimum tenure of six months. Read the language carefully regarding the notice period to see if the lease permits termination at six months or permits you to give notice of termination at six months. In the latter case, termination will occur at seven or eight months depending on the required notice period.

- Do you have an option to renew? You may want an option to extend for a second or third year.

2

- What is the level of annual rent increase? It is likely to be no less than the Retail Price Index (i.e., inflation) but a minimum of either 3 per cent or 5 per cent. A maximum percentage can also be negotiated.

### Be prepared

- Rent is expressed on a per week basis. As there are 52 weeks in a year, your monthly rent is equivalent to 4.3 weeks – not four weeks.

- The deposit required against dilapidations is normally six weeks. If pets are allowed, this may go up to eight weeks. The deposit may not be returned until you have proved you have settled your utility bills.

- If you are asked for a holding deposit to secure a tenancy, make sure it is refundable against the full deposit.

- Sort out your wish list at the negotiation stage (e.g., redecoration, linens or a microwave). It is difficult to go back to the landlord later.

- There may be additional charges for related matters, such as drawing up tenancy agreements and check-ins.

### Best practice

- Set up a Standing Order Mandate (direct debit) to pay the rent. You are obliged to pay on time.

- You have no legal right to withhold rent, whatever your grievance, so discuss any problems with your agent.

- Ensure your check-in is conducted by an independent inventory clerk, as this will form the basis of the dilapidation charges. Take photographs of any existing damages, no matter how minor, and keep them with your copy of the inventory check.

- Take care with picture hooks or you may end up redecorating. Review the terms of your tenancy agreement to make sure you are complying with any specific requirements.

- Make sure the utilities (e.g., gas, water, electricity, telephone, television licence and council tax) are transferred into your name at the onset and out of your name when you leave.

- Get to know your managing agents and be realistic about what they can achieve – that way you will get the best out of them. It is rare in the UK for a tenant to talk directly to the landlord during negotiations. The normal process is for the tenant to talk to his or her agent, who then talks with the landlord's agent, who then talks with the landlord.

- Protect your belongings with tenant's contents insurance. Normally, the landlord insures the property and its contents (if furnished) and the tenant is responsible for his or her own belongings. Insurance quotes can be lower if certain security devices such as locks and security alarms are installed. If possible, obtain an insurance quote before finalising the tenancy agreement so that you can request that the landlord install the proper devices. To find an insurance broker the website of British Insurance Brokers Association at **www.biba.org.uk** is a good starting place.

- Always get your property professionally cleaned when you leave. Domestic cleaning is no substitute. Ensure that your tenancy agreement includes the requirement that the property be professionally cleaned before you move in.

- There are now Tenancy Deposit Protection schemes in place for many rental properties to ensure your deposit is kept safe. For more information, including advice on resolving disputes, visit **www.direct.gov.uk**.

Know your neighbourhood

- Proximity to schools/parks/playgrounds.
- Proximity to amenities (shops, restaurants and pubs).
- Is there a local supermarket?
- Proximity to the bus, tube and/or train – is there an easy link to work?
- Availability of on-street or off-street parking.
- Level of crime in the area – check with local police if necessary.

Household tips

Look for:

- Storage space and bedroom wardrobe space.

- Electrical points for appliances, PC, TV & video, stereo, etc.

- Burglar and smoke alarms.

- Separate washing machine and dryer (they are often combined). If you do a lot of laundry and have a combination machine, you may want to ask your landlord to install a separate dryer if space permits.

- Refrigerator/freezer size (UK appliances are often smaller).

- Shower pressure (power showers).

- Access – are there too many stairs? Are the common areas of a good standard?

- Height and width of the corridors and stairwells (especially in conversions) for moving furniture in and out.

- Outside space – do you have access to the garden or will you have to share? Who is responsible for maintenance?

## Council tax

Council tax is a local tax set by each local council to help pay for local services such as rubbish collection and street cleaning. There will be one bill per dwelling to be paid by the resident (or by the owner where the property is untenanted). The amount paid will be based on the value of the dwelling.

**DID YOU KNOW?**

Single occupants receive a 25 per cent discount on council tax. Full-time students do not have to pay council tax, but must apply for an exemption from the council.

## Buying property

For those not familiar with buying property in London, the experience can be daunting, distressing, time consuming and expensive. But if you are planning on being in London longer term is can definitely be a worthwhile investment. It will pay dividends to acquaint yourself with basic procedures and terms and to obtain good professional advice. One of the most common reasons that sales of property in the UK fail is that no deposits are required and until contracts are exchanged, the buyer is under no legal obligation to buy the property, the seller is under no legal obligation to sell and neither the buyer nor the seller have to compensate the other for any of the costs that the other party may have incurred.

## Acquisition costs

### Finder's fee

The fee paid to a property search or purchase management company for representing you (the buyer) and finding your property. You do not have to pay this fee if you register with a normal estate agent and/or reply to an advertisement for a property. Remember that an estate agent represents the seller's interest – not yours.

### Land Registry fees

The cost of registering the buyer as the new owner at the Land Registry, visit **www.landregistry.gov.uk**.

### Legal fees

The solicitor's fee for acting on your behalf in the purchase. The fee can vary quite significantly so it is advisable to obtain a quotation from several solicitors before proceeding.

### Lender's arrangement fee

Lenders may charge you for organising your mortgage. This may be a flat fee or a percentage of the total advance. They may also require legal representation using a solicitor from their designated panel. Some lenders will make a contribution towards legal fees.

### Local searches

These are searches undertaken by your solicitor with the local council to ensure there are no apparent reasons for not proceeding with the purchase. The searches take about four weeks and cost approximately £300.

### Stamp duty

A government tax levied on the purchase price of a property. If the purchase price is below a certain threshold, you don't pay any stamp duty. If it is above the threshold, you pay between 1 and 4 per cent of the entire purchase price on a sliding scale. For further details, visit the HM Revenue and Customs website at **www.hmrc.gov.uk**.

### Survey fees

The cost of the survey conducted to determine that the property has no significant structural faults. The lenders may insist on a particular type of survey, but they may make a contribution towards the cost of it.

## Conveyancing (legal) process

### Estate agent

The selling agents, who receive a fee from the seller to achieve a sale at the best possible price.

### Formulating the offer

Your bid will be given to the estate agent, who will forward it to the seller for acceptance. Your ability to negotiate will depend on the current market. If you offer the asking price, you should ask for a period of exclusivity (when another contract cannot be issued) but this is not legally binding.

### Exchange of contracts

At this stage, which takes place approximately one month after the initial offer, providing you have received your mortgage offer, you will enter into a legally binding contract with the seller, who can no longer accept other offers. You will normally pay a 10 per cent deposit.

### Completion

This usually occurs within one to four weeks after the exchange of contracts, at which time you become the legal owner of the property and obtain possession.

### Gazumping

The seller agrees a price with the buyer and then sells to another buyer for a higher price.

### Gazundering

The buyer drives down the agreed price by threatening to pull out of the agreed purchase just before exchange of contracts.

### Insurance

If you are buying a house, you are responsible for buildings insurance from the exchange of contracts. With flats, you pay for this via the service charge. You will require contents insurance at completion to cover your belongings.

## Mortgages
The term for a housing loan, normally up to 70 to 80 per cent of the purchase price and for a period up to 30 years.

### Capital repayment
In this type of mortgage, the instalment payment covers interest as well as repaying the capital borrowed.

### Endowment
This mortgage uses the maturity value of an endowment policy to pay off the borrowing at the end of the term. Be aware that at maturity, the assurance policy may not cover the full loan sum.

### Interest only
This type of mortgage payment only covers the interest that is accumulating on the loan. In this case it is advisable to have collateral security to pay off the capital at the end of the term.

## Surveys

### Homebuyer's report and valuation
Normally used by the homebuyer to obtain basic structural information.

### Full structural survey
A more expensive but comprehensive report highlighting significant faults which may lead to further negotiation on the property purchase price.

### Mortgage valuation
A visual inspection carried out by the bank to confirm the property valuation.

## Types of property charges

### Ground rent
The sum paid to the owner of the freehold for use of the land over which your property is built.

### Service charge
Flat owner's annual contribution to the running costs of a building (e.g., porter, lift, lighting, cleaning).

### Sinking fund
Reserve fund collected annually to provide for major works (e.g., external redecoration).

### Types of tenure

Freehold

The outright purchase of a building, normally a house, and land 'in perpetuity'.

Leasehold

The purchase of a right to occupy a house or, more normally, a flat, for a specified number of years, up to 999 years. The land and main structure of the property is owned by the freeholder, who charges ground rent. Leases confer obligations on the lessee and the landlord. Property values diminish as leases shorten but owner-occupiers have a statutory right, subject to certain terms, to extend their lease for a further 90 years. For purposes of making a sound investment, it is typically recommended to obtain a property with at least 80 years on the leasehold.

Share of freehold

In some cases, the building lessees combine together to buy the freehold. A management company is normally set up to purchase it and the lessees take a share. Among other benefits, it is then possible to extend the lease term without the payment of a premium.

# Online resources

FindaProperty

www.findaproperty.com

This website lists all the properties available per area, regardless of which estate agent represents the property.

House Prices

www.houseprices.co.uk

This website allows you to search a postcode or area to determine historical property sales prices.

Money Supermarket

www.moneysupermarket.com

This website has an excellent mortgage search engine.

Mouse Price

www.mouseprice.com

This website allows you to search by post code to receive a local guide of an area or free valuation of a home or flat.

Nestoria
www.nestoria.co.uk
This website is a useful search engines for properties to sell and rent.

Our Property
www.ourproperty.co.uk
This website gives free house price information from Land Registry databases.

Primelocation
www.primelocation.com
A property portal that lists up-market properties in the UK and abroad. It accepts property listings only from estate agents, letting agents and new homes developers.

Property Snake
www.propertysnake.co.uk
This website allows you to search for reduced house prices across the UK.

Right Move
www.rightmove.co.uk
This website is a useful search engine for properties to sell and rent.

# British terminology

The following list of real estate terminology will hopefully eliminate any confusion in communication and help you interpret your property's particulars.

### A home by any other name

There is a host of different descriptions for property, especially in London. Here are a few of the most common:

| | |
|---|---|
| Bedsit | Single room rented accommodation combining bedroom and sitting room with shared bathroom. |
| Bungalow | One-level ground floor house; very rare in Central London. |

| | |
|---|---|
| Conversion | A flat in a house that was originally built for single-family occupancy. |
| Cottage | Small rustic-style house, generally old, often with garden. |
| Detached house | A house that stands apart from any others, generally surrounded by its own garden. |
| Edwardian | Period property built between 1901 to 1910. |
| Flat | An apartment, usually on one floor, that may be in a clock or in a large converted house. |
| Georgian | Period property built between 1714 to 1830. |
| Maisonette | An apartment arranged over two or more floors usually with its own separate entrance. |
| Mansion block | Period apartment building, often Victorian, Edwardian or Art Deco, built specifically to provide flats. |
| Mansion flat | Large, traditionally old-fashioned apartment, usually in a good area; often possessing large rooms, good storage space and lacking modern conveniences until refurbished. |
| Mews house | Converted carriage house with smaller rooms and lower ceilings than a typical period house, lots of character and often with garage. |
| New build | A new development of flats or houses. |
| Period property | A property built before 1911 and named after the period in which it was built. |
| Purpose-built block | A modern building of flats built specifically for this purpose. |
| Semi-detached house | A house that is joined to another house on only one side, often with its own garden. |
| Studio flat | A one-room flat with a separate bathroom and kitchen or kitchenette. |

| | |
|---|---|
| Terraced house | One of a row of similar houses joined together mainly built in Victorian times. |
| Townhouse | Typical Central London home, often located in a Georgian or Victorian terrace, usually two to five storeys high. |
| Victorian | Period property built between 1837 to 1901. |

## The ABCs of property

Know your abbreviations. These are some of the most commonly used.

| | |
|---|---|
| CH | Central heating. |
| CHW | Constant hot water. |
| F/F | Fully furnished: equipped with furniture, soft furnishings and accessories for immediate occupation. |
| GFCH or GCH | Gas-fired central heating (as opposed to oil-fired). |
| OSP | Off-street parking which is free and unrestricted. |
| Respark | Residents' parking: council-approved on-street parking. Usually unrestricted access in allocated areas for two vehicles per household for a small annual fee. |
| U/F | Unfurnished: no furniture but generally with carpets, light fixtures and appliances. |
| WC | Literally 'water closet', but really a room with toilet and wash basin. |

3

MONEY, BANKING AND TAXATION

# 3

# Money, banking and taxation

When moving to London, one of the first tasks you will find yourself confronted with (after sorting out all the different pound notes and various coins) is opening a UK bank account. When choosing a bank, consider the services you will need, for example, direct deposit, bill payment, international transfers, credit cards or different currency accounts. All banks and building societies in the UK that accept sterling deposits must guarantee all deposits up to £50,000. As an international centre of finance with hundreds of thousands employed in the industry, London offers a wealth of information. As you organise your finances, remember to consider tax implications and consult an expert where necessary.

## IN THIS CHAPTER...

- British currency
- European Union
- The euro
- UK banking
- Offshore banking
- Taxation

45

# British currency

British currency, normally referred to as **sterling**, is comprised of two monetary units: the pence and the pound. One pound equals 100 pence. Coins include the 1 pence, 2 pence, 5 pence, 10 pence, 20 pence, 50 pence, the 1 pound coin, and the 2 pound coin. The bills are called **pound notes** and come in denominations of 5, 10, 20 and 50 pound notes. There are no paper versions of the 1 and 2 pound coins. Pence are commonly abbreviated as **p** (e.g., 10p), and the pound sign is **£** (e.g., £10) while the currency code is **GBP**. You may hear a pound called a **quid**.

> **DID YOU KNOW?**
>
> The term **quid** comes from the Latin expression quid pro quo meaning one thing in return for another, no doubt dating back to the Roman occupation of Britain.
>
> Many services, particularly shops, buses, minicabs and taxis, don't like to or can't change large notes. Asking for smaller notes when banking will make life easier.

# European Union

The European Union (**EU**) is an institutional system comprising 27 countries (called **Member States**) that aims to represent its members on issues of interest to all. The idea was suggested by France and came to fruition in the 1950s because Europeans were determined to prevent the killing and destruction that occurred in World War II from happening again. In the beginning, the cooperation was between six countries, concerned primarily with trade and the economy. The current 27 Member States' objectives include: establishing European citizenship; ensuring freedom, security and justice; promoting economic and social progress; and asserting Europe's role in the world. The Member States are: Austria, Belgium, Bulgaria, Cyprus, the Czech Republic, Denmark, Estonia, Finland, France, Germany, Greece, Hungary, Ireland, Italy, Latvia, Lithuania, Luxembourg, Malta, the Netherlands, Poland, Portugal, Romania, Slovakia, Slovenia, Spain, Sweden and the UK.

Life has become much easier for the traveller in the EU, with the removal of most passport formalities between countries and the sharing of a common currency (the **euro**), which makes price comparisons easy and eliminates the need to carry and convert different forms of money.

## The euro

The euro is the legal tender of 16 of the 27 countries that make up the European Union. The symbol for the euro is € and the currency code is **EUR**. As of this printing, euro notes and coins have replaced the national currencies of the following EU countries: Austria, Belgium, Cyprus, Finland, France, Germany, Greece, Ireland, Italy, Luxembourg, Malta, the Netherlands, Portugal, Slovakia, Slovenia and Spain. Estonia is due to join in January 2011. The UK has chosen not to use the single currency.

One euro is divided into 100 cents, with coins and notes issued in a similar fashion to the British pound. In addition to the cent coins (issued in denominations of 1c, 2c, 5c, 10c, 20c and 50c), there is a 1 euro coin and a 2 euro coin. Bills are issued in denominations of 5, 10, 20, 50, 100, 200 and 500. Euro notes are identical in all countries but each country issues its own coins with one common European side and one side displaying a distinctive national emblem. All of the notes and coins can be used anywhere in the euro area. Some retail outlets in countries outside the euro area will accept payment in euro as well as the national currency, but they are not legally obliged to do so.

There has been, and continues to be, fierce debate in the UK regarding participation in the euro. Although many of the British support strengthening ties between European states in a political sense, many question the merits of joining the monetary unit of the euro. The main cause for concern is the historic strength of the British pound compared to the euro. To many, abandoning the pound and joining the euro is synonymous to propping up Europe's economy at the expense of the UK.

## UK banking

Many of your banking needs will likely be determined by your main source of income. If you are moving to the UK as an expatriate, your company may choose to continue to pay your salary in your local currency and provide an adjustment for the difference in the cost of living. If this is the case, please speak with a financial advisor prior to moving to London and look into options of opening an offshore banking account for tax implications. See sections on *Offshore banking* and *Taxation* below for more information.

It is generally a good idea to open a local currency account with a UK bank. The major banks offer essentially the same services (and can provide accounts that hold multiple currencies). Therefore, you will probably choose the bank with which your company has a business relationship, or the bank located nearest to your home or office. Some of the largest UK and international banks, with branches throughout London and the UK, are:

**Barclays Bank**
www.bank.barclays.co.uk, www.barclayswealth.com/international.htm

**Citibank**
www.citibank.co.uk, www.citibank.com/ipb/europe

**Coutts**
www.coutts.com

**HSBC**
www.hsbc.co.uk, www.offshore.hsbc.com

**Lloyds TSB Bank**
www.lloydstsb.com, www.lloydstsb-offshore.com

**National Westminster Bank**
www.natwest.co.uk, www.natwestinternational.com

**Royal Bank of Scotland**
www.rbs.co.uk, www.rbsinternational.com/offshore.ashx

Banks in the UK are acutely aware of the risk of fraud and money laundering and take several measures to prevent such crimes, which are particularly noticeable to persons opening accounts. Sometimes it can take up to six weeks to open an account.

The verification of the identity of new customers may be a rigorous process, including requiring original identity documents (i.e., passport, identity card and/or utility bills) or certified copies of the same. A letter of introduction from your firm helps and, if you require immediate credit facilities, copies of your previous country's bank statements or a letter of introduction from your previous bank will also help to speed the process.

## Banking services

The UK banks offer two basic types of accounts: current (chequing) accounts and deposit (savings) accounts, although there are variations of each type of account. Building societies (similar to the US savings and loans associations) also offer current accounts. Most British banks now offer interest on select current accounts and will provide free banking for personal customers who remain in good credit standing. Some banks will also provide sweep accounts. This means that the bank will automatically transfer excess funds from your current account to your deposit account. In reverse, the bank will move funds from your deposit account to your current account to maintain the agreed credit balance. You should obtain a direct debit/cheque guarantee card for your current account (see *Cheques and debit cards* below). At the request of the customer, statements are sent quarterly or monthly. Cancelled cheques are returned only if requested and a fee is frequently charged.

Monthly or quarterly bills (e.g., telephone, electricity, gas, water and council tax) may be paid at your bank by three methods. One method is to use the giro slips attached to most bills. The giro slips can be grouped together and all paid with a single cheque. The bank stamps your bill to provide a record of payment, proving beneficial as cheques are not normally returned by the bank. The second method is paying electronically online each month or quarter. The third method of payment is the use of standing orders or direct debit. With a standing order, you instruct your bank to pay a fixed amount to a specified payee at regular intervals, usually on a certain day each month (e.g., £1,000 rent on the 15th of every month to the landlord or estate agent). With a direct debit, you authorise your bank to pay on demand varying amounts as specified by a particular supplier (e.g., whatever the electricity company states is your monthly or quarterly bill). For additional information on paying utilities, see *Chapter 5: Utilities.*

## Bank hours

Regular banking hours are 9:00-17:00 or 9:30-16:30 Monday through Friday. Saturday hours (usually 9:30-12:00) are currently being offered by some UK banks. This is mainly in, but not limited to, their suburban locations.

All banks are closed on holidays (hence the term bank holiday). Please see *Chapter 17: Annual events* for a listing of bank holidays in the UK. Many banks close at 12:00 on Christmas Eve and do not reopen until after Boxing Day. All major banks have cash machines that operate 24 hours a day at most of their branches and, increasingly, elsewhere.

You can ask for **cashback** when paying for your items with a debit card at UK supermarkets. Cashback is usually not charged and is handy if you need cash without having to go to a cash machine. Cash machines in the UK do not accept deposits.

### Cheques and debit cards

Writing a sterling cheque may differ slightly from writing cheques elsewhere. When drafting a cheque there are two important points to remember:

1. The date is written with the day, the month and then the year (e.g., 5 March 2007 or 5-3-07). Do remember either to put the day first or spell out the month.

2. To write the amount, you must write 'pounds' and 'p' or 'pence'. For example, £10.62 is written: 'Ten pounds and 62p' or 'Ten pounds and sixty-two pence'.

Sterling cheques are usually crossed, meaning they have two vertical lines running down the middle. A crossed cheque is for deposit only and cannot be cashed by a third party. Hence, cheques are not endorsed for cash in the UK.

All UK banks are now on a three- to five-day clearing cycle at the bank's discretion. Most banks, however, credit cash deposits immediately.

Importantly, in addition to any credit cards you may apply for, you should obtain a direct debit/cheque guarantee card for your current account. Well-known versions of the direct debit card are Maestro and Visa. This card will let you pay for goods and services wherever you see the Maestro or Visa logo and gives you access to your money from cash machines across the UK, as well as guaranteeing your cheque up to the amount shown on the card. Although you may cash a cheque for any amount at your own bank branch (where you opened the account), you will be required to show your cheque card when cashing a cheque at either another branch of your bank or at another chain of banks. If the cheque amount is over the limit stated on your card, you will often need to make prior arrangements even within your own branch in order to cash it.

Whenever you use your direct debit/cheque guarantee card, the transactions will appear on your account statement, so you will have a clear audit trail of your transactions. Purchases are limited, however, to available funds (or an agreed overdraft).

Most establishments in the UK use **Chip and PIN** as a more secure way to pay with credit or debit cards. Instead of using your signature to verify payments, you must enter a four-digit Personal Identification Number (PIN) known only to you. If you do not know your PIN, you will be asked to use an alternative method of payment.

### Credit cards

Most major banks issue credit cards in the form of a Visa or MasterCard, which can be used throughout the UK and in Europe where the appropriate sign is displayed. Similar cards from other countries are also accepted. Attaining a UK credit card can be difficult initially if you do not already have a credit history in the UK. A letter or phone call from your company can help speed the process. American Express also offer credit cards in the UK. If you hold an American Express card in your home country, they may be able to assist you in transferring your card to the UK. Please keep in mind that many places in the UK do not accept American Express cards so it is helpful to also own a Visa or MasterCard or debit card. In addition, many services in the UK charge you a fee when you use a credit card.

### Traveller's cheques

Traveller's cheques and foreign currency can be purchased from all major UK banks, however, it is usually necessary to give a few days' notice and order ahead. Traveller's cheques can also be obtained from Thomas Cook and American Express offices located throughout the UK. Importantly, foreign currency can also be ordered at most UK Post Office branches (but not often at the postal counters that can be found in retail stores like your local chemist or newsstand).

### Transferring money

If you want to transfer money from your previous home country to your UK current account you can have it sent by wire transfer with the help of your previous banker; or a transfer by telex can be completed in 48 hours. Alternatively, you can purchase sterling from your UK bank with a foreign currency cheque (e.g., in dollars drawn on your US bank account). The time it takes for the foreign cheque to clear and be credited to your UK account will vary by type of currency and the size of the cheque. If timing is important, be sure to check with your bank before you proceed.

If you wish to remit money to another foreign country, you can ask your UK bank to draw a draft on your behalf against the sterling in your current account or to transfer the amount to a foreign bank account by mail, cable or telex.

**DID YOU KNOW?**

As an expatriate living in the UK, you pay UK taxes on any money you bring into the country, especially if it comes from an interest-bearing account. It is advised to open an offshore account and transfer funds prior to moving to the UK. Speak with a financial or tax advisor for more tips.

### Safety deposit boxes

Although local commercial banks often provide 'strong rooms' for storing their customers' valuables, they do not have facilities for individual safety deposit boxes. Privately run safety deposit centres offer these boxes instead. *Metropolitan Safe Deposits* is one of the UK's leading independent safe deposit companies. There are two locations in London: Knightsbridge and St. John's Wood. Visit the website **www.metrosafe.co.uk** for more details.

# Offshore banking

Several banks provide an offshore banking option in addition to local services. The rationales for obtaining and utilising an offshore account vary according to your individual situation. They may include tax savings, shelter from monetary instability or an investment opportunity.

As a UK resident, offshore banking may provide a tax benefit because any income earned while you are physically located in another country is not subject to UK tax provided that the money is deposited into an offshore account and does not make it back to the UK. For example, if you spend two months working in Germany for your company, you would not be liable to pay UK income tax on those two months of wages provided that the wages were deposited in an offshore account and are not brought into the UK.

To make tax reporting easier, it is recommended when opening up your accounts to also open an interest account, thereby all interest earned on your bank accounts is separate.

MONEY, BANKING AND TAXATION

3

# Taxation

When you come to reside in the UK, your tax status changes and HM Revenue & Customs (**HMRC**) – the UK's tax office – has primary jurisdiction over your income. Their website is **www.hmrc.gov.uk**. Depending on where you have come from, you may have a tax obligation to your 'home' country and may be required to report and pay income tax there as well. (This is true for American citizens who can refer the section American taxes below). In almost all cases, however, you will want to consult a tax accountant soon after you arrive regarding your tax status and filing requirements.

## UK taxes

The UK tax year runs from 6 April to the following 5 April. If you send in a paper tax return, it must reach HMRC by midnight on 31 October. If you send your tax return online, it must reach HMRC by midnight on 31 January. Interest and penalties may be charged on tax not paid by the due date and penalties will be levied for tax returns filed late.

If you are employed by a firm in the UK, the tax on your earnings will be calculated and withheld at source via the **PAYE** (Pay As You Earn) system. If you are self-employed, your accountant can advise you on how to make estimated payments or you may consult with your nearest HMRC office, which is listed in the telephone directory. In addition to wages, you will be taxed on any investment income that is sourced in the UK, along with any income from your investments outside the UK that is remitted to the UK. Publication HMRC6 *Residence, Domicile and Remittance* is available from HMRC or at **www.hmrc.gov.uk/cnr/hmrc6.pdf**; it addresses many of the issues of individual taxation in the UK.

National Insurance taxes (similar to the US Social Security tax) in the UK are payable through withholding if you are an employee and payable with your income tax or by direct debit if you are self-employed. If you are an American working in the UK, you will be required to pay either Social Security tax to the US or National Insurance tax to the UK, but not both. The length of your anticipated stay in the UK should determine which plan to pay.

Finally, **VAT** (Value Added Tax) is a tax that you pay as a consumer when purchasing goods and services in the European Union. Each country in the EU has its own rate for VAT. In the UK the standard rate is currently 17.5 per cent, but is set to rise to 20 per cent in January 2011. Some items, like domestic power, are charged at a reduced rate of 5 per cent. You do not pay VAT on items such as newspapers, children's clothing and most groceries.

## American taxes

American citizens are taxed by the US government on their worldwide income, but are given a tax credit, subject to limitations, for foreign income taxes paid. In general, American citizens, wherever they live in the world, must file a tax return if their income exceeds a certain amount. Filing dates are automatically extended for Americans abroad from 15 April to 15 June – and can be extended even further by application – but penalties and interest are applied from 15 April for tax due but not paid.

Publication 54, *Tax Guide for US Citizens and Resident Aliens Abroad*, is available at the IRS office of the US Embassy, 24 Grosvenor Square, W1A 1AE, ✆020 7894 0477, or find it online at **www.irs.gov/publications/p54/index.html**.

Importantly, US taxpayers living in the UK are entitled to two potentially sizeable exclusions/deductions on their foreign earned income if they meet one of two conditions involving the length of their stay in the UK: the *bona fide residence test* or the *physical presence test* (spelled out in detail on Form 2555). The exclusions are as follows:

1. *Foreign earned income exclusion*: If your tax home is a foreign country (e.g., the UK) and you qualify under either the bona fide residence test or the physical presence test, you can exclude the actual amount of foreign income earned during the year, up to a current maximum of $91,400. If both husband and wife work, the foreign earned income exclusion is computed separately, even if they file jointly.

2. *Housing cost amount exclusion*: A qualified taxpayer may also choose to exclude from gross income any qualified housing costs in excess of a specified base amount.

After these deductions, any remaining earned income and all unearned income is taxed as if it were the only income and, therefore, will generally be taxed at a lower effective tax rate.

When it comes time to compute your US tax liability, you may be able to take a credit for some, if not all, of the foreign income taxes paid to HMRC. Although you are generally subject to tax both in the UK and the US, this credit has the potential to limit your US liability.

In terms of state and local taxes, depending on the state from which you have moved, you may be liable for these income taxes while living abroad. Check with your tax accountant to be sure. However, you remain liable for any taxes on property (real estate or personal property) that generates income in the US.

## Tax assistance

For further information on your UK or US tax obligations, you may contact HMRC, your UK or US accountant or lawyer, or your company's personnel or expatriate employee departments. For UK tax enquiries, there are various local enquiry offices in London which you can find on the HMRC website (**www.hmrc.gov.uk**). The IRS office in the US Embassy can assist you, at no cost, in filing your US returns and the Consular Office of the US Embassy has lists of American accountants and lawyers who can assist you for a fee (**www.usembassy.org.uk**).

There are a few small UK firms who specialise in US expatriates residing in the UK. These include:

Buzzacott LLP
12 New Fetter Lane, EC4A
✆020 7556 1200, www.buzzacott.co.uk

Expatriate Tax Management
16 Brune Street, E1
✆020 7721 7993

MacIntyre Hudson
30-34 New Bridge Street, EC4V
✆020 7429 4100, www.macintyrehudson.co.uk

## Canadian taxes

In general, if you can establish that you are no longer a resident of Canada you do not have to pay taxes in Canada on income earned outside Canada. Specific questions can be directed to the International Tax Services Office, ✆+1 613 952-3741. Information may also be accessed on the Canada Revenue Agency website **www.cra-arc.gc.ca**.

# Working

Many readers of this book, possibly the majority, have come to live in London because of their work or their partner's work. As a cosmopolitan city and financial centre, it can sometimes seem that every other person you meet in London is an expat lawyer or banker. Although in recent years, the tide of expats flowing into and out of London has slowed, there are still a great number of companies transferring their employees here. This chapter gives an overview of information that may be helpful to those already employed, but may be particularly useful to those looking to find work in London.

For those looking to earn a living in London, your two most important assets will be the Internet and your network of people who can help give you access to job opportunities. If you are new to London, a great way to begin networking is through the many organisations here, including alumni associations, professional and social groups (see *Chapter 18: Organisations*). If you are unsure about whether or not you have the right to be employed in the UK, this chapter lists some of the visas and work permits available (see *Visas and work permits* below), but you should also visit the UK Border Agency website at **www.ukba.homeoffice.gov.uk/workingintheuk** or consult an expert.

## IN THIS CHAPTER...

- Job seeking
- Volunteering
- Visas and work permits
- Settling in the UK
- Employment rights
- National Insurance numbers

# Job seeking

If you haven't arrived in London as a result of work and need to look for employment, job hunting in London can be a creative task that requires considerable initiative from the individual. It is a frequently quoted claim that only 80 per cent of job openings are advertised, so creative efforts are rewarded. Recruiters and employment consultants will universally tell you that the best way to find a job is through networking.

In addition to any connections you may have been able to make through referrals from your home country, former employers and friends, listed below are some resources that can help start your career search in London.

FOCUS

13 Prince of Wales Terrace, W8

© 020 7937 7799, www.focus-info.org

FOCUS is a not-for-profit, membership-based organisation providing services and resources for internationals in the UK. The staff and volunteers are all expatriates. Among its services, FOCUS operates a comprehensive Career Development Programme, including job workshops, one-to-one coaching and career seminars designed for a variety of different stages of a career search. The *FOCUS Career Guide*, which can be purchased via the website, is a resource for understanding what is required in the UK job market. Topics include preparing your CV (résumé), job websites, resource lists, networking groups and tips, interviewing strategies and more. FOCUS membership is £100 for one year and includes full access to their website.

## Online resources

The best and most-used resource for job searching is the Internet. Below are a few of the larger UK job search websites:

**www.efinancialcareers.co.uk** – for jobs in financial industry

**www.jobsearch.co.uk** – all job sectors covered

**www.jobserve.com** – all job sectors covered

**www.jobsite.co.uk** – upload your CV for all job sectors, provides for charity and volunteer roles

**www.monster.co.uk** – for job seekers and recruiters

**www.reed.co.uk** – 'the UK's biggest job site'

**www.totaljobs.com** – jobs by sector and location

**www.totallylegal.com** – for jobs in the legal sector
**www.workthing.com** – jobs from employers

## Newspapers

The UK's newspapers publish sections aimed at job seekers and many post job vacancies for particular sectors on a regular schedule. The classified job advertisements can also be found on most UK newspapers' websites.

Times/Sunday Times – **www.timesonline.co.uk/jobs**
Financial Times – **www.exec-appointments.com**
Evening Standard and Metro – **www.londonjobs.co.uk**
Guardian – **www.guardian.co.uk/jobs**
Independent – **www.londoncareers.net**
Daily Telegraph – **www.jobs.telegraph.co.uk**

## Recruitment consultants

Executive Grapevine is a publisher and information service for the executive talent management sector. Executive Grapevine publishes a monthly magazine as well as *The UK Directory of Executive Recruitment Consultants*, an annual publication that will help you identify the top recruitment consultants in the UK by salary range, function, industry and location. This book can often be found at major libraries in the careers section or can be purchased directly from the publisher's website at **www.askgrapevine.com** for £299. There is also an *International Directory of Executive Recruitment Consultants*.

The distinctions between different types of recruitment firms may not always be clear to a job searcher. Recruitment consultants often work in at least one of the following ways:

### Executive search

Executive search firms (often referred to as head hunters) are retained by a corporate client on a fee basis to find an appropriate candidate to fill a particular role. This type of search is typically for senior-level positions for which the pool of suitable candidates is relatively small. Executive search firms target the best candidates for a position, whether or not they are actively looking for a new job.

### Advertised selection

Recruitment firms are retained by a corporate client to advertise in the press to find candidates for a particular role. This approach relies on job candidates actively searching newspapers and trade publications to find job listings that may be of interest to them. Usually the recruitment firm will review all cover letters and CVs received, and then interview the most relevant candidates. A short list of interviewed candidates is then presented to the client for the next stage of the interview process. Advertised selection is most frequently used for hiring middle-management positions.

### Contingent recruitment

Fees charged to a corporate client by a contingent recruitment firm are conditional on a job placement being made. This type of recruitment relies on job seekers registering their CV with the recruitment firm or job seekers responding to an advertised position. Typically, corporate clients will select more than one contingent recruitment firm for a particular search to find the best pool of candidates at a given time. This type of recruitment is most common with lower salary bands, as well as temporary and contract positions. Contingent recruitment is also used for more senior roles in markets where there is a large supply of suitable candidates.

It is important to understand how the firm will use any personal information that you provide. It is a good idea to make sure your personal details are not passed on to a potential employer without your approval.

### DID YOU KNOW?

In the UK, a CV will often contain personal information such as date of birth, marital status, nationality and whether or not the applicant has a UK driving licence. A CV should always include: contact information, education, relevant experience, key skills (e.g., computer programmes or languages) and extracurricular activities where relevant. It should be no more than 2 to 3 pages in length (one page is preferred, when possible).

### Libraries

A visit to a large reference library can be helpful in finding information on companies, industries and recruitment firms. Libraries can be a great source for trade journals, newspapers and other periodicals. Listed below are three of the best reference libraries in London for a job search:

The British Library
96 Euston Road, NW1
✆ 0843 208 1144, www.bl.uk

City Business Library
Aldermanbury London, EC2
✆ 020 7332 1812, www.cityoflondon.gov.uk

Westminster Reference Library
35 St. Martin's Street, WC2
✆ 020 7641 1300, www.westminster.gov.uk/libraries

## Networking

Networking is often a key aspect of any job search. Most jobs are never advertised and are filled by word of mouth and personal recommendation. Friends, relatives, former employers, former colleagues, members of professional organisations and neighbours are all potential networking contacts. It may be helpful to have business or social cards printed with your name, phone number and email address to pass out to contacts.

Alumni associations and clubs in London can often be good sources for networking. There are also numerous networking groups in the UK that welcome newcomers. FOCUS (see *Job seeking* above) maintains an extensive list of networking organisations for its members. This book also lists professional, charitable, social and service organisations in *Chapter 18: Organisations*.

Maintaining a good network is demanding work and needs constant development. Acquaintances that do not have employment information today may have some tomorrow. Some key networking tips are to:

- Keep good records of all networking contacts in one place.

- Keep in touch with networking contacts regularly, but not obtrusively.

- Make sure you are a good networker for others, as networking benefits should go both ways.

- Try to ask at the end of networking efforts whether the individual knows of anyone else who may be able to give you advice or help with other contacts.

# Volunteering

Volunteering for an organisation can be a temporary or long-term alternative to full-time, paid employment. Volunteering offers a great way to build your CV while you look for paid employment, as well as another source for networking contacts.

The following organisations can help you identify an appropriate volunteer position for your needs and interests:

Do-it
50 Featherstone Street, EC1
© 020 7250 5700, www.do-it.org.uk
National database of volunteering opportunities in the UK; can advise you where to find your local volunteer bureau.

Reach
89 Albert Embankment, SE1
© 020 7582 6543, www.reachskills.org.uk
Enables voluntary organisations to benefit from the business, managerial, technical and professional expertise of people who want to offer their career skills working as volunteers.

TimeBank
Downstream Building, 1 London Bridge, SE1
© 0845 456 1668, www.timebank.org.uk
National charity for local, regional and international volunteering opportunities.

Volunteering England
Regent's Wharf, 8 All Saints Street, N1
© 0845 305 6979, www.volunteering.org.uk
National volunteering development agency for England.

# Visas and work permits

This section provides a general overview to visas and work permits in the UK and is not intended to be a complete guide to getting authorisation to work in the UK or to obtaining necessary visas. Advice specific to a situation should be sought when pursuing permission to work in the UK. General advice about the various types of visas available and their application processes may be found on the website of the UK Border Agency at **www.ukba.homeoffice. gov.uk**.

Most citizens living in the European Economic Area (**EEA**) and Switzerland are entitled to take employment in the UK without a visa or a work permit. Nationals of the Czech Republic, Estonia, Hungary, Latvia, Lithuania, Poland, Slovakia or Slovenia must register under the Worker Registration Scheme when they accept with a UK employer for more than one month. Once they have completed 12 months of continuous employment in the UK they can obtain a residence permit. Bulgarian and Romanian nationals may apply for permission to work in the UK but cannot start work until they receive permission.

Non-EEA persons will need to obtain a visa that allows them to work in the UK. If a person does not qualify for a visa that permits them to seek work in the UK, then they will have to obtain a work permit through a UK employer. The employer will have to make an application to the Home Office, providing detailed information about the position and why the non-EEA person is the best person to fill it.

Guidelines for visa requirements to work in the UK can be found on the UK Border Agency website at **www.ukba.homeoffice.gov.uk/workingin theuk**. The visa system continually undergoes changes, so always check the website for the most up-to-date information. The following is a selection of the most common visas that allow a person to work in the UK.

## UK ancestry visa

Commonwealth citizens who can prove that they are a citizen of a Commonwealth country and one of their parents or grandparents were born in the UK are entitled to an ancestry visa for up to five years, which allows the visa holder to seek employment in the UK. A condition of this visa is that the applicant is able to work in the UK and intends to do so and can adequately support and accommodate themselves without help from public funds.

## Highly skilled workers

The application is assessed on points. You do not need to have a specific job offer but will need to demonstrate you are highly skilled, have money to support yourself and are able to speak English. Unlike sponsored skilled workers (see below), you do not need a job offer to apply under the highly skilled worker category. When you apply, you are awarded points based on your qualifications, previous earnings, UK experience, age, English language skills and available funds for maintenance.

## Entrepreneurs

The entrepreneur category is for those investing in the UK by setting up or taking over, and being actively involved in the running of, one or more businesses in the UK. This category is designed to allow high net worth individuals make a substantial financial investment in the UK and the application is assessed on points that are awarded based on the ability to access £200,000 in the UK.

## Post-study workers

Under the points system, you may be eligible to work in the UK as a post-study worker. This category is designed to allow the UK to retain the most able international graduates who have studied in the UK, enabling post-study workers to be free to look for work without having a sponsor for the length of the visa. It is expected that the applicant will switch to a highly skilled or other visa as soon as they are eligible.

## Sponsored skilled worker

If you have a job offer from a UK-based employer who is prepared to sponsor you for a specific role, you can apply for permission to enter or stay in the UK. The employer needs to apply for a work permit on the prospective employee's behalf and must show that the employee will fill a skilled position that cannot be filled by another settled worker. The work permit will apply to a specific role and is not transferable to other positions within the company. Points are awarded based on qualifications, future expected earnings, sponsorship, English language skills and available funds for maintenance. The employer has responsibility for proving it has gone to all reasonable lengths to find an EEA worker before looking elsewhere. Work permits typically are for a five-year period.

The application process for a work permit is fairly rigorous. The employer will need to provide information about the prospective employee, including work references, education, career history and professional qualifications, as well as the company's annual reports and accounts. The employer will also need to provide a job description and information about its recruitment advertising or other efforts made to fill the position. Work permits are rarely granted for manual, secretarial or domestic positions or for salaries of less than £20,000 per year.

After a work permit has been obtained, work permit holders who wish to come to the UK for more than six months must obtain entry clearance before travelling. Entry clearance is the formal term used to describe the application process for a visa that will allow a person to remain in the UK. The entry clearance certificate (the visa) is placed in the passport or travel document.

This is not an exhaustive list of visas to work in the UK. For more information on this complex subject, refer to:

British Foreign & Commonwealth Office (FCO)
King Charles Street, London, SW1
℡ 020 7008 1500, www.ukvisas.gov.uk
Jointly run by the UK Border Agency and International Group to handle UK visa services through diplomatic posts overseas.

UK Border Agency
Lunar House, 40 Wellesley Road, Croydon, CR9
℡ 0870 606 7766 (general information) or ℡ 0114 207 4074 (work permit information), www.ukba.homeoffice.gov.uk/workingintheuk

# Settling in the UK

Many UK immigration categories lead, after a period of time, to indefinite leave to remain (permission to settle in the UK). In addition, those legally living and working in the UK for a certain length of time (usually between two to five continuous years) may be eligible to apply for indefinite leave to remain. Being granted indefinite leave to remain removes restrictions on the work or business you may do in the UK and eliminates any time limits on your stay in the UK. In addition, the holder is entitled to certain public benefits. However, be aware that lengthy delays are probable, and it is not at all unusual to wait longer than six months for the Home Office's decision. It may be possible to expedite the process by applying in person at the UK Border Agency (see contact information above), or by hiring the services of a solicitor or lawyer. Before going to the Home Office in person, be prepared to spend the entire day there and ensure that you have all the correct information with you. For more information regarding extending your stay once in the UK, visit the UK Border Agency website at **www.ukba. homeoffice.gov.uk/settlement**.

# Employment rights

All UK employers need to provide a statement of employment to the employee that clearly indicates the following information:

* The names of the employer and employee.
* The job title or a brief job description.
* Where the employee is expected to work.
* The date the employment started (or is to start).
* Details of salary and when payment will be made (e.g., weekly or monthly).
* Hours of work, and any related issues such as overtime. An employee may be expected to work beyond the contractual hours for no additional pay if more work is required.
* Holiday entitlement (most UK workers receive 20 to 25 days per year).
* Sick pay entitlement and procedures.
* Notice of termination period – standard notice is one month, but this can vary between industries and positions within a company.
* Pension scheme details.
* The length of the contract if the employee is working for a fixed time period.
* Details of the existence of any relevant collective agreements that directly affect the terms and conditions of employment.

More information on employment rights is available at the public services website **www.direct.gov.uk**. If you need help with employment rights, including employment disputes, you can contact the Advisory, Conciliation and Arbitration Service (**Acas**) helpline for advice on © 08457 474 747 or visit **www.acas.org.uk**.

# National Insurance numbers

National Insurance (**NI**) numbers are unique numbers assigned to individuals who reside in the UK for use when dealing with the Inland Revenue and the Department of Work and Pensions. The NI number ensures correct credit and a record of National Insurance benefits. Employers use the number for deducting taxes and National Insurance contributions from employees' pay. The NI number is also used for National Health Services registration (see *Chapter 7: Healthcare – National Health Service (NHS)* for further details).

If you are working in the UK, you will have to obtain an NI number promptly. If you are employed, your company will usually obtain your NI number for you. Should need to obtain an NI number yourself, you can find information on the Department for Work and Pensions website **www.dwp. gov.uk**. You can also telephone Jobcentre Plus on *℃* 0845 600 0643. Jobcentre Plus will arrange and evidence of identity interview or send you a postal application. You will have to provide various documents to prove your identity and employment in the UK.

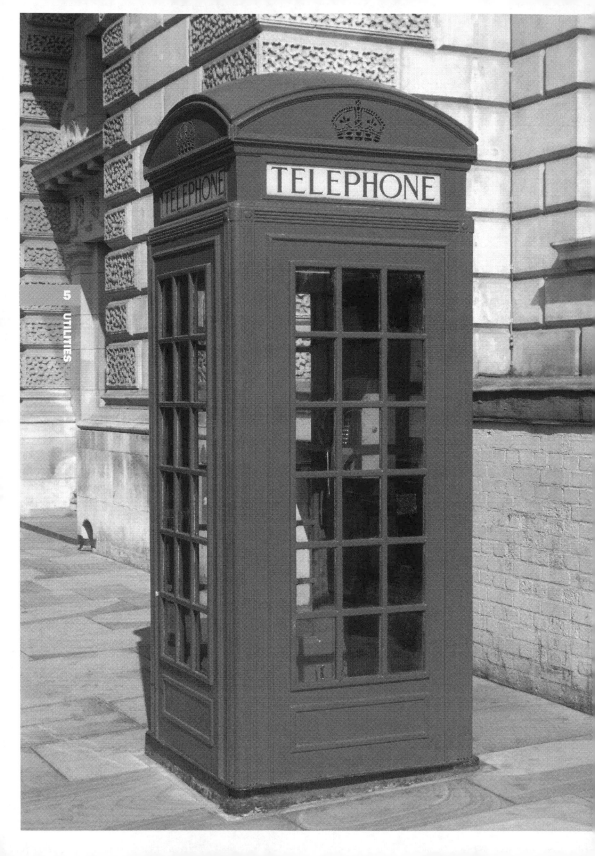

# Utilities

Upon moving to London, one of the first, and sometimes the most frustrating tasks will be to set up all of your utility accounts: from paying your local council taxes, gas, water and electric bills, to getting internet, telephone and television up and running. Often your letting or estate agent can help you with contacting various utilities.

With the exception of water, consumers in the London area have a variety of utility suppliers. For electricity and gas, a wide range of services and price structures is available. Moreover, switching from one supplier to another is relatively easy. To compare major utility prices and services in your area, visit the following websites:

**www.buy.co.uk**
**www.saveonyourbills.com**
**www.unravelit.com**
**www.uswitch.com**

Telephone, television and broadband services often come in packages. These websites offer comparisons:

**www.broadband-tv-phone.com**
**www.digitalchoices.co.uk**

## IN THIS CHAPTER...

- Useful telephone numbers
- Local councils
- Telephone
- Internet
- Television
- Electricity & gas
- Water
- Recycling & waste
- Post Office & Royal Mail

**DID YOU KNOW?**

Many utility contracts, including telephone contracts, have inflexible terms and you may be liable for payments until the end of the contract period so look out and read the fine print.

# Useful telephone numbers

| | |
|---|---|
| Ambulance, Fire, Police (for immediate danger) For non-urgent incidents – contact your local police station* | 999 or 112 |
| Crimestoppers (anonymous) | 0800 555 111 |
| Electrical Emergency (London) (EDF) | 0800 096 9000 |
| Gas Emergency | 0800 111 999 |
| Directory Enquiries, UK | 118 500/118 118/118 247 |
| Directory Enquiries, International | 118 505 |
| Operator Assistance, UK | 100 |
| Operator Assistance, International | 155 |
| Telephone Repairs | 151 |
| Time (from area codes 0207/0208) | 123 |
| London Underground | 0845 748 4950 |
| National Rail Enquiries | 0845 748 4950 |
| National Bus Service (National Express) | 0870 580 8080 |
| Racial Harassment Reporting Hotline | 0800 138 1624 |

*Contact your local council for other key numbers specific to your area.

# Local councils

Each council works to meet the needs of residents and to provide various community services, including:

• operating some of the best schools in London

**5**

UTILITIES

- maintaining roads and pavements

- ensuring rubbish is promptly collected

Whether you are renting or own your property, you are responsible for paying the council tax, which covers these services.

Below are the local council contact details for central London:

London Borough of Camden
Camden Town Hall, Judd Street, WC1
www.camden.gov.uk
General: ✆ 020 7278 4444
Recycling: ✆ 020 7974 6914/5
Refuse collection and street cleaning: ✆ 020 7974 6914/5

Corporation of London
PO Box 270, Guildhall, EC2P
www.cityoflondon.gov.uk
General: ✆ 020 7606 3030
Recycling: ✆ 020 7606 3110
Refuse collection and street cleaning: ✆ 020 7606 3110

London Borough of Hackney
Hackney Town Hall, Mare Street, Hackney, E8
www.hackney.gov.uk
General: ✆ 020 8356 3000
Recycling and refuse collection: ✆ 020 8356 6688

London Borough of Hammersmith and Fulham
Town Hall, King Street, Hammersmith, W6
www.lbhf.gov.uk
General: ✆ 020 8748 3020
Emergencies (out of hours): ✆ 020 8748 8588

London Borough of Islington
Islington Town Hall, 222 Upper Street, Islington, N1
www.islington.gov.uk
General: ✆ 020 7527 2000
Recycling: ✆ 020 7527 2000
Refuse collection: ✆ 020 7527 2000

Royal Borough of Kensington & Chelsea
The Town Hall, Hornton Street, W8
www.rbkc.gov.uk
General: ✆ 020 7361 3000
Recycling: ✆ 020 7361 30001
Refuse collection & street cleaning: ✆ 020 7361 3001

London Borough of Lambeth
Lambeth Town Hall, Brixton Hill, SW2
www.lambeth.gov.uk
General: ✆ 020 7926 1000
Refuse collection and street cleaning: ✆ 020 7926 9000

London Borough of Southwark
Southwark Town Hall, Peckham Road, SE5
www.southwark.gov.uk
General: ✆ 020 7525 5000
Recycling: ✆ 020 7525 2000
Refuse collection and street cleaning: ✆ 020 7525 2000

Westminster City Council
PO Box 240, Westminster City Hall, 64 Victoria Street, SW1
www.westminster.gov.uk
General: ✆ 020 7641 6000
Recycling, refuse collection and street cleaning: ✆ 020 7641 2000

# Telephone

### Public phone boxes

London's red telephone boxes are iconic and luckily there are still a few of them around. Phone boxes (public telephones) can be found in larger shops, in pubs and along the street. The minimum charge is 60 pence. Coin-operated telephones generally take 10p, 20p, 50p and £1 coins and in some cases £2 coins, and/or phone cards. Some payphones also accept 50c, €1 and €2 coins. Most new phones require you to insert the coin before dialling. When using older phones, dial the number and wait for the beeping sound before inserting coins. If an additional coin is required, ample warning is given by another beeping sound. Do not ask someone to ring you at the payphone unless you are certain that it will accept incoming calls.

Many new public telephones operate on phone cards available from most newsagents and post offices. These phone cards are composed of units of 10p and come in values of £3, £5, £10 and £20. If you plan on using the public telephones, it is useful to buy and carry a phone card with you, as coin-operated phones are being phased out.

## Mobile telephones

Mobile phones are very popular in the UK. Common providers include O2, Orange, T-Mobile, Virgin Media and Vodafone. Most of these companies offer services that will work throughout Continental Europe. To help decide on the right provider and plan, consider how often and where you will use your mobile phone (the UK, Europe or the rest of the world), how long you want your service contract to last and the ease of ending the contract.

Many mobile providers have stand-alone shops on most high streets and throughout London. If you change providers it is usually possible to keep your mobile number. However, this is based on agreements between mobile phone companies. You do not have a legal right to keep the same number.

The month-to-month contracts tend to be cheaper, but may not be available to customers without local credit history. Some providers are more flexible than other to provide month-to-month services to expats and you may need to provide a three to six months deposit. Prepaid mobile phone plans may be a good alternative.

## Land lines

While in some countries you can get away with only a mobile phone, in the UK some services may only be accessible if you have a fixed phone line (land line). You can choose from a large variety of fixed-line telephone service providers, including:

BT (British Telecom)
℡ 0800 800 150, www.bt.com

Virgin Media
℡ 0845 650 4545, www.virginmedia.com

Talk Talk
℡ 0800 049 7802, www.talktalk.co.uk

Tesco
℡ 0845 600 4411, www.tesco.com

For help and advice on telephone companies and services, the UK's independent regulator and competition authority for the UK communications industries, Ofcom, has a useful website at **www.ofcom.org.uk**.

It is fairly easy to switch phone companies. In the UK, if you change your phone line and stay at the same address, you can keep your phone number. However, phone companies may make a reasonable charge for this number portability.

Before making any final decision, it is recommended that you check with the individual telephone companies for their latest prices, and other factors such as services offered and quality of service. Bundling telephone services with another utility service provider, such as broadband, pay TV services or gas, might enable you to take advantage of some special discounts. A little research can go a long way, as the packages and costs differ across providers.

Calculating the cost of various phone services can be complicated because you need to consider:

- line rental
- cost of calls
- discount packages
- number of calls you make and when
- type of calls you mostly make (local, national, international or internet).

Currently, most calls, including local calls, are charged on a per-minute and per-unit basis. Telephone charges are based on metered units. The unit charge varies according to the time the call is made for local, national and international calls. Calls tend to be less expensive between 18:00 and 08:00.

Some free numbers include those with prefixes of 0800, 0808 or 0321. Numbers with the prefix 0345 or 0845 are charged at local rates. Numbers with the prefix 0900 or 0870 are charged at the national rate even if you make a local call.

New telephone equipment is available at local BT (British Telecom) shops, any high street electronics retailer, such as Currys or Maplin, or at online retailers such at Dixons (**www.dixons.co.uk**) or Argos (**www.argos.co.uk**). New telephone equipment can also be rented from several of the telephone service suppliers, including BT. You can also purchase a phone adapter that will enable you to use a foreign telephone in the UK.

Telephone directories, including *Yellow Pages*, are published for London and the other cities and towns in the UK. The dialling codes for all UK cities and towns are listed in the front of each directory.

If you need flexibility, be careful when selecting a telephone contract, as some may have inflexible terms and you may be liable for payments until the end of the contract period.

### Voice-over-internet protocol

A growing service for long distance and international calls is the voice-over-internet protocol (VoIP). Several companies provide this service and, if you make frequent international or long distance calls, this service may prove to be less expensive than mobile phone or land line calls. The quality of the lines varies (usually depending on the time of day and the speed of your internet connection) but services are improving.

Some companies that provide this service include:

BT Anytime Call Plan
✆ 0800 800 150, www.bt.com

Skype
www.skype.com

Tesco Internet Phone
✆ 0906 301 8000, www.tesco.com

VOIPCheap
www.voipcheap.co.uk

Vonage
✆ 0808 008 600, www.vonage.co.uk

# Internet

There are three different Internet services you can subscribe to: dial-up, broadband or wireless.

Dial-up is the oldest and definitely the slowest. There is no reason to use dial-up Internet access in the UK since broadband and wireless options are plentiful with roughly the same price for better quality of service.

Broadband (cable/ASDL) service is faster. In the UK broadband is often tied to your home phone line – so you will need to have a home phone line. By choosing a bundled service by the likes of Virgin Media or Talk Talk you can get home phone, broadband, and cable television services together for best value. The monthly fee for ADSL broadband is typically between £15 to £40 depending on which services you require. Sometimes, additional equipment and set-up charges are added on top of the monthly fee. Watch out for long-term contracts as they are not required by all vendors.

Wireless (**Wi-Fi**) Internet allows you to access the Internet anywhere in your house or, if provided by mobile operators, anywhere within the coverage area. This is particularly useful if you have more then one home computer or prefer to use a notebook computer. Some providers may supply a wireless router with your service. Service providers such as O2 and T-Mobile offer bundled Wi-Fi services with mobile phone plans.

Some of the common Internet providers include:

AOL
✆ 0800 376 5599, www.aol.co.uk

BT
✆ 0845 601 5190, www.btopenworld.com

Orange
✆ 0800 072 5563, www.orange.co.uk

Sky
www.sky.com

Talk Talk
✆ 0800 049 7802, www.talktalk.co.uk

Tesco
✆ 0906 301 8000, www.tesco.com

Virgin Media
✆ 0845 650 1000, www.virginmedia.com

# Television

All users of television sets must possess an annual TV licence, obtainable from any Post Office or through TV Licensing at **www.tvlicensing.co.uk**. One licence, which is valid for 12 months, covers all of the television sets in a household. The charge for a colour television licence is £145.50, and one for black and white televisions is £49.00. Fines for not having a TV licence can be as much as £1,000. There is no charge for a television licence if you are over 75 years old. Radios do not require a licence.

For more information about television licences, call © 0300 790 6131 or visit **www.tvlicensing.co.uk**. If you leave the country before the expiry of the licence, you can obtain a refund by contacting the Refund Centre, PO Box 140, Bristol, BS99 5HP or by completing a form on the website.

## Digital and satellite

Digital television is replacing analogue across the UK with the official switch to digital already begun. London is scheduled to switch in 2012 (the analogue signal will be turned off upon completion). A full schedule and advice on how this may affect you are available at **www.digitaluk.co.uk**.

One of the benefits of digital television is that in addition to the five terrestrial channels available with your television licence (i.e., BBC 1, BBC 2, ITV, Channel 4 and Channel 5), a digital Freeview box (visit **www.freeview. co.uk**) will allow you access to a host of free digital channels (see *Freeview* section below). Additional cable, digital and satellite television may be available in your area through a service provider.

Digital providers include Virgin Media and Sky Digital. Digital offers several advantages to the viewer, such as wide-screen pictures, CD-quality sound and video-on-demand. Interactive services such as home banking, home shopping and connection to the Internet are also now available digitally through the television in some areas.

Packages of televisions and DVD accessories are available to rent from Boxclever (© 0870 5546 563, **www.boxclever.co.uk**).

In order to receive satellite communications, you may either purchase or rent an individual satellite dish to be installed at your residence. You must then subscribe to a plan, which will be payable on a monthly basis. Satellite dishes are available from many local high street electronic and appliance shops as well as from signal suppliers. To subscribe to channels such as CNN, MTV and Sky, contact Sky (© 0844 241 1268, **www.sky.com**) or Virgin Media (© 0845 840 7777, **www.virginmedia.com**).

### DID YOU KNOW?

Some residential estates offer satellite TV reception via a central dish. Other buildings do not allow satellite dishes at all. Be sure to check before purchasing this service.

### Freeview

A less expensive alternative to pay for digital television services or satellite television is called Freeview. This digital TV service requires that you purchase an electronic Freeview box (usually starting from £20), which you hook up to your television and aerial. There is no contract and no additional fees other than the cost of the Freeview box. Freeview boxes are available at your local electrical retailer.

Freeview digital television includes access to nearly 50 television channels, including all-day children's programming and round-the-clock news as well as several digital radio stations. Other options are Freeview+, which allows you to record digital television, and Freeview HD for high definition digital television viewing. Some newer digital televisions include Freeview and a separate box does not need to be purchased.

For more information, visit **www.freeview.co.uk**.

**5**

UTILITIES

# Electricity & gas

Electricity and gas meters are generally read quarterly and bills are sent following the reading. The bill will include electricity units used and their unit price, plus a quarterly standing charge. Electricity and gas services are not disconnected between renters. Make sure to take a gas and electricity meter reading during the move-in inspection to avoid being liable for chargers incurred prior to move-in. Many gas and electric companies offer a dual fuel plan which provides price reductions and is usually less expensive than separate gas and electricity plans.

Gas is the least expensive method of heating. If you intend to install gas appliances, you should choose a gas fitter who is registered with:

The Council of Registered Gas Installers (CORGI)
1 Elmwood, Chineham Business Park, Crockford Lane,
Basingstoke, Hants, RG24
✆ 0870 401 2200, www.trustcorgi.com
CORGI will provide the names of members in your area.

If you have individual gas and water heaters for bathrooms or the kitchen, you must have them serviced every year and make sure the rooms are well ventilated. A significant number of fatal accidents have occurred because of defective gas heaters.

The electrical supply in London is 240V AC. Each electrical outlet has a switch to turn electricity on and off at the individual outlet. The UK has several types of electrical plugs, the most common of which is a square-shaped, three-pin plug. This plug requires a fuse and has a ground wire (an intentionally grounded wire). The fuse is located inside the plug itself rather than at a central box.

The UK has several types of light bulbs, including a screw in and a pin variety. When purchasing replacement bulbs, you will need to know the type of bulb the lamp requires and it is often useful to bring the old bulb with you as there are a great variety of bulbs.

For more information on electricity, see *Chapter 1: Moving – Electrical appliances.*

## Water

Thames Water supplies water for much of London (✆ 0845 9200 888; **www.thameswater.co.uk**). Many water bills are not based on a consumption rate, but on the value of the property plus a standing charge. Usually, you can improve on your water bill if your home is fitted with a water meter, which Thames Water will fit free of charge. You may not use a sprinkler to water your garden unless you have a water meter.

Water bills are sent semi-annually and include charges for water plus sewage services. You can call Thames Water to change your bills to quarterly or monthly cycles. If you rent your property, the landlord may pay this charge.

In most houses, the only drinkable tap water is from the tap in the kitchen. Water from other taps comes from storage tanks on the premises, rather than from the main line. Water in London is very hard so you will need to use a decalcification liquid to rid appliances such as kettles, irons and washers from the limescale that accumulates with use. For your washing machine, water-softening tablets are available. For your dishwasher, salt is used to soften and prevent the deposit and stain of lime on kitchen utensils.

If your water looks cloudy, discoloured, tastes different or smells funny, contact the Drinking Water Inspectorate (✆ 030 0068 6400, **www.dwi.gov.uk**).

# Recycling & waste

Recycling centres for bottles, cans, clothes and paper products are widespread in London. Several methods of recycling are available to most London residents, including doorstep recycling collection, blue bins (larger recycling bins found throughout London neighbourhoods in designated areas), mini recycling centres and composting.

Most residents receive one or two domestic waste collections each week and one weekly recycling collection. Normal refuse should be put in strong plastic bags and securely tied. There are usually no domestic collections on New Year's Day, Easter, May Day, Christmas and bank holidays. Most local councils also operate a Too Big for the Bin service for items that are too bulky to fit in with your normal refuse. Payment must be made in advance, and usually can be made by credit and debit card, cash, cheques or postal orders. This service tends to be fairly popular, with waiting times of up to four weeks. For specific details on all of the recycling and waste services available in your area, contact your local council (see *Local councils* section above).

# Post Office & Royal Mail

Royal Mail Holdings is a public corporation owned in part, but not managed, by the UK Government. Royal Mail Holdings includes three separate businesses: Post Office, Royal Mail and Parcelforce Worldwide. **Post Office** manages the post office outlets; **Royal Mail** is the branch that handles the delivery of all mail within the UK; and **Parcelforce Worldwide** handles the movement of mail to and from overseas destinations.

## Post Office

The Post Office has a very helpful website at **www.postoffice.co.uk**. Here you can locate your local Post Office branch, track and trace mail posted in the UK, locate a UK address and learn about all of the services provided at your local Post Office.

The Post Office has a nationwide network of about 12,000 offices. Most are open Monday to Friday from 09:00 to 17:30 and on Saturday from 09:00 to 12:30. Neighbourhood Post Office hours vary, some are open later on Saturday. The Post Office near Trafalgar Square at 24/28 William IV Street, WC2; ✆ 020 7484 9307, is open on Saturday from 09:00 to 17:30. Some post offices in the airports are also open on Sundays.

The **Post Office Helpline** is © 0845 722 3344 and is open on weekdays from 08:15 to 18:00, and on Saturdays from 08:30 to 19:00.

The UK postal service provides a wider range of functions than in most other countries, offering over 170 products and services that include the following (note that services may vary from branch to branch):

* *Banking*. Basic banking services are available to customers at most high street branches of the Post Office.

* *Certifying documents*. Photocopies of identity documents certified as being a true likeness of the original.

* *Credit cards, mortgages and personal loans*. Credit cards, mortgages and personal loans, from £2,000 to £25,000, available.

* *Driving licences and car tax*.

* *Home phone and broadband plans*.

* *Insurance*. Car, home, travel and pet insurance available, among others.

* *Pay household bills*. All payments such as phone, digital TV, utilities and council tax can be processed.

* *Pay Self Assessment*. Make your Self Assessment (tax return) payment by cheque, cash or debit card without charge. Be sure to take the Self Assessment payslip with you, or else you will be charged for this service.

* *Postal orders*. Available at all branches of the Post Office. These can be used to pay household bills, pay someone who does not have access to a current (cheque) account, and to send money domestically or internationally.

* *Transferring money overseas*. MoneyGram is a fast and safe way to send and receive money around the world in minutes, although this service can be quite expensive and is best suited for urgent small transfers.

* *Travel services*. Foreign currency exchange and/or pre-order currency service, American Express traveller's cheques, travel insurance and passport validation service.

## Other Post Office services

### Mail Redirection Service

The Post Office enables you to have mail redirected for one, three, six, or 12 months for a variable fee. This service is renewable for up to two years. Mail can be redirected to a permanent or temporary address, either within the UK or abroad. Fill out a redirection form at the post office (or download it from the website) at least a couple of weeks in advance of your move.

### Keepsafe

The Post Office can hold your household's mail safely while you are away for up to two months, and then deliver it on a day that you specify. The Post Office requires at least one week's notice for this service and charges a fee.

### PO Box

As an alternative to receiving mail at home, you can set up a PO Box. You will be required to have a permanent UK home or work address. You can apply for a PO Box and find out about the full terms and conditions of the service by contacting your local Sales Centre on ℂ 0845 795 0950.

### Poste Restante (holding mail)

Mail can be received free of charge via the main Post Office of any town in the UK. The mail will be returned to the sender if you do not collect it within 14 days (one month if sent from abroad). Photo identification is necessary when you collect the mail. This service can be quite useful if you are going to be living at a certain address for a short amount of time. Letters should be addressed as follows:

> **Your Name**
> **Poste Restante**
> **Address of Post Office, including postcode**

Several American Express offices, including the branch at 30-31 Haymarket, SW1, ℂ 020 7484 9610, also provide poste restante services for its customers' letters for up to 30 days. The service is free to American Express cardholders and traveller's cheque holders; all others pay a small fee.

### Royal Mail

Royal Mail collects, sorts and delivers the mail. Royal Mail provides a wide range of services, including signature on delivery, guaranteed next working day delivery, and extra compensation cover for loss, damage or delay. The Royal Mail General Personal Enquiry number is ℂ 0845 774 0740 and their website is **www.royalmail.com**.

### Sending mail

Postage stamps can be bought at the Post Office, grocery stores, newsagents and even some petrol stations. A pre-paid envelope can be recognised by the two thick vertical bars it has on the top right-hand side.

### Sending mail within the UK

Two rates apply for sending letters in the UK up to 100 grams. First Class post will usually arrive the next business day within the UK. Second Class post is used for sending less-urgent items and usually takes about three business days for delivery.

Recorded Signed For post provides additional reassurance by allowing for confirmation of delivery of important (but not valuable) items. You will receive proof of posting, signature on delivery, online confirmation of delivery and up to the value of 100 First Class stamps in compensation. You can track the progress and check if an item has been delivered by visiting **www.royalmail.com**.

Special Delivery is available for next day and by 09:00 the next working day. Special Delivery is recommended for valuable and time-critical items. This service provides the following benefits:

- up-to-date delivery tracking
- a record of time and signature upon delivery (not necessarily the addressee's)
- confirmation of delivery by visiting **www.royalmail.com**
- compensation up to £500 and you can buy additional cover

### Sending mail abroad

Airmail items need a blue airmail sticker (supplied for free by the Post Office), or BY AIRMAIL – PAR AVION written in the top left corner on the front of the item.

The maximum weight for overseas postcards or letters is 2 kg and all post goes by air.

A convenient and economical way to send goods and gifts is via the small packet service. When using this service, write SMALL PACKET in the top left corner on the front of the item. A customs declaration form must also be attached (most EU destinations are exempted). The maximum weight you can send is 2 kg (except for Saudi Arabia, which only accepts small packages of 1 kg or less).

A cost-effective way to send printed papers, such as pamphlets, books, magazines and newspapers, abroad is the printed papers service. When using this service, write PRINTED PAPERS in the top left corner on the front of the item. You can't include personal correspondence. The maximum weight for most places is 2 kg, or 5 kg for books and pamphlets.

International Signed For service allows you to send insured packages and ensure a signature is recorded upon delivery. This service is not available for all countries and the maximum compensation may be lower for some countries. Visit **www.royalmail.com** for more details.

Airsure is Royal Mail's fastest international tracked service. Mail is placed on the next available flight to the required destination. Airsure does not guarantee delivery times as postal standards vary from country to country.

A variety of parcel services are offered depending on how fast you want the package to be delivered. A customs declaration form must be attached to the parcel (EU destinations are exempt). Parcelforce Worldwide provides a worldwide delivery service to over 200 countries. The Parcelforce Worldwide National Enquiry Centre can be contacted on ✆ 0870 850 1150 or visit the website at **www.parcelforce.com**.

**DID YOU KNOW?**

Postal services get a surge in the volume of mail they handle during the holiday period, so post Christmas and holiday packages and cards by the end of November to non-EU destinations to ensure they will arrive in time.

Sending goods into the UK

Care should be taken regarding the shipment of goods into the UK. Customs services may stop incoming shipments and levy VAT charges and import duties on the value of the incoming shipment.

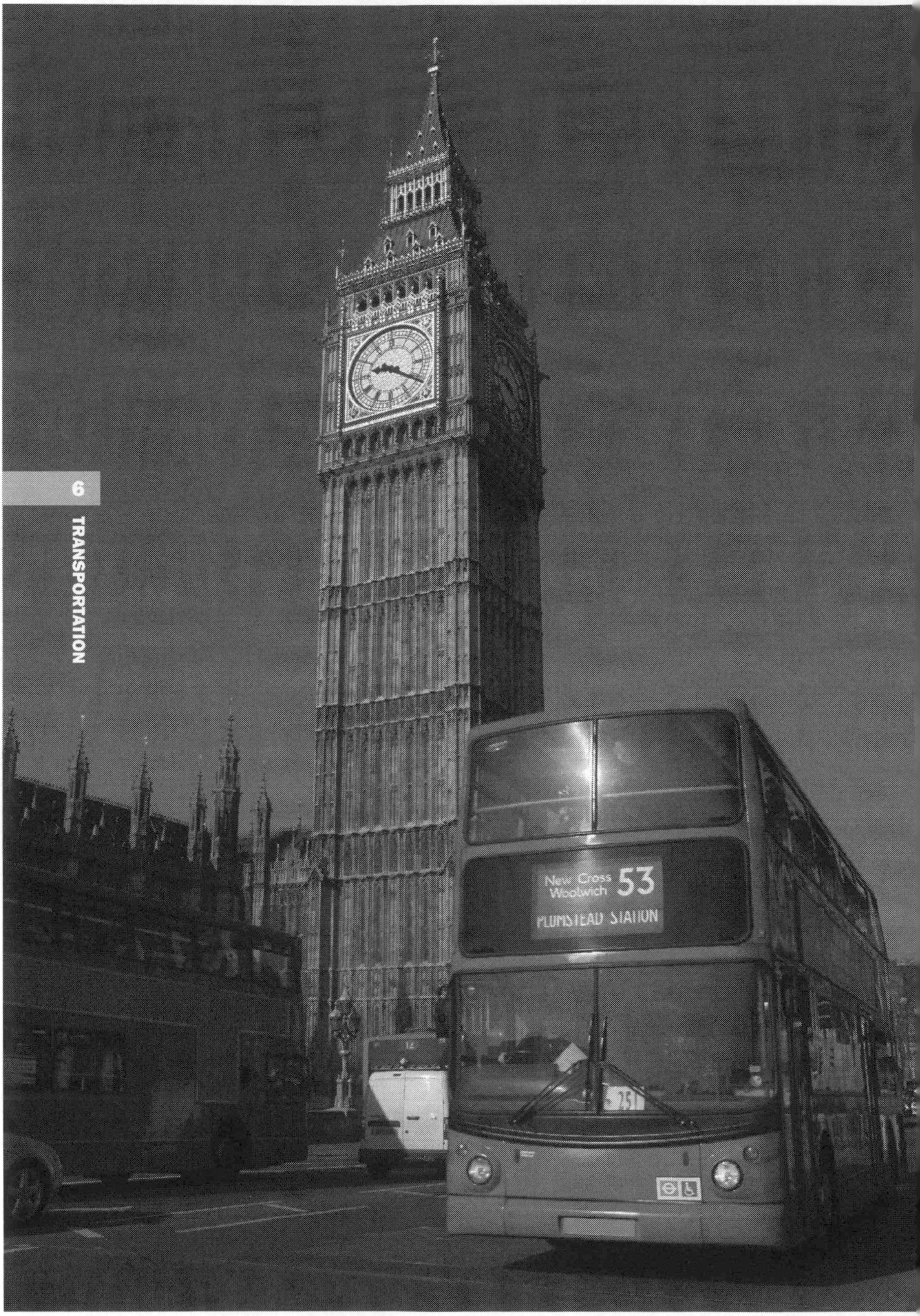
New Cross
Woolwich
53
PLUMSTEAD STATION

# Transportation

There are a myriad of options for getting to London and getting around London. Getting around London is probably easiest and most enjoyable when wandering the streets and taking in the sights, smells and sounds.

For longer journeys, the public transportation system is quite comprehensive and is made easier to manage by Oyster cards and Travelcards (London's electronic ticketing systems). The Underground rail system (**Tube**), trains and bus systems can take you almost anywhere you want to go. The most useful resource for planning a trip by public transportation is the Transport for London (**TfL**) website found at **www.tfl.gov.uk**. The TfL phone number for general enquiries is ✆ 020 7222 1234 (24 hours a day).

Like most major cities, London is often congested with traffic and travel by car, bus and taxi can be quite slow and frustrating at peak times.

Finally, London's five airports are among the busiest in the UK and it is worthwhile knowing your options on how to access them.

## IN THIS CHAPTER...

- Walking
- Cycling
- Oyster cards and Travelcards
- Buses
- Trains
- Riverboats
- Black cabs
- Minicabs
- Driving in the UK
- London airports

# Walking

The best way to get to know London is on foot. Buy a good street guide (such as *London A to Z Street Atlas*, available in any bookshop or newsagent) or look up the address on the Internet (e.g., **www.streetmap.co.uk** or **www.multimap.com**) and off you go! Just remember that cars travel on the left side of the road, so pay attention when crossing to the writing on the street telling you to 'look right' or 'look left', as traffic may not be coming from where you expect it. Also, pedestrians do not have the right of way, except at a zebra crossing (a pedestrian crosswalk), which is clearly marked with black and white stripes painted on the road surface or on poles and a flashing yellow light.

When exploring London, the city offers many guided walking tours. In addition to having a good street map, **www.walklondon.org.uk** details walking routes in London. Another good reference is *City Walks: London: 50 Adventures on Foot* by Craig Taylor, which provides 50 cards detailing places of interest and attractions by neighbourhood.

# Cycling

Cycling is a great way to explore London's many parks and neighbourhoods, visit the Saturday farmers' markets and even commute to work. In the past few years there have been great improvements made to London's cycle network thanks to the efforts put forth by the Mayor of London to create fast, safe and convenient cycle routes throughout the city. By 2026, the Mayor aims to increase cycling by 400 per cent while making two-wheeled transport safer, more attractive and more convenient – so expect to see even more improvements to the cycle network in coming years.

> **DID YOU KNOW?**
>
> Many work places have a shower and locker room facilities available to employees, so check with your employer to see if there is one available at your company.

London is currently rolling out a new cycle hire scheme that will make cycles more widely available to London residents. Barclays Cycle Hire, launched in summer 2010, is a public bicycle sharing scheme for short journeys in and around central London. You can pick up a bicycle, use it as you like, then drop it off, ready for the next person. For additional details and to sign up for a cycle hire membership visit **www.tfl.gov.uk/ barclayscyclehire**.

Transport for London (**TfL**) offers a through guide to cycling which covers everything you need to get around London on a cycle, including purchasing a bicycle, safety, lock security, and travel on the underground or train with your bike. Visit **www.tfl.gov.uk**. You can also order free local cycle maps from TfL which detail the best roads for cycle travel and advise of areas that are highly congested with motor vehicles. Once ordered, TfL will send your map to your address by post, free of charge. These cycle maps are also available at many cycle shops.

Sustrans, a sustainable transport charity, also offers a comprehensive online guide to cycling in London as well as the greater London area at **www.sustrans.org.uk**.

## Oyster cards and Travelcards

Public transportation tickets can be purchased as either a single use ticket or by using an Oyster card, London's travel smartcard. Generally, travel on tubes and buses within London will cost you less if you use an Oyster card. The Oyster card is valid on the Tube, buses, Docklands Light Railway (**DLR**), London Overground and trams. It can be topped up (added to) when your season ticket expires or your pre-pay runs out. If you are making multiple journeys in one day, the Oyster card will cap the price you pay and will be slightly cheaper than a one-day Travelcard or Bus & Tram Pass. Oyster cards can be ordered online at **www.oyster.tfl.gov.uk** and both single use tickets and Oyster cards can be purchased at Underground and National Rail ticket windows and machines or newsagents displaying a red 'Pass Agent' sign. Oyster cards require a small deposit, however, this (as well as any remaining value) is refundable if you return the card at any ticket window (handy for weekend visitors). Make sure you register your Oyster card at the website above to protect it in case your card is lost or stolen.

Various types of tickets and passes can be purchased ranging from single-ride tickets to Travelcards as either a paper ticket or using your Oyster card.

Travelcards are recommended if you want flexibility and unlimited travel to multiple destinations. They can be purchased for one day, three days, one week, one month and any longer period up to a year. Anytime and off-peak options are also available depending on your time of travel. Please note that day Travelcards are only available as paper tickets.

Travelcards are best if you are travelling on the Tube, but are also valid on the bus, tram, DLR, London Overground and National Rail services, and for one-third off riverboat services. If you do not plan to use the Tube, a Bus & Tram Pass or DLR Rail & River Rover may be a preferred pass. Travelcards and passes can be purchased at the ticket and Oyster sales locations noted above. Tickets purchased after 09:30 and before 16:00 weekdays and all day Saturday and Sunday, are considered off-peak and, therefore, are less expensive than peak fares.

The Oyster card is really very smart. It can store your Travelcards, Bus & Tram Passes and Pre-Pay (pay-as-you-go travel), or a combination of all three and will automatically work out when to switch from your Travelcard to pay as you go, for example if you go outside the zones covered by your Travelcard. To ensure you pay the correct fare when using your Oyster card, on the Tube and DLR, you must touch the yellow reader at the start and end of each journey. (On the buses and trams, you only need to touch in at the start of the journey.) Note that Oyster pay-as-you-go is valid on most National Rail routes within greater London (please verify before travelling).

## DID YOU KNOW?

You can plan your journey online before you head out the door. If you want to plan a journey online, to include the Tube, buses, tramlink, DLR or riverboat services, visit www.tfl.gov.uk or www.tubejp.co.uk. These useful sites include both a journey planner and real-time travel updates.

### Underground rail (Tube)

London's Underground rail network consists of 12 Tube lines, along with the DLR. Free paper maps are available at all London Transport ticket offices and the majority of the routes are clearly colour coded.

In order to purchase Tube ticket, go to the ticket window in Underground stations and ask for a ticket to your destination or use the self-service ticket machines that exist in most stations. Newer machines accept cash, debit and credit cards; older machines require coins, rather than notes, and occasionally exact change is required. Tickets must be put through the scanner at the barrier at both the beginning and end of your journey, so remember to keep your ticket in order to exit at your destination. If you are travelling with children, be sure to hang on to their tickets as well. If you are using an Oyster card, the card must touch the yellow reader at the start and end of each journey.

Fares are based on the distance travelled. London is divided into six concentric bands called travel zones for Tube fares. Zones 1 and 2 are considered central London while Zone 6 is the outer edges of London. The more zones you cross, the higher the fare. Free and discounted Tube travel is available for children under 18 and discounted travel is also available to students over 18. In some cases, a free Oyster photocard may be required to receive the discount. Free or discounted travel may be available to adults who are older or have a registered disability (Freedom Pass), unemployed (New Deal), veterans, or on income support.

The Tube operates from approximately 05:00 until midnight, Monday to Saturday, with reduced schedules on Sunday and public holidays. Rush hours (for peak fares) are from 05:00 and before 09:30 Monday to Friday (excluding public holidays). Smoking and drinking alcohol are not permitted on the Underground trains or in the stations. Dogs are allowed to travel on the Underground and bicycles are allowed on most lines. For restrictions to bicycles on the tube, visit **www.tfl.gov.uk**.

Often stations close due to construction/engineer works so it is wise to check before you begin your journey, especially at weekends. If you forget to check for closings before you depart, look for the white boards at the station's entrance. These boards should list current service disruptions, however, you can also ask any station workers (at the ticket window or in the station wearing an orange vest) or press the green button on the round information box if more information is needed.

## Buses

Buses are less expensive than the Underground. Most buses run from approximately 06:00 to midnight with different timetables on Sunday and public holidays. Several night bus routes operate after midnight until 06:00 to cover the period between when the Tube closes and the start of the daytime bus services. Trafalgar Square is the hub for most night bus routes.

Most bus stops have placards indicating which bus routes stop there. Some stops are 'request stops', which are marked with red signs. At a request stop, you must signal the driver from the road to stop the bus by holding out your hand. If boarding a bus at a central London bus stop, a bus ticket must be purchased before boarding or an Oyster card must be used. There are red ticket machines that are located at most central London bus stops and require exact change. If you are outside of central London, on most buses you pay the driver as you enter. Bus drivers and fare collectors may not be able to make change for large bills so carry small change whenever possible. Pay the fare to the driver and he or she will hand you a ticket. If you are using an Oyster card, press one side of the card to the electronic scanner next to the driver. Make sure you always keep your ticket during your ride, as inspectors occasionally conduct checks. You cannot transfer from one bus to another without paying an additional full fare unless you have an all-day ticket, however, if using an Oyster you will never exceed the daily maximum bus fare no matter how many buses you ride.

As with the Tube, free and discounted bus travel is available for children under 18 and discounted travel is also available to students over 18. In some cases, a free Oyster photocard may be required to receive the discount. Adults may be eligible for free or discounted travel based on senior age or registered disability.

Victoria Coach Station, London's main coach station, is located at 164 Buckingham Palace Road, SW1W. The station supports all forms of coach activities, including scheduled express and commuter services, coach holidays and private hire. It is the base for many coach operators and is equipped with services including a travel counter and luggage storage facilities.

The following are a few of the major coach operators:

National Express Coaches
✆ 0871 781 8181, www.nationalexpress.com/coach
and Eurolines
www.eurolines.co.uk
These companies link London with other cities in the United Kingdom, Ireland and Continental Europe.

Green Line

© 0844 801 7261, www.greenline.co.uk

Coaches serve communities within a 40-mile radius of central London. The company also runs coaches to Luton Airport. There are stops within London, indicated by green bus stop signs.

Oxford Espress

© 0186 578 5400, www.oxfordbus.co.uk

and Oxford Tube

© 0186 577 2250, www.oxfordtube.com

24-hour bus services between London and Oxford with several pick-up and drop-off points en route.

---

**DID YOU KNOW?**

If you have lost something on the buses, Tube, trains, trams, black cabs, or in Victoria Coach Station, make sure you fill out a TfL Lost Property Enquiry Form at **www.tfl.gov.uk/lpo**. Lost property may be held locally at the station for a few days before being sent on to TfL's Lost Property Office, typically arriving between two and seven days after it was lost. You can also use the TfL lost property form to find out if your property has been found. Lost property enquiries are searched for a period of 21 days from the submitted date of loss. All enquiries will be responded to whether or not they have been successful. If you have questions, call © 0845 330 9882.

# Trains

Modern, high-speed trains (mainline service) link the major cities in the UK. There are also commuter lines (local service) between towns and outlying areas. Tickets can be purchased at any train station, online or by phone and at most travel agencies. There are various ticket schemes: Anytime fares are flexible tickets with no time restrictions on when you can travel; Off-peak fares are cheaper tickets for travelling on trains during off-peak hours on specified dates; and Advance fares are single (one-way) tickets that offer great value, but require reservations and are subject to availability. Several discount Railcards (i.e., 16-25, Family & Friends, Network, Senior, Disabled and HM Forces) are sold for an annual fee where holders get one-third off all standard class tickets, subject to certain restrictions. You should ask about the most economical way to get to your destination before purchasing a ticket. If your journey involves both National Rail and Tube or DLR services, you can pay a Through fare that is valid for the entire trip. When you buy your ticket, you will need to give your final destination and say that you plan to travel using a combination of services. Hold on to your ticket throughout your journey. If you have a Travelcard, it may be valid for train journeys that are within the zones covered by your Travelcard (ask a ticket agent).

For more information, the 24-hour telephone number for all national train times and fares is ℂ 0845 748 4950 or visit **www.nationalrail.co.uk**.

Trains for various destinations in the UK depart from the following London stations:

| The North & Central Britain, Scotland & Paris: | Euston<br>King's Cross<br>St. Pancras International |
|---|---|
| The South & Southeast: | Charing Cross<br>London Bridge<br>Victoria<br>Waterloo |
| The West Country, Wales & South Midlands: | Paddington<br>Waterloo<br>Marylebone |
| The East, East Anglia & Essex: | Liverpool Street<br>Victoria<br>Fenchurch Street |

**Eurostar**

The Eurostar high-speed train conveniently connects London to France and Belgium, offering great potential to continue travelling through Europe by train. All Eurostar trains depart from St. Pancras International station and travel seven days a week. The website **www.seat61.com** is worth consulting for local train operators, routes, best ways to book and tips on cheap fares. Note that similar to airfare, prices increase significantly when purchased closer to the date of travel – so if possible book in advance.

### Express trains to London airports

The fastest way to get to most of London's airports is by express train and these are listed below. See *London airports* below for more detailed information regarding transportation to London airports.

| | |
|---|---|
| Gatwick Express | Victoria, Blackfriars, Moorgate, Farringdon and London Bridge stations |
| Heathrow Express | Paddington station |
| Stansted Express | Liverpool Street station |

Note: its also quite easy and very inexpensive to take the underground directly to Heathrow on the Piccadilly Line.

# Riverboats

London's river services provide reliable transportation for both commuter and leisure journeys along the Thames River. Commuter services are available from Woolwich Arsenal Pier in the east to Embankment Pier in the west, as well as Blackfriars Pier in the City to Putney Pier in the west. Many operators offer one-third off the normal advertised adult and child fares with a valid Travelcard or Oyster card, loaded with a valid Travelcard, subject to certain restrictions. Oyster cards with pay-as-you-go are not accepted.

There are two primary riverboat operators that offer commuter services:

Thames Clippers (✆ 08707 815 049, **www.thamesclippers.com**) has a fleet of hi-speed catamarans that leave the major piers every 20 minutes, starting at approximately 06:00 and ending around 01:00 the following day. Its commuter service runs from Woolwich (east) to Millbank (west) with stops at the following piers (from east to west): Woolwich, QEII, Greenwich, Masthouse, Greenland, Canary Wharf, Tower, London Bridge, Bankside, Blackfriars, Embankment, Waterloo and Millbank. Thames Clippers also offers the O2 Express, a limited stop service from Waterloo London Eye Pier to the QEII Pier that departs every 30 minutes from Waterloo Pier, 3 hours prior to an arena event start time at The O2. After the event, the first departure from QEII Pier is 15 minutes after the event finishes.

Thames Executive Charters (℡ 01342 820 600, **www.thamesexecutive charters.com** or **www.thamesrivertaxi.com**) specialises in Thames river cruises, boat parties and special events on the River Thames. The company operates weekday commuter river taxis between Putney (west) and Blackfriars (east) with stops at the following piers (from west to east): Putney, Wandsworth, Chelsea Harbour, Cadogan Pier, Embankment and Blackfriars. These river taxis only operate during peak hours, approximately 06:30 to 10:00 in the morning and 16:45 to 20:00 in the evening.

## Black cabs

The familiar black London taxi (now often painted in other colours yet still commonly referred to as the black cab) is the most expensive but often the most convenient and reliable form of transportation. All licensed London taxi drivers need to pass a special test (the Knowledge), which usually takes between two and four years, before they can drive a black cab.

Taxis are strictly controlled by law and all areas within London are regulated by meters. The meter calculates the maximum fare based on time of day, distance travelled and taxi speed. Some taxis can now accept credit or debit cards, however there is typically a surcharge of 10 to 15 per cent on the metered fare. During periods of fare increases and before meters are adjusted, your fare may be higher than the meter indicates but the new fares will be explained and posted inside the cab. It is customary to tip by rounding up the charge (e.g., pay £6 for a £5.50 fare) or by giving approximately 10 per cent. Taxis are limited by law to carrying five adults. You can hail a taxi that has a lit 'for hire' sign on its roof, queue (line up) at an appointed taxi stand or ring one of the taxi companies directly.

## Minicabs

London also has minicabs, taxis that can be both licensed and unlicensed. Minicabs cannot be hailed in the street and must be booked ahead of time. Any minicab journey that isn't booked by phone or in a minicab office is illegal and risky. If a minicab stops you in the street and offers you a ride, you should always refuse the offer.

Booking your minicab guarantees that your trip will be carried out by a licensed driver in a licensed vehicle. It is important to verify or even negotiate a minicab price when you book and it is helpful to have a good idea of where you are going, as minicab drivers (unlike black cab drivers) are not required to know London streets and directions.

If you use a reputable minicab company, and become comfortable with them, not only will they offer a courier service (pick-up and delivery of goods, packages and food), but they will also take your children to and from school and home or wherever necessary. Personal and corporate accounts can be set up.

One of the most popular, reputable and trustworthy minicab services is Addison Lee, which can be booked by phone or online (✆ 020 7387 8888, **www.addisonlee.com**). For more minicab recommendations, see *Chapter 11: Services – Taxis and minicabs*.

> **DID YOU KNOW?**
>
> Text CAB to 60TFL (60835) to get the numbers of one taxi and two licensed minicab firms, in the area from which you are texting. You can also contact TfL's 24-hour travel information centre on ✆ 020 7222 1234 to get phone numbers for licensed operators.

# Driving in the UK

Owning a car is not essential in central London because of the comprehensive public transportation. If you prefer the convenience of a car, you can buy, lease or rent a vehicle easily. It is strongly recommended that you purchase and read *The Highway Code*, the official road user guide for Great Britain (available in most bookshops or online, which outlines the British driving regulations before beginning to drive in Britain. The differences do not end with driving on the left-hand side of the road!

> **DID YOU KNOW?**
>
> Even London taxi drivers and natives keep good maps of London in their automobiles. Some of the most useful are *London A to Z Street Atlas*, *Nicholson's London Street Guide*, *Geographer's* and *One Way London*. You can also plan your route in advance on line at **www.mapquest.co.uk** or **www.streetmap.co.uk**.

## Congestion charge

As in any other major city, traffic and congestion are problems in London. In an effort to reduce congestion and encourage the use of other modes of transport in London, certain vehicles must pay a congestion charge when driving within central London between 07:00 and 18:00, Monday to Friday. The Congestion Zone is clearly marked with traffic signs, including a large letter 'C' in a red circle, and there are cameras monitoring every entrance and exit. It covers the following areas: Bayswater, Notting Hill, North and South Kensington, Knightsbridge, Chelsea, Brompton, Belgravia, Pimlico, Victoria, St. James's, Waterloo, Borough, City of London, Clerkenwell, Holborn, Finsbury, Bloomsbury, Soho, Mayfair and parts of Marylebone.

You can pay the congestion charge either in advance or on the day of travel before, during or after the journey. The charge is £8 if you pay by midnight on the day of travel. The charge increases to £10 if you pay the charge by midnight of the day after you have travelled into the Congestions Zone. If you forget to pay by midnight on the following charging day, a notice will be issued to the vehicle registrant and you will be subject to a penalty charge of £60. The Congestion Charge does not apply on weekends, bank holidays, or the three working days between Christmas and New Year. Residents who live within the congestion zone receive a discount on the charge. Certain vehicles (e.g., alternative fuel and electrically propelled vehicles) are exempt from the congestion charge.

The Congestion Charge can be paid online, by email, text message, or phone, by post or at newsagents, petrol stations and any other shop displaying the 'C' sign. For more detailed and up-to-date information regarding the congestion charge, exemptions and to pay online visit **www.cclondon.com**.

## Driving licences

It is important to obtain a proper driving licence, because driving without one is illegal and will affect your insurance. For more information, contact the Driver and Vehicle Licensing Agency (**DVLA**), part of the Department of Transport, on ✆ 0300 790 6801 or **www.dvla.gov.uk**.

Generally, if you hold a valid driving licence or International Driving Permit (and are not barred from driving in the UK) you may drive vehicles covered by your licence in the UK for up to 12 months. If you are in the UK as a visitor, the 12 months begins on the date that you last entered Great Britain. If you are a new resident, the 12 months begins on the date you took up residence in the UK.

If you hold a valid driving licence from an EC/EEA country you can drive in Great Britain until you are 70 or for three years after becoming resident, whichever is the longer period. If that driving licence has been previously exchanged from a non-EC/EEA country, at the end of the 12 months after becoming a resident, you will need to exchange your licence for a British one. If you hold a valid driving licence from Gibraltar, Australia, Barbados, British Virgin Islands, Canada, Falkland Islands, Faroe Islands, Hong Kong, Japan, Monaco, New Zealand, Republic of Korea, Singapore, South Africa, Switzerland or Zimbabwe, you can drive in the UK for up to 12 months from the time you first became a resident. At the end of the 12 months, you can exchange your licence for a British one, subject to certain conditions. If you hold a valid driving licence from any other country, you can drive in the UK for up to 12 months from the time you first became resident. At the end of the 12 months you will not be able to exchange your licence for a UK licence and will need to get a UK provisional driving licence and sit a theory and practical driving test if you wish to continue driving in Great Britain.

To obtain a provisional licence (similar to a learner's permit in the US) or exchange your licence, providing you meet the requirements, you will need to submit a driving licence application either online at **www.direct.gov.uk/drivinglicence** or via the post. The application form is available at many Post Office branches. You should allow at least three weeks for the licence to be issued.

To schedule your theory and practical driving tests either call DVLA Customer Service Centre on ℂ 03002 001 122, Monday to Friday, or book the appointments online at **www.direct.gov.uk/drivingtest**. There are often delays in scheduling a test appointment. If you wish to expedite the application process, you might state that you are willing to take the test at any time and at any location.

If you need to sit for a theory and practical driving test, make sure you prepare for the exams. *The Driving Test*, published by the Department of Transport, is a useful tool. It lists available driving instructors and test centres, and breaks down the driving test components. The driving test begins with a written theory test, which consists of multiple-choice questions and a hazard perception skills test. To help prepare, *The Highway Code* and *The Official DSA Complete Theory Test for Cars and Motorcycles* can be purchased at most bookstores or online. Free practice exams can be accessed at **www.theory-tests.co.uk**. In addition to the written theory test, there is an eye exam, some vehicle safety questions and a 40-minute practical driving test.

There are many firms offering driving lessons. Motoring schools can advise you on the requirements, handle applications and instruct you in techniques required to pass the British driving test. The best-known school is BSM (the British School of Motoring), which can be reached on ✆ 0845 727 6276 or at **www.bsm.co.uk**. Another service is International Drivers Service, which can be reached on ✆ 020 8570 9190 or at **www.international driversservice.com**.

If you wish, your driving school instructor can accompany you to the test and acquaint you with the test route. It is important to remember that if you take the test while driving a car with an automatic transmission, your licence will be restricted to automatic transmissions. However, if you take the test on a vehicle with a manual transmission, your licence will be valid for vehicles with automatic and manual transmissions. There is no limit to the number of times that these tests can be taken.

### Insurance

In the UK the driver needs to be insured to use a specified vehicle rather than the vehicle being insured for use by specified persons. Third-party insurance is compulsory and it is advisable to have comprehensive insurance as well. No claims reductions and other options are available. You might bring a letter from your previous insurance agency stating that you are entitled to no claims insurance for the past five years. It is recommended that you contact several insurance companies regarding types of coverage and cost. You should also have a clear understanding with your insurance company regarding claims and the kind of licence you possess.

### Purchasing a car

Purchasing a car in Britain is expensive but there is a good market for second-hand cars. The London evening papers, Sunday papers, specialised car magazines (*The Auto Trader*, or *Loot* and *The American*) are all good sources. Auto Trader also has an easy to use website at **www.autotrader.co.uk**. There is also a monthly magazine called the *Motorist's Guide to New and Used Car Prices* and several large resale lots in London (e.g., **www.cargiant.co.uk**). Both the Automobile Association and the Royal Automobile Club will thoroughly inspect and value second-hand cars for their members for a fee. See *Automobile associations* below.

A compulsory Road Tax must be paid each year for each car. Upon paying your Road Tax, you will receive a round sticker (tax disc) to display inside your windscreen. If you are buying a car through a dealer, they will generally take care of this detail as part of the sales procedure but it is up to you to renew it for subsequent years. If you have brought a car with you to the UK, registration forms are available at your local Post Office. Annual renewal forms will be sent to you automatically.

If your car is more than three years old, you must have a Ministry of Transport (**MOT**) test each year to prove its roadworthiness. Garages licensed by the Ministry of Transport to conduct this test can perform the test within 24 hours or while you wait. There is a fee for this service. You must present your MOT certificate along with proof of insurance when paying your Road Tax.

## Leasing, renting and sharing cars

Leasing cars is a common practice in the UK and dealers can supply details of the various lengths of time and conditions. Car hire firms provide the usual services. Cars with manual transmission are most common and less expensive than those with automatic transmissions.

Car rental companies are listed in the Yellow Pages of the phone directory under *Car Rental* or *Car Hire – Self Drive*. Hertz, Avis, Budget, Enterprise, Europcar, Kenning and Thrifty are well-known rental agencies.

Car sharing is another option that enables you to hire a car by the hour (or longer stretches) with pickups available all over most London neighbourhoods. These self-service car hire companies require you to become a member by paying an annual fee. You can then reserve a car online, via phone or iPhone app and for pick up at one of the many convenient locations all over London. In addition to use of the car, rates generally cover petrol, insurance and congestion charge. Available cars vary in size from a Smart car to family size. For more details see **www.zipcar.co.uk** or **www.streetcar.co.uk**. Note: At the time of printing, Zipcar UK recently acquired Streetcar. Existing members can still reserve cars through the separate company sites however to register for a new Zipcar membership you will now get redirected to the Streetcar site. It is unclear at this time whether future combined operations will operate under the Zipcar or Streetcar name.

## DID YOU KNOW?

If you are a member of Zipcar in the United States or Canada, your membership can be used to hire cars here in the UK. Similarly, you have a UK membership and travel to the US or Canada the same reciprocity applies.

## Automobile associations

You may consider becoming a member of the Automobile Association (**AA**) or the Royal Automobile Club (**RAC**). These organisations offer emergency services, breakdown insurance for trips to the Continent and can even provide legal service in court.

### The Automobile Association

✆ 0870 600 0371, www.theaa.com

For car problems, call the Automobile Association 24-hour Emergency Breakdown line on ✆ 0800 887 766.

### The Royal Automobile Club Motoring Services

✆ 0800 051 4868, www.rac.co.uk

For car problems, call the Royal Automobile Club's 24-hour Emergency Breakdown line on ✆ 0844 891 3111.

For national traffic information and live motorway traffic updates, call the traffic line on ✆ 0906 470 1740.

## DID YOU KNOW?

If you are a member of AAA in the United States or Canada, your membership can be transferred to the AA and the RAC here in the UK.

## Parking

Parking is limited to car parks (parking lots) or meters for non-residents in certain areas, and street parking in these restricted areas is only possible for residents with permits (resident's parking). In many areas of London, you are entitled to purchase a Resident's Parking Permit (check with your council for eligibility). Traffic wardens regularly patrol residents' areas and fines are given if you are in a restricted area without the proper parking permit. Resident parking regulations vary from area to area so it is imperative to read signs thoroughly.

If you are not fortunate enough to locate a parking meter on the street, you may opt for a car park. Blue signs with a white 'P' direct you to public parking in unfamiliar surroundings. Some central public parking garages are:

NCP (National Car Parks)
✆ 0845 050 7080, www.ncp.co.uk
Multiple locations around London.

Westminster City Council Car Parks
✆ 0800 243 348, www.westminster.gov.uk/carparks
Multiple locations around London.

### Clamping

Parking violations may result in fines, towing or clamping (where a triangular metal trap is fitted over one car wheel preventing the car from moving), all of which involve considerable expense and inconvenience. In the unfortunate case of getting clamped, you can call your local council to get it removed. Vehicles may also be clamped or removed as a result of TfL's congestion charging scheme. Visit **www.tfl.gov.uk** or call ✆ 0845 900 1234 for details. Drivers unsure of whether a vehicle has been clamped and towed may call the TfL TRACE line on ✆ 020 7747 4747. TfL hold details all of vehicles removed within the London area.

# London airports

There are five airports conveniently located to London: Heathrow, Gatwick, Stansted, London City, and Luton. The British Airport Authority (**BAA**) operates the two of the largest airports (Heathrow and Stansted) and has a very informative website at **www.baa.com** for real-time arrivals and departures information, directions, methods of public transport available and more.

Below is information regarding the five London airports and the types of travel available to and from each of them. Please note that prices of travel are as at the time of printing and may have changed.

**Heathrow (LHR)**

The Compass Centre, Nelson Road, Hounslow, TW6

℗ 0870 000 0123, www.heathrowairport.com

Heathrow, located 20 miles (32 km) to the west of London, is one of the busiest international airports in the world. It is also very large with five terminals. Terminals 4 and 5 are a considerable distance by road from the others and extra time should be allowed to reach them, or to transfer between terminals. Check your departure terminal before you begin your journey to Heathrow by checking the website above, calling ℗ 0800 183 9474 or texting your flight number to 64222.

Train

The Heathrow Express (**www.heathrowexpress.com**) is the fastest way to reach the airport from central London. The journey takes 15 minutes from Paddington Station to Terminals 1, 2 and 3, 30 minutes to Terminal 4, and 20 minutes to Terminal 5. Trains run every 15 minutes between 05:00 and midnight. A one-way fare is £16.50 (£32 return) if bought on-line, £18 if bought at the station. A return ticket is £32 on-line and at the station. Tickets are available on board the train at a premium. If you own a Rail Card or International Student Identity Card, please check at the station because discounted tickets may be available. If you have heavy luggage, be warned that there may be a long walk after arriving at the airport to reach the terminal. Passengers for Terminal 4 should change at Terminals 1, 2, 3 for a free and frequent transfer service to Terminal 4.

The Heathrow Connect (℗ 0845 678 6975, **www.heathrowconnect. com**) provides local service to London Paddington station. The journey takes 25 minutes from Paddington Station to Terminals 1, 2, 3 and 33 minutes to Terminal 4. Trains run every 30 minutes, calling at Ealing Broadway, West Ealing, Hanwell, Southall, Hayes & Harlington, between 04:30 and midnight. A one-way ticket costs £7.90. If you own a Rail Card, please check at the station because discounted tickets may be available. Passengers for Terminal 5 should change at Terminals 1, 2, 3 for a free and frequent transfer service (Heathrow Express) to Terminal 5.

At Paddington Station near Platform 12, there is a secure place where you can leave luggage for collection later. For more information, call ℗ 020 7262 0344 or visit **www.excess-baggage.com**.

## Tube

The Piccadilly Line connects central London and Heathrow's three tube stations (one station for Terminals 1, 2 and 3, one for Terminal 4 and one for Terminal 5). Trains run every ten minutes, from 05:00 to midnight, and the journey time is roughly one hour from central London. The Heathrow stations are located in Zone 6. Prices depend on zones travelled, time of day and if an Oyster card is used.

## Bus

National Express Coaches offer service to Heathrow from various pick-up points throughout London starting from Victoria Coach Station. Journey time takes between 40 minutes to 1 hour and 30 minutes depending on the route, with the estimated single fare of £5. If you own a Coachcard, please check at the station because discounted tickets may be available. Passengers travelling to Terminal 4 will need to transfer at the Central Bus Station to a free Heathrow Connect train. Visit **www.nationalexpress.com/coach** or telephone © 0871 781 8181 for details.

Between midnight and 05:30, the N9 night bus runs from Heathrow Airport to central London (Aldwych) every 30 minutes. The journey time is approximately 65 minutes. For more information visit the TfL website at **www.tfl.gov.uk**.

## Taxi

In central London a black cab will always take passengers to Heathrow. The fare will vary on traffic and time of day but is generally £40 to £70 from central London. The average journey time is 45 minutes to one hour depending on traffic. Only some black cabs will accept pre-booked trips for a set fare whereas most mini-cab companies offer fares to Heathrow for a set price. See *Chapter 11: Services – Taxis and minicabs* for recommendations.

## Parking

The airport is located almost at the intersection of the M4 and M25 Motorways. Pre-book your airport parking directly on the Heathrow Airport website. With the Meet & Greet Valet service, a representative can collect your vehicle from you at the terminal, and have it waiting for you upon your return. For an additional fee, they will wash, wax and service your car while you are away. For other parking options, visit **www.airport-parking-shop.co.uk**.

6

TRANSPORTATION

## Gatwick (LGW)

Crawley, West Sussex, RH6

© 0844 335 1802, www.gatwickairport.com

Gatwick, 28 miles (45 km) to the south of London, is the second largest airport in the UK. Although it is farther from central London than Heathrow, many consider travelling from Gatwick to be a more pleasant experience.

There are two terminals at Gatwick: the north terminal, mainly dedicated to British Airways scheduled flights, and the south terminal, from which most other scheduled services and all holiday charter flights depart. The two terminals are linked by a monorail service that leaves every three to six minutes and has a journey time of approximately two minutes. Check your departure terminal before you begin your journey to Gatwick by checking the website above.

### Train

The fastest and best value way to reach Gatwick is via the Gatwick Express, a non-stop service to and from Victoria Station and Gatwick South Terminal. Trains leave every 15 minutes between approximately 03:30 and midnight. Journey time is 30 to 35 minutes and the one-way fare is £16.90 (£28.70 return). Booking in advance is not necessary; you can purchase your ticket on the train at no extra cost. If you own a Rail Card or International Student Identity Card, please check at the station because discounted tickets may be available. Visit **www.gatwickexpress.com** or call © 0845 850 1530 for the latest schedules and further information.

There are a few other rail services that call at Gatwick Airport. First Capital Connect trains run every 15 minutes to Brighton (via Mid Sussex) and to Bedford via East Croydon, London Bridge, St Pancras International and Luton. Southern northbound trains run to London Victoria via East Croydon and Clapham Junction, and to London Bridge via East Croydon. Southern southbound services run to Brighton, Eastbourne, Portsmouth and Southampton. You should buy these tickets before boarding the train. For more details, visit **www.firstcapitalconnect.co.uk** or call © 0845 748 4950 or visit the National Rail website at **www.nationalrail.co.uk**.

### Bus

National Express Coaches offer service to Gatwick from various pick-up points throughout London, starting from Victoria Coach Station. Journey time takes between 90 minutes to 1 hour and 45 minutes depending on route, with the estimated single fare of £7.50. If you own a Coachcard, please check at the station because discounted tickets may be available. Visit **www.nationalexpress.com/coach** or call © 0871 781 8181 for details.

EasyBus offers low-cost, non-stop service between Fulham Broadway Tube station and Gatwick Airport North Terminal. The journey time is 1 hour and 10 minutes and bus services run every 20 minutes from 06:00 to midnight. Fares start at £2 one-way online and are based on demand. You can also buy tickets at non-internet prices from the easyBus driver on the day at the London departure points or from the easyBus ticket sales desks located in airport arrivals after baggage re-claim, subject to availability. Visit **www.easybus.co.uk** for details.

Local bus services also run direct to and from both Gatwick terminals into Crawley, Horley and Redhill, as well as other local destinations. Visit **www.gatwickairport.com** for details.

### Taxi

The black cab fare to Gatwick is roughly £70 to £80 from central London and takes about 65 to 90 minutes depending on traffic. Checker Cars (© 01293 567 700, **www.checkercars.com**) has booking offices in the North Terminal arrivals area and in the South Terminal entrance building. They charge approximately £77 one-way (plus £8 congestion charge if your destination is within the charging zone). Most minicab companies also offer fares to Gatwick for a set fare that should run you much less than the prices above. See *Chapter 11: Services – Taxis and minicabs* for further recommendations.

### Parking Services

Gatwick is directly linked to the M23 at Junction 9 and to the A23 London-Brighton Road. Just a ten minute drive away, the M25 further connects with the UK's extensive road and motorway network. Pre-book your airport parking directly on the Gatwick Airport website. For other parking options visit **www.airport-parking-shop.co.uk**.

## Stansted (STN)

Enterprise House, Stansted, Essex, CM24

© 0870 000 0303, www.stanstedairport.com

Stansted is a very modern airport, 40 miles (64 km) northeast of London, and is the third busiest airport in the UK. Several low-cost airlines, including Ryanair, have made Stansted their hub.

### Train

Stansted Express (© 0845 850 0150, **www.stanstedexpress.com**) is a fast and convenient way to reach the airport from Liverpool Street Station, with trains departing every 15 or 30 minutes from approximately 03:30 to midnight, with an average journey time of approximately 45 minutes. The one-way fare is £19 (£28.70 return) and slightly cheaper if travel is booked online. If you own a Rail Card or International Student Identity Card, please check at the station because discounted tickets may be available.

### Bus

Stansted Airport's coach station is opposite the main terminal entrance. National Express Coaches offer service to Stansted from various pick-up points throughout London starting from Victoria Coach Station. Journey time takes between 85 minutes to 1 hour and 40 minutes depending on the route, with the estimated single fare of £10. If you own a Coachcard, please check at the station because discounted tickets may be available. Visit **www.nationalexpress.com/coach** or telephone © 0871 781 8181 for details.

EasyBus offers low cost non-stop service between London Victoria station (with a popular pick-up and drop off point at Baker Street Underground) and Stansted Airport. The journey time is 1 hour and 30 minutes and bus services run every 20 to 30 minutes from approximately 03:00 to 22:00. Fares start at £2 one-way online and are based on demand. You can also buy tickets at non-internet prices from the easyBus driver on the day at the London departure points or from the easyBus ticket sales desks located in airport arrivals after baggage reclaim, subject to availability. Visit **www.easybus.co.uk** for details.

### Taxi

Stansted airport is conveniently situated just off the M11 motorway and Junction 8. The train is the fastest and most reliable route to Stansted. Checker Cars (© 01279 661 111, **www.checkercars.com**) has booking offices on the international arrivals concourse and a courtesy telephone in the UK and Ireland baggage reclaim hall. They charge approximately £99 one-way. Most minicab companies also offer set fares to Stansted that should run you less than the prices above. See *Chapter 11: Services – Taxis and minicabs* for further recommendations.

## London City (LCY)

City Aviation House, Royal Docks, E16
✆ 020 7646 0088, www.londoncityairport.com

London City Airport is situated just 6 miles (9.5 km) east of central London and 3 miles (4.8 km) from Canary Wharf. The airport handles short-haul flights with a strong emphasis on business travel.

### Tube and DLR combined

The recommended route for the London City airport is to take the Tube and connect with the Docklands Light Railway (**DLR**). The DLR connects London City Airport to the City (Bank) and Canary Wharf. Trains leave every 10 to 15 minutes and the journey time is about 7 minutes from Canning Town and 22 minutes from Bank station. The London City airport is located in Zone 3. Prices depend on zones travelled, time of day and if an Oyster card is used. Visit the airport or TfL website at **www.tfl.gov.uk** for more details.

### Bus and parking services

Local buses (numbers 473 and 474) will also take you to the airport, as well as black cabs. If you choose to drive, there is a choice of short-term and long-term car parks, which are conveniently located adjacent to the terminal. Refer to the airport website for more details.

## Luton (LTN)

Navigation House, Airport Way, Luton, Bedfordshire, LU2
✆ 0158 240 5100, www.london-luton.co.uk

London Luton Airport is about 32 miles (51km) northwest of central London and is one of the UK's fastest growing airports.

### Train

An airport shuttle bus service connects Luton Airport and Luton Airport Parkway train station. This service runs every 10 minutes from 05:00 and midnight and the journey time is approximately 5 minutes.

Regular rail services to St. Pancras International station take approximately 20 minutes with East Midlands Trains and 25 minutes with First Capital Connect. Rail passengers will be able to purchase through tickets to London Luton Airport. For more details, visit **www.firstcapitalconnect.co.uk** or call © 0845 748 4950 or visit the National Rail website at **www.national rail.co.uk**.

## Bus

National Express Coaches offer service to Luton from various pick-up points throughout London. Visit **www.nationalexpress.com/coach** or call © 0871 781 8181 for more details.

Green Line 757 provides an express coach link between Luton and several locations in central London, starting from Victoria Coach Station. This coach service runs 24 hours a day every 15 to 20 minutes during the day and every 30 minutes in the evening, with a journey time of 1 hour and 15 minutes. For more information call © 0844 801 7261 or visit **www.greenline.co.uk**.

EasyBus, in partnership with Greenline Service, offers low cost 24-hour service between London Victoria station (with popular pick-up and drop off points at Brent Cross, Finchley Road, Baker Street and Marble Arch) and Luton Airport. The journey time is 1 hour and 20 minutes and bus services run every 15 to 30 minutes depending on the time of day. Fares start at £2 one-way online and are based on demand. You can also buy tickets at non-internet prices from the easyBus driver on the day at the London departure points or from the easyBus ticket sales desks located in airport arrivals after baggage re-claim, subject to availability. Visit **www.easybus.co.uk** for details.

## Taxis and parking services

Luton Airport is located close to the M1 and M25. The train and bus provide the fastest and most reliable route to Luton. The black cab fare is roughly £70 to £80 from central London, and takes about 60 minutes depending on traffic. If you choose to drive, there is a choice of priority, short-term, mid-term and long-term car parks, located minutes from the terminals. Priority Parking is Luton's official Meet & Greet service. Refer to the airport website for more information on the parking options.

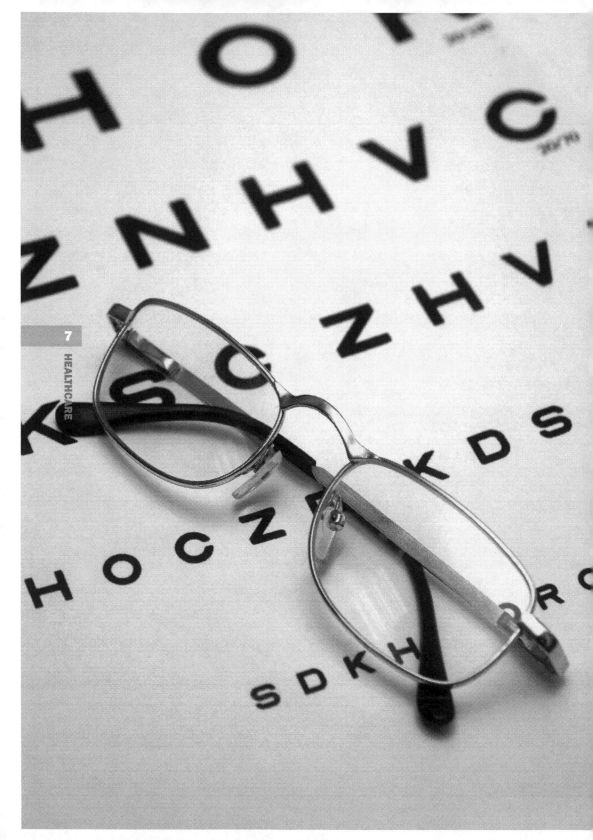

# Healthcare

Healthcare in the UK is exceptionally good and is low cost or free of charge for UK citizens and, in most cases, foreign residents. Healthcare providers in the UK fall into two categories: National Health Service (**NHS**) providers, most of whose services are free of charge, and private medical practitioners, who charge a fee. Some doctors see patients both privately and under the NHS.

This chapter explains the services provided by NHS and private healthcare centres and lists contact details and information for both. It is essential to have healthcare in the UK, so if you do not qualify for healthcare under the NHS, you should ensure that you are covered privately. Many Londoners, even if they do qualify for NHS healthcare, choose to be covered privately as well since there are often long waiting lists for non-urgent operations and specialists.

Should you need a visit from a private doctor at a place and time that is convenient to you, 24 hours a day, seven days a week, contact Doctors Direct (✆ 0800 9889 999, **www.doctorsdirect.co.uk**) or Doctorcall (✆ 0844 257 9507, **www.doctorcall.co.uk**).

## IN THIS CHAPTER...

- **Emergency facilities and casualty units**
- **National Health Service (NHS)**
- **Private medical care**
- **Prescriptions and late night chemists**
- **Dental care**
- **Eye care**
- **Maternity care**
- **Paediatric care**
- **Family planning**
- **Counselling**
- **Complimentary medicine**

# Emergency facilities and casualty units

If an emergency does arise, proceed immediately to a hospital with an Accident & Emergency (**A&E**) department. It is most important to know the nearest A&E department in your area. **IN A SERIOUS EMERGENCY, DIAL 999** and ask for the ambulance service. Emergency service to a resident is provided free of charge by the NHS and is available to anyone, including tourists.

For minor injuries and illnesses, NHS Walk-in Centres provide treatment seven days a week. You do not need an appointment and will be seen by an experienced NHS nurse. To locate the Walk-in Centre nearest you (located in Soho, Fulham, Whitechapel, Parsons Green, Tooting and Charing Cross), visit the NHS website at **www.nhs.uk**.

Each police station keeps a list of emergency doctors and chemists who are available on a 24-hour basis.

Nearly all London NHS hospitals have a 24-hour A&E department. Listed below are some of the larger ones throughout London. Check **www.nhs.uk** for a full list.

## Central

St. Mary's Hospital
Praed Street, Paddington, W2
✆ 020 3312 6666, www.st-marys.nhs.uk

University College Hospital
235 Euston Road, NW1
✆ 0845 155 5000, www.uclh.nhs.uk

## South & West

Charing Cross Hospital
Fulham Palace Road, W6
✆ 020 8846 1234, www.hhnt.org

Chelsea & Westminster Hospital
369 Fulham Road, SW10
✆ 020 8746 8000, www.chelwest.nhs.uk

St. Thomas's Hospital
Westminster Bridge Road, SE1
✆ 020 7188 7188, www.guysandstthoms.nhs.uk

### North

Royal Free Hospital
Pond Street, NW3
✆ 020 7794 0500, www.royalfree.nhs.uk

### East

Royal London Hospital
Whitechapel Road, E1
✆ 020 7377 7000, www.bartsandthelondon.nhs.uk

### Eye emergencies

Moorfields Eye Hospital
162 City Road, EC1
✆ 020 7253 3411, www.moorfields.nhs.uk

Western Eye Hospital
Marylebone Road, NW1
✆ 020 3312 6666, www.imperial.nhs.uk/westerneye
24-hour emergency care.

### Children's emergencies

Chelsea & Westminster Children's Hospital
369 Fulham Road, SW10
✆ 020 8746 8000, www.chelwest.nhs.uk

### Dental emergencies

Royal London Hospital
New Road, Whitechapel, E1
✆ 020 7377 7151, www.bartsandthelondon.nhs.uk/dentalhospital
Call to speak to a dentist for free advice and help finding
emergency treatment.

### Ambulance services

London Ambulance Service (NHS)
✆999

St. John's Ambulance Service
✆020 7258 3456
Provides non-emergency (private) services.

# National Health Service (NHS)

The UK has a government-subsidised national health service. If you pay National Insurance (**NI**) as a resident of the UK, you are entitled to medical coverage at little or no additional cost. This service includes:

- doctor care, including home visits if necessary
- specialist and hospital care
- dentistry and orthodontia
- eye examinations and glasses
- child-care clinics for under-fives
- maternity care
- well-man and well-woman clinics
- marriage counselling
- family planning services

While most of the services are free of charge, there are some (e.g., prescriptions, sight tests and dental treatments) that incur a supplementary charge. The NHS produces several leaflets explaining its different services. They are usually available at your doctor's surgery or through the Department of Health Publications Orderline at **www.orderline.dh.gov.uk**.

The NHS is also available to foreign visitors on an emergency basis. UK taxes paid by you or your employer go towards these services, so eligibility should be verified. Advice on eligibility is available from the Department of Health (✆020 7210 4850, **www.dh.gov.uk**). Please consult the website for various help-lines and information.

**DID YOU KNOW?**

NHS Direct is a free 24-hour service available 365 days a year for any health advice and information. NHS Direct provides a service whereby a nurse will advise on particular symptoms or medical treatment for adults and children confidentially over the telephone allowing you to get early advice without leaving home. Call the NHS Direct helpline on ✆**0845 4647** or visit **www.nhsdirect.nhs.uk**.

The Citizens' Advice Bureau provides free information and advice about the NHS. Check their website at **www.citizensadvice.org.uk** for the nearest office location or ask at a local library.

### NHS Registration

All permanent UK residents are eligible to register with the NHS. Eligibility for temporary residents depends on whether you or your spouse is paying UK income tax and National Insurance (**NI**). For an expatriate and his or her family, the individual's company will often obtain an NI number, which is needed in order to apply for NHS registration.

Matters relating to social security (including the allocation of NI number) are managed by the Department of Work and Pensions (**www.dwp.gov.uk**). If you have a right to work in the UK and you are looking for, starting work or setting up as self-employed, telephone Jobcentre Plus on ✆ 0845 600 0643. Jobcentre Plus will arrange an Evidence of Identity interview or send you a postal application.

To obtain an NHS number, you must register with a doctor or General Practitioner (**GP**) who has vacancies for NHS patients. The doctor's surgery must be in the same postcode that you live in. (Note: not all GPs handle NHS patients, some handle only private patients.) It is up to the discretion of the GP to register temporary residents with the NHS. If the GP decides to accept you as a patient, he or she will take your personal details (including your NI number and length of stay in the UK) and then apply to the local Primary Healthcare Trust (**PCT**) for your NHS number.

For a complete listing of GP surgeries in your area, visit **www.nhs.uk**. The website will provide an address, phone number and map, and may identify whether or not the GP is accepting new NHS patients. As an alternative, contact your local council's PCT for the names, addresses and telephone

7

HEALTHCARE

numbers of GPs in your area. Lists of doctors can also be found at local libraries, main post offices, Community Health Councils and the Citizens' Advice Bureau. Local chemists may have a list, but they are not officially permitted to make specific recommendations.

There are often waiting lists for many NHS doctors. In those cases, it may be easiest to sign up with a local GP practice as a private patient and ask to be placed on their NHS waiting list. This may be the best way to get into the local practice of your choice.

For medical attention other than general family care, you must be referred by your GP. Known in the UK as a consultant, the specialist is anyone other than a GP. Most consultants practise under the NHS and privately.

A drawback of the NHS is that if your complaint is not an emergency, you may be required to wait before receiving attention (this includes non-emergency operations). In these instances, consulting a private doctor may be an advantage as there would be no waiting list. Under certain circumstances, both NHS and private doctors are willing to make house calls.

## DID YOU KNOW?

In the UK, specialists and general practitioners are addressed as **Doctor**. Surgeons, including dental surgeons, obstetricians and gynaecologists, are referred to as **Mr, Mrs** or **Miss**. The **surgery** or **operating room** in a hospital is called a **theatre**, and the office of a medical professional is called a **surgery**. In some instances the surgery is located in a home instead of a clinic or office building. Patients go **'to hospital'** rather than **'to the hospital'**.

# Private medical care

An alternative to NHS medical care is private treatment. Although much more costly, it allows you to have control over when treatment should take place and who should perform it. Visit **www.privatehealth.co.uk** for more information.

Employer-sponsored group health plans issued in other countries may be extended to the UK with employer consent. Any questions regarding the extent of coverage should be directed to your employer's personnel department. You may wish to consider subscribing to a British form of medical insurance. BUPA and PPP are two of the most popular plans. These insurance plans generally cover hospital and specialist treatment, but not routine visits to the GP or dentist, as the NHS covers these.

**DID YOU KNOW?**

There are several **Medicentres** (privately-run, walk-in clinics) throughout London, including locations at Victoria station and Liverpool Street station. Many are open seven days a week. They are an option for conditions that are not quite A&E emergencies. They are also useful to visitors who might need a doctor's aid. For a list of locations and services, telephone ✆ 0870 600 0870 or visit **www.medicentre.co.uk**.

There are around 50 privately staffed and run hospitals in the London area. These facilities are available to private-care patients only. These hospitals are usually modern, offer private rooms and overall good facilities. They may not offer the emergency care of the NHS hospitals and are not subject to the same regulation as NHS hospitals. As few of the more well known are listed below. See *Maternity care – Hospitals* below for hospitals with maternity wards.

The Harley Street Clinic
35 Weymouth Street, W1
✆ 020 7935 7700, www.theharleystreetclinic.com
Specialists in cancer and cardiology treatments.

The Lister Hospital
Chelsea Bridge Road, SW1
✆ 020 7730 7733, www.thelisterhospital.com
Known for its assisted conception and fertility clinic.

The London Clinic
20 Devonshire Place, W1
✆ 020 7935 4444, www.thelondonclinic.co.uk
Largest single private hospital in the UK.

The Princess Grace Hospital
43-52 Nottingham Place, W1
✆ 020 7486 1234, www.theprincessgracehospital.com

# Prescriptions and late night chemists

Doctors write prescriptions to be filled at the chemist. You will be required to pay a fixed cost for each prescription unless the patient for whom the prescription is written in is within a class of persons who receive prescriptions at no cost, including, but not limited to, persons under 16 years old, full time students under 19 years old, and pensioners. Oral contraception is free in most cases and you may ask your doctor if you are eligible. In addition, women holding a Maternity Exemption Certificate (obtained from your doctor during pregnancy) will receive free prescriptions during pregnancy and for one year after the birth of the baby.

People with regular prescriptions may find it cost-effective to buy a prepayment certificate (**PPC**). Consult **www.nhsbsa.nhs.uk** or call ✆0845 850 0030 for details.

If you need a prescription filled outside of normal opening hours, below is a list of chemists open late.

Bliss Chemists
50-56 Willesden Lane, Kilburn, NW6
✆020 7624 8000
Open 09:00-22:00, 364 days a year. Christmas Day 09:00-14:00.

Bliss Chemists
5 Marble Arch, W1
✆020 7723 6116
Open 09:00-24:00, 365 days a year.

Boots The Chemist
West Concourse, Victoria Station
✆020 7834 0676
Open 07:00-24:00 Monday to Friday and 09:00-24:00 Saturday.

Dajani
92 Old Brompton Road, SW7
✆020 7589 8263
Open 09:00-22:00 Monday to Friday, 09:00 to 20:00 Saturday and 10:00-20:00 Sunday. Also open 10:00-20:00 on Bank Holidays.

HEALTHCARE

Warman Freed

45 Golders Green Road, NW11

✆ 020 8455 4351

Open 08:30–24:00, 365 days a year.

Zafash

233-235 Old Brompton Road, SW5

✆ 020 7373 2798, www.zafash.com

Open 24 hours.

# Dental care

Dental care is available through the NHS (much the same as medical care) at a reduced cost. As an NHS dental patient you are expected to pay a percentage of the cost of the procedures needed. There is an upper limit set on the contribution you will be asked to make for one course of treatment. Expect to be asked to pay all or part of the charge in advance. Before each and every visit you must ascertain that the dentist will treat you as an NHS patient, otherwise you could be treated as a private patient. The difficulty, however, is that the majority of dentists in London are private, meaning that you will be asked to pay the full cost of your dental treatment (and will only be reimbursed if you have alternative private dental insurance coverage).

If you are interested in trying to locate a dentist using the NHS, lists of NHS dentists are posted in the same fashion as NHS doctors at **www.nhs direct.nhs.uk**.

You are automatically entitled to free dental healthcare through the NHS if:

- You are under 16 years of age, or a student under 19 years of age and still in full-time education.
- You are expecting a baby and were pregnant when the dentist accepted you for treatment.
- You have had a baby during the 12 months before your treatment began.

A few recommended private dentists are listed below. Others in your area can be obtained from your GP.

Carnaby Street Dental Practice

31 Carnaby Street, W1

© 020 7734 6421, www.carnabystreetdentist.co.uk

Dental practice offering very high-quality dentistry using the latest technology.

The Q Clinic

139 Harley Street, W1

© 020 7317 1111, www.qclinic.com

A full-service, state-of-the-art dental practice which offers a broad range of procedures and services.

John F. Roberts

33 Weymouth Street, W1

© 020 7580 5370

Paediatric dental specialist.

Swiss Smile Dental Clinic

10 Brook Street, W1

© 020 7290 1180, www.swiss-smile.co.uk

General and cosmetic dentistry, with emergency service 365 days a year.

**DID YOU KNOW?**

Tap water in London is not fluorinated. It is especially important to see if your young children may need to have vitamins with fluoride prescribed in a fluid or tablet form.

# Eye care

Your eyes can be tested only by a registered ophthalmic optician (optometrist) or an ophthalmic medical practitioner. If you want to find an optician, go to your local library for a list of registered opticians in your area, ask at your local Citizens' Advice Bureau or look in the *Yellow Pages* under 'Opticians'.

Free sight tests are available to some, including those less than 16 years of age (or under 19 years of age if still in full-time education), diagnosed diabetics, the registered blind and partially sighted.

The optician must give you a prescription (or a certificate that you do not need glasses), even if your sight has not changed. You cannot be asked to pay for your sight test until you have been given your prescription. You are under no obligation to buy your eyeglasses from the same optician who gave you the test. Your prescription is valid for two years.

If you need to consult with an opthamologist (a medical doctor with knowledge on diseases of the eye), contact Moorfields Eye Hospital on © 020 7566 2345 or visit **www.moorfields.nhs.uk**.

## Maternity care

If you are expecting a baby, it is necessary to notify your GP promptly. Your GP can recommend an obstetrician and you must decide on whether to have your baby with the NHS or privately. If you have private health care insurance, check to see what maternity care is covered as many UK insurance providers do not consider pregnancy a medical condition and will not cover private healthcare costs unless you have a scheduled C-section or other high-risk condition. Some private health insurance policies that specialise in coverage for expats living in the UK will cover maternity care, or a portion thereof.

If you decide to use the NHS, you will have free care throughout your pregnancy and delivery. In the case of a normal delivery, the NHS provides a midwife to attend your birth, along with an obstetrician and full medical support staff on call at the hospital in case of complications. You will have a private birthing room, but during recovery you will be on an NHS ward, which usually has four to eight beds. Private or semi-private rooms may be available but only if you make prior arrangements with the hospital.

A midwife is a specialist in pregnancy, birth and the post-natal period. As well as performing ante-natal checks, she can deliver your baby, perform ultrasound scans and care for you once you have had your baby. She may work in the hospital or be based in the community. In some areas, you can book directly with a midwife instead of your GP. Telephone the Director of Midwifery at your local hospital and ask if there is a midwives clinic or a GP/midwives clinic in the community.

Traditionally, you are booked under a consultant at the hospital and receive your ante-natal care from members of his or her team, including midwives. You visit the clinic for all of your ante-natal care, and your baby is delivered by labour-ward midwives or the obstetrician on duty at the time you arrive to deliver your baby. Although the consultant leads the team, you may never actually see him or her unless your pregnancy is complicated.

There are many options for delivery within the NHS. Call your local hospital or speak to your GP to see whether these options are available in your area:

### Shared care

You visit the hospital two or three times during your pregnancy and for any special ultrasounds and tests. The rest of the time, you are cared for by your GP and/or your community midwife. When you go into the hospital to have your baby, your baby will be delivered by hospital midwives.

### Midwives clinic

Most of your antenatal care is done by a team of midwives at the hospital who may work in teams under a consultant. Your baby is delivered by the same team of midwives who then take care of you on the post-natal ward.

### GP/midwife care

Your antenatal care is done by your GP or community midwife at the surgery or local health centre. When you go into labour, you are cared for by community midwives and your GP is informed. If complications arise, you will be transferred to consultant care.

### Domino scheme/midwife care

Your antenatal care may be shared between the community midwife and your GP, or done by the community midwife at the surgery or local health centre. The midwife may visit you at home for antenatal checks and you may go into hospital for any special tests. When you go into hospital to deliver your baby, your midwife or another on her team will attend the birth and provide your post-natal care once you have returned home.

### Home birth

Home births are becoming more common in the UK as they are gaining support from the medical community. Your antenatal care may be undertaken entirely by your community or independent midwife with your own GP or another doctor acting as back-up. The midwife will deliver your baby at home and also provide your post-natal care.

### Private care

If you choose private care, you are assured that your obstetrician and a midwife will assist your delivery. In the case of an unexpected emergency situation, there is always an obstetrician on call in both private and NHS hospitals. Private doctors may use both NHS and private hospital facilities. It is important to book early with a private obstetrician as they only take a limited number of patients per month and it is critical that you are comfortable with the style of the obstetrician. If you need to change obstetrician it is better to do so earlier rather than later.

If your pregnancy is considered 'high risk', you may not be allowed to delivery your baby at a private hospital. Instead, you may have to deliver your baby at an NHS hospital that has more appropriate facilities to care for you and the baby in the case of an emergency. One may feel more comfortable knowing that at an NHS hospital there is more staff and facilities to handle unforeseen emergencies.

**DID YOU KNOW?**

Black cabs may refuse to transport you to hospital once in labour. If you are planning to deliver at a private hospital and need transportation, contact the hospital to arrange for a private ambulance. If you call 999 for an ambulance, they must take you to the nearest hospital.

### Hospitals

Whether you choose the NHS or private care, your choice of hospitals for your delivery will be limited to the hospital or hospitals at which your obstetrician is registered. In the case of a private hospital, accommodation must be reserved well in advance of your baby's due date. Hospitals may also request a deposit at the time of reservation.

In London, most large hospitals offer good maternity facilities. Some hospitals with exceptional maternity facilities are listed below. Note that not all hospitals have neonatal intensive care units.

Chelsea & Westminster Hospital
369 Fulham Road, SW10
☎ 020 8746 8000, www.chelwest.nhs.uk
Has excellent childbirth facilities including birthing pools and a private maternity wing that opened in August 2008. NHS and private.

Portland Hospital for Women and Children
209 Great Portland Street, W1
© 020 7580 4400, www.theportlandhospital.com
Private.

Queen Charlotte's Maternity Hospital
150 Du Cane Road, W12
© 020 8383 1111, www.imperial.nhs.uk
NHS and private.

The Wellington Hospital
8a Wellington Place, NW8
© 020 7483 5148, www.thewellingtonhospital.com
Private.

The NHS and most private hospitals offer parents birth and parenting preparatory classes at local hospitals and clinics. A listing of independent antenatal courses and refresher courses for repeat mums is available through your GP or obstetrician.

The National Childbirth Trust (**NCT**) is a non-profit organisation formed expressly for the purpose of education for pregnancy, birth and parenthood. Contact the NCT for information on what parenting and birth preparation courses are offered in your area (© 0300 330 0770, **www.nctpregnancyand babycare.com**). You must contact them early in your pregnancy if you are interested in antenatal classes in London. Many of the neighbourhood branches of the NCT have produced wonderful information packs on having a baby in London that can be a great help to a pregnant expatriate.

After you have had your baby, whether using the NHS or private healthcare, a midwife will come to your home after you have given birth to check that you and your baby are healthy and adjusting to life at home. The midwife will schedule visits with you for up to ten days after the birth.

Following a new mum's discharge from the midwife's services, a **health visitor** (a specially trained nurse concerned with the health of the whole family) will visit the home to offer help and support. You may continue to see the health visitor periodically for general questions on the baby's growth, feeding and other common baby questions.

### Birth registration

All births taking place in the UK must be registered. The hospital where the birth occurs will notify the local Registrar of Births, Deaths and Marriages with details of the birth. The parents (mother or father, if the parents are legally married) must register the child at the local office within 42 days of the birth. Either a short- or long-form of birth certificate is available for a fee. The long form is more detailed and, in some countries, it is considered to be the only 'official' birth certificate. Therefore, it is often helpful to obtain several official long-form birth certificates at the time of registration so that they are readily available when required (there is a discounted fee on the day of registration).

It is recommended that babies born in the UK to resident foreign nationals register at the appropriate foreign embassy or high commission to receive proper citizenship papers and passports. Each country's laws differ, so it is best to check with your embassy's website (see *Chapter 18: Organisations – Embassies and high commissions* for a partial list of foreign embassies in London). There is usually a fee for this service.

In certain circumstances, it will also be possible to register a child born in the UK as a UK national and obtain a British passport for the child. (This may or may not affect the child's primary citizenship.) Parents interested in this possibility should contact the UK Home Office Nationality Contact Centre on © 0845 010 5200.

# Paediatric care

Your local health clinic or GP offers a full service of paediatric care, as well as Child Health Clinics, which specialise in children only. Check with your local PCT for one close to you. The following services are available:

- Immunisations and boosters.
- Developmental checks (i.e., hearing, vision, weight, height) at six weeks, eight months, 18 months, three years and four years (pre-school). The service then continues via the school system.
- Psychotherapy, educational psychology for learning and behaviour problems, speech therapy and orthopaedics.
- Health visitors who run clinics and/or make house calls to answer any questions you may have, discuss problems, remind you of injection dates and help orient you to local play groups, and registered childminders in the area.

All clinics have emergency numbers to be used after hours. GPs or their deputies will make house calls in emergency situations.

A recommended private paediatric centre for round-the-clock, one-stop child healthcare is the Harley Street Paediatric Group (78 Harley Street, W1, ℭ 020 7034 8950, **www.theharleystreetpaediatricgroup.com**).

### Immunisations and vaccinations

Immunisations for babies are available free of charge through your local GP or Child Health Clinic. The current immunisation schedule for babies in the UK is very similar to the schedule in other countries. The NHS immunisation information website at **www.immunisation.nhs.uk** provides comprehensive, up-to-date and accurate sources of information on vaccines and immunisation in the UK.

Immunisations that are not included in the NHS protocol are available for a fee, in some cases at your GP's office, but more commonly at private providers. One such provider is the Children's Immunisation Centre Limited (139 Harley Street, W1, ℭ 0207 486 8162, **www.childrensimmunisation. com**), which is a private practice specialising in single jabs for measles, mumps and rubella, but offers a variety of jabs including chicken pox and tetanus.

When travelling, many countries require you to have certain immunisations and vaccinations. Please see *Chapter 15: Travel – Before you travel* for details.

# Family planning

A full range of family planning services is available through your GP or local clinics as well as specific family planning clinics run by the NHS. The larger clinics will offer all types of birth control for men and women, well-women clinics, psycho-sexual counselling, termination referrals and follow-up and post-natal examinations. All services are available free of charge on a walk-in basis. To find your nearest clinic and further information contact:

The Family Planning Association
50 Featherstone Street, EC1
ℭ 0845 122 8690, www.fpa.org.uk

# Counselling

To find information about where to receive counselling locally, start by asking your GP. Some useful addresses and telephone numbers:

Al Anon/Al ateen

✆ 020 7403 0888

24-hour telephone service to help relatives and friends of problem drinkers.

Alcoholics Anonymous

✆ 0845 769 7555, www.alcoholics-anonymous.org.uk

24-hour telephone service to discuss an alcohol-related problem.

British Association for Counselling and Psychotherapy (BACP)

✆ 01455 883300, www.bac.co.uk

Nationally, the BACP supplies information about counselling services and specialist organisations, including counsellors in your local area. Publishes a nationwide directory of counselling and psychotherapy resources.

Counselling Directory

www.counselling-directory.org.uk

Use the website to find a counsellor or psychotherapist near you.

Cruse Bereavement Care

✆ 0844 477 9400, www.cruse.org.uk

Services are free to bereaved people and anyone can contact Cruse if they want to talk about themselves or someone they know who has been affected by a death.

Narcotics Anonymous

✆ 0300 999 1212, www.ukna.org

Primary service is local meetings for recovering addicts.

Relate

✆ 0300 100 1234, www.relate.org.uk

Provides relationship support, including relationship counselling for individuals and couples, family counselling, counselling for children and young people and sex therapy. Visit the website to find the nearest centre.

HEALTHCARE

The Tavistock Centre for Couple Relationships
✆ 020 7380 1975, www.tccr.org.uk
Leading charity provider of highly-specialised and affordable couple and
parent counselling and psychotherapy. The organisation offers a range
of other relationship, parenting and psychosexual support services
throughout London.

# Complimentary medicine

Your local health food store or chemist can be a good resource for
complimentary therapies and health products (e.g., herbal supplements,
vitamins and homeopathic products). Some of these products are untested
and may have been tested showing effects other than what they are sold as, so
it is important to inform your health care provider if you are using any
chemicals or herbs. Below is a list of resources and centres where you may
find a variety of complimentary medicine products and practitioners,
including acupuncture, homeopathy, osteopathy and reflexology.

AcuMedic Centre
101-105 Camden High Street, NW1
✆ 020 7388 6704, www.acumedic.com
Founded in 1972, offers Chinese medicine, acupuncture and traditional
herbal treatments. Doctors trained in both Western medicine and
Chinese medicine.

Culpeper
Unit 8, The Market, Covent Garden, WC2
✆ 020 7379 6698, www.culpeper.co.uk
A 17th century apothecary and herbalist; the oldest chain of herbal shops
in England.

The Hale Clinic
7 Park Crescent, W1
✆ 020 7631 0156, www.haleclinic.com
Well-known clinic with emphasis on preventative medicine and over
60 practitioners based there. Shop sells books, vitamins, minerals and
herbal supplements.

Holland & Barrett
www.hollandandbarrett.com
The UK's leading retailer of vitamins, minerals and herbal supplements.
Multiple locations.

Neal's Yard Remedies
2 Neal's Yard, WC2
✆ 020 7379 7662, www.nealsyardremedies.com
Own beauty and healthcare products, herbs and homeopathic remedies.
Multiple locations, some with therapy rooms.

The Royal London Homeopathic Hospital
60 Great Ormond Street, WC1
✆ 0845 155 5000, www.rlhh.eu
Walk-in clinic and homeopathic dispensary.

Sloane Health Shop
27 King's Road, SW3
✆ 020 7730 7046
Vitamins, nutritional supplements and homeopathic remedies.

7

HEALTHCARE

# 8

# Children

If life with children is an adventure, living in London with children is an even bigger one! Whether you already have children or are having a child here for the first time, the resources in this chapter will get you and your little ones started on exploring London and taking advantage of all it has to offer.

There is no shortage of things to do in London for the younger set – it's just a matter of becoming familiar with all of the options and narrowing down the choices. Despite all of the various venues, activities and special events, you will not find one source that lists everything to do. Some key websites, magazines and guidebooks are listed at the end of this chapter in *Resources for parents*. You should also contact your local council and visit your local library, community centres, parks, playgrounds and schools for more information. You will be amazed at what isn't advertised in the local newspaper or magazine!

## IN THIS CHAPTER...

- Baby care products
- Mummy speak
- Medical needs
- Pregnancy

- Childcare
- Shopping and services
- Entertaining your children
- Resources for parents

# Baby care products

Many popular foreign brands are widely available in the UK; however, you will find that the selection can vary depending on the store or chemist, which means you may have to visit a few different places in order to find everything you're looking for.

Johnson & Johnson, Pampers and Huggies products are carried by most supermarket and chemist chains in the UK. Large supermarkets and chemists such as Sainsbury's, Tesco and Boots also carry their own lines of wipes and nappies.

Vaseline and A+D ointment are sold in the UK. There are also several British-made nappy rash ointments such as Sudocrem and Kamillosan that work very well.

### Formula/breastfeeding

Ready-to-feed or powdered infant formulas are commonly offered in the following brands: SMA, Cow & Gate, Aptamil, SMA Wysoy (a soya milk formula) and Hipp Organic. It is possible to find specialised formulas (such as hypoallergenic), but you may need to search a bit more, as these items are generally not carried in most chemists or supermarkets.

The most popular and widely distributed brand of feeding accessories is Avent, offering everything from bottles and nipples to breast pumps, shields and storage bags. Dr Brown's and Tommee Tippee are additional popular feeding accessory brands. Medela breast pumps, a well-regarded brand, can be ordered through selected chemists or on **www.breastpumps.co.uk**.

In addition, the MAM and Nuk brands all have breastfeeding accessories, bottles and pacifiers.

### Baby food/feeding items

Popular UK brands of baby food include Heinz and Beechnut, as well as organic brands Hipp Organic, Plum Baby and Organix.

Beaker cups, bibs, feeding bowls and accessories made by Avent, Tommee Tippee and Dr Brown's are readily available.

### Detergents

Fairy, Ariel and Persil are common detergent brands found in stores and offer both biological and non-biological formulas. Good detergents for young babies and people with sensitive skin are Ecover and Filetti. There is also a handy product called Napisan, which safely removes germs and stains from children's clothes.

## Mummy speak

| British | American |
|---|---|
| antenatal | prenatal |
| beaker | sippy cup |
| cot | crib |
| crèche | daycare centre/nursery |
| crib | cradle |
| dummy | pacifier |
| flannel | washcloth |
| fringe | bangs |
| half term | school vacation |
| Moses basket | bassinet |
| mummy | mommy |
| nappies | diapers |
| plaster | band aid |
| pram | buggy |
| pushchair | stroller |
| rubber | eraser |
| sellotape/sticky tape | scotch tape |
| tea | children's supper/dinner |
| teat | nipple (baby bottle) |
| vest | t-shirt/undershirt |

**DID YOU KNOW?**

UK bed and linen sizes (including those for baby cots) may vary from store to store, as well as from any standard sizes in your home country. If moving to the UK with your bed and linens, remember to bring everything you will need.

# Medical needs

### Baby first aid/safety

Below are some helpful contacts for baby first aid and safety information and training.

### Child Alert

www.childalert.co.uk

A comprehensive reference/guidance website that focuses on addressing a variety of child safety topics and parenting concerns. There is a section on child-proofing, plus the opportunity to arrange for a child-proofing survey.

### The Parent Company

6 Jacob's Well Mews, W1

℗ 0845 094 4220, www.theparentcompany.co.uk

Offers classes in first aid and basic life support and can arrange private sessions in your home.

### The Portland Hospital

Physiotherapy Department, 234 Great Portland Street, W1

℗ 020 7390 6553, www.theportlandhospital.com

Offers a baby/toddler first aid class taught by a midwife. Topics include how to make your house safer, what to do in emergencies and how to administer CPR, with practice on a dummy. Classes are held monthly.

### R.E.D.I. Training

℗ 020 7348 7117, www.redi-training.co.uk

Offers courses in accidents and illnesses, and emergency care.

### Healthcare/immunisations

You will see a National Health Service (**NHS**) or a private General Practitioner (**GP**) for your child's routine or emergency medical care. Paediatricians are considered specialists and generally are seen when referred by a GP. You can make an appointment directly if you wish, although there may be a fee for doing so if you do not have comprehensive private health insurance.

Immunisations for babies and regular health checks are available free of charge through your local NHS well-baby clinic. The current immunisation schedule for babies in the UK is very similar to the schedule in other countries. See **www.immunisation.nhs.uk** for more information.

For more information on the NHS and paediatrics, see *Chapter 7: Healthcare.*

## Medicines

Over-the-counter medicines for children's health are readily available although they may carry different brand names than you are used to. Most chemist shops have a pharmacist on duty that can help you find the medicine you need for your situation. See *Chapter 7: Healthcare – Prescriptions and late night chemists* for late night chemists.

Popular children's medicines and products include:

| | |
|---|---|
| Aqueous Cream | dry skin |
| Calpol | pain reliever containing paracetamol |
| Canesten | antifungal cream |
| Dentinox | teething pain |
| Dioralyte | rehydration powder (to be mixed with water) |
| E45 Cream | dry skin |
| Gripe water | colic and hiccups |
| Infacol | colic |
| Nurofen | pain reliever containing ibuprofen |
| Oilatum | cradle cap, eczema |
| Piriton Syrup | antihistamine |
| Sudacrem | nappy rash |
| Zinc and castor oil lotion | nappy rash |

# Pregnancy

Having a baby in the UK is an exciting proposition, but the antenatal care may differ from the common practice of your home country. Pregnancy is discussed in more detail in *Chapter 7: Healthcare – Maternity care,* but one of the first decisions you will have to make when you become pregnant is whether you plan to use the NHS or private healthcare. Most British health insurance policies, such as BUPA, do not consider pregnancy a medical condition and will not cover private healthcare costs unless you have a scheduled C-section or other high-risk condition. Some private health insurance policies that specialise in coverage for expatriates living in the UK will cover maternity care. Always check with your policy provider for details. If you are working, the Working Families group may be helpful. They have a free help line and fact sheets on issues such as maternity rights, legal and practical advice for returning to work, establishing a flexible work schedule and helping working parents with a disabled child. This group's goal is to help working parents find a better balance between home and work responsibilities. They can be reached on ℂ 0800 013 0313 or **www.workingfamilies.org.uk**.

### The National Childbirth Trust

For recent arrivals to the UK or anyone with young children, the National Childbirth Trust (**NCT**) is a tremendous resource. The NCT is a non-profit organisation and a registered charity full of excellent information on all matters relating to childbirth and early parenting. Many of the neighbourhood branches of the NCT have produced wonderful information packs on having a baby in London that can be a great help to a pregnant expatriate. For information on branches all over London, contact ℂ 0300 330 0770 or visit **www.nctpregnancyandbabycare.com**.

The NCT, as well as your local council, will offer resources on children in London. Contact your local NCT branch or your local council for more information on what they offer for your area. See *Chapter 5: Utilities – Local councils* for contact information.

### Antenatal classes

The NHS offers free antenatal classes, but other resources offer private classes (for a fee), which may be more convenient. The following centres offer various antenatal preparatory classes and post-natal exercise classes for a cost:

Active Birth Centre
25 Bickerton Road, N19
ℂ 020 7281 6760, www.activebirthcentre.com
Pregnancy yoga and therapies, active birth courses and postnatal classes for breastfeeding.

The Life Centre
15 Edge Street, W8
ℂ 020 7221 4602, www.thelifecentre.com
Offers pregnancy and postnatal yoga. Also offers baby massage classes.

NCT
ℂ 0300 330 0772, www.nctpregnancyandbabycare.com
For general information and also to organise pregnancy support groups.

Triyoga
6 Erskine Road, NW3
© 020 7483 3344, www.triyoga.co.uk
Offers antenatal Pilates, yoga classes and treatments. Multiple locations.

## Maternity wear

The following stores sell a variety of maternity clothes. In addition, some major department stores and high street stores, such as Topshop and H&M, offer a selection of maternity clothes – be sure to check locations to make sure there is a maternity department. In addition, stores children's stores such as Blooming Marvellous, JoJo Maman Bébé, Mothercare and Mamas & Papas also sell maternity clothing (see *Shopping and services* section below).

9 London
8 Hollywood Road, SW10
© 020 7352 7600, www.9london.com
Offers a range of designer maternity jeans and fashion; located downstairs to Emily Evans, which also offers designer maternity wear.

Blossom Mother and Child
69 Marylebone High Street, W1
© 020 7486 6089, www.blossommotherandchild.com
High fashion maternity wear, especially good for jeans and party wear.

Great Expectations and Night Owls
50 Fulham Road, SW3
© 020 7584 2451, www.greatexpectationsmaternity.co.uk
Designer maternity clothes and underwear.

Isabella Oliver
© 0844 844 0448, www.isabellaoliver.com
Online store for stylish maternity essentials in easy, wearable fabrics.

Rigby & Peller
22A Conduit Street, W1
© 0845 076 5545, www.rigbyandpeller.com
Good source for nursing bras and maternity underwear. Multiple locations.

Séraphine

28 Kensington Church Street, W8

© 002 7937 3156, www.seraphine.com

Comfortable and fashionable maternity wear staples and occasional wear. Multiple locations.

# Childcare

Once you arrive in the UK, you may wish to take advantage of the wonderful childcare that seems to be readily available. Before deciding on help with the children, it is helpful to be aware of the distinctions amongst the following:

### Au pair

A girl in her late teens or early 20s who live with a family in order to learn the English language. She will help around the house and do some babysitting for up to 35 hours per week in exchange for her room and board and pocket money. She is usually a student and may not speak fluent English.

### Babysitter

Will come to your house and look after the children for a few hours, day or night.

### Childminder

Self-employed persons who looks after children up to 12 years old in the childminder's home. Childminders must be registered with the Office for Standards in Education, Children's Services and Skills (**Ofsted**), the government's regulatory body.

### Crèche

Provides occasional care for children under 8.

### Mother's helper

A non-professional who will do housework and care for children either full- or part-time.

### Nanny

Provides childcare in your own home. She generally does not do housework or meal preparation for the family but will take care of all the children's needs, including laundry and meal preparation. She can live in or out. A nanny will be an employee of yours and as such, will require an employment contract.

### Nursery

Day nurseries and nursery schools provide care for children, usually up to age 5. Nurseries are often integrated with early education and are registered with Ofsted.

### Agencies for childcare

When working with an agency, make sure that you have a complete understanding of the fees charged. There are membership fees, engagement fees and booking fees depending on the situation and agency. These fees vary widely. It is advisable to contact more than one agency. Finding a good match for your specific needs will depend on the sort of people a given agency has on its books at the time you call. Help can be found to suit most permanent and part-time requirements.

*The Good Nanny Guide*, by Charlotte Breese and Hilaire Gomer, is a resource book outlining the traditional duties and pay scales for all types of help.

Below is a short list of agencies:

### Emergency Childcare
✆ 0845 676 7699, www.emergencychildcare.co.uk
A resource for getting last-minute nannies, childminders or nursery places.

### Greycoat Placements
✆ 020 7233 9950, www.greycoatchildcare.co.uk
Permanent and temporary childcare.

### Kensington Nannies
3 Hornton Place, W8
✆ 020 7937 2333, www.kensington-nannies.com
Nannies and mother's helpers, both live-in and live-out.

### The Nanny Service
6 Nottingham Street, W1
✆ 020 7935 3515, www.nannyservice.co.uk
Specialises in Australian, New Zealand and British nannies on a temporary or permanent basis – both daily and live-in.

Night Nannies

3 Kempson Road, SW6

✆ 0207 731 6168, www.night-nannies.com

Experienced night nannies; also offers maternity nurse services.

Sitters

✆ 0800 389 0038, www.sitters.co.uk

Babysitting service/evening childcare, child daycare, temporary short-term nannies, emergency nanny service.

In addition to the agencies listed above, these online resources can be helpful:

Best Bear

www.bestbear.co.uk

Good resource for all types of childcare in the UK. This agency rates and recommends nanny agencies and other childcare services. They pose as interested childcare workers and conduct interviews with services to see what type of childcare workers they hire.

Gumtree

www.gumtree.com

Post advertisements for childcare and potential nannies will contact you.

Nannyshare

www.nannyshare.co.uk

Puts you in touch with other local parents so that you can share the cost of a nanny.

**Nanny tax**

If you employ a nanny on a part- or full-time basis, you are required by law to pay regular tax and National Insurance contributions to the Inland Revenue on the nanny's behalf, as well as provide the nanny with regular pay slips. There are payroll service companies that will take care of all the details for a fee including but not limited to Nannytax (✆ 0845 226 2203, **www.nannytax. co.uk**) and Taxing Nannies (✆ 020 8882 6847, **www.taxingnannies.co.uk**).

**Gym crèches**

For mums who like to get a bit of exercise, there are several London sports clubs that have crèche (nursery) facilities for children, including but not limited to certain leisure centres, as well as private health clubs such as David

Lloyd, Esporta and Virgin Active. The amenities vary between locations and companies, so telephone or visit before making your decision. See *Chapter 14: Sports and leisure – Fitness and sports facilities* for contact information.

## Shopping and services

### All-rounders

These stores and services offer pretty much everything for babies, children and mums-to-be, including baby and children's clothing and supplies, toys, nursery furniture, pushchairs, linens, home and car safety equipment, as well as maternity clothing and other items for new mums.

### Babylist

50 Sulivan Road, SW6

✆ 020 7371 5145, www.babylist.co.uk

Fee-based consultation service offering a large variety of brand name nursery and baby items at recommended retail prices. They will help you create a list (and/or a wish list) of complete nursery needs and deliver them all to you at your convenience.

### Blooming Marvellous

✆ 0845 458 7405, www.bloomingmarvellous.co.uk

Multiple locations.

### Harrods

87-135 Brompton Road, SW1

✆ 020 7730 1234, www.harrods.com

### John Lewis

278-306 Oxford Street, W1

✆ 020 7629 7711, www.johnlewis.com

Multiple locations.

### JoJo Maman Bébé

101 Westbourne Grove, W2

✆ 020 7727 3578, www.jojomamanbebe.co.uk

Multiple locations.

Mamas & Papas
256-258 Regent Street, W1
℃ 0845 268 2000, www.mamasandpapas.co.uk
Multiple locations.

Mothercare
526-528 Oxford Street, W1
℃ 0845 650 515, www.mothercare.com
Multiple locations.

Peter Jones
Sloane Square, SW1
℃ 020 7730 3434, www.peterjones.co.uk

## Books

The large bookstores such as Waterstones and independent bookshops, such as Foyles and Daunt (see *Chapter 12: Shopping – Books* for contact information) have extensive children's book areas.

Barefoot Books
℃ 0800 328 2640, www.barefoot-books.com
Speciality bookseller that offers books that focus on our cultural differences; themes that encourage independence of spirit, enthusiasm for learning, and sharing of the world's diversity.

Children's Bookshop
29 Fortis Green Road, N10
℃ 020 84444 5500
Fantastic range of books, roomy and lovely staff.

Tales on Moon Lane
25 Half Moon Lane, SE24
℃ 020 7274 5759, www.talesonmoonlane.co.uk
Books and reasonably priced gifts and cards, delightful window displays.

## Children's wear

Most department stores such as John Lewis, Peter Jones and Debenhams have children's departments with a large selection. Stores such as H&M, Gap

8

CHILDREN

Kids and Baby Gap are also excellent for competitively priced, unfussy clothes for boys and girls. Other stores with recommended children's clothes are:

Caramel Baby & Child
77 Ledbury Road W11
✆ 020 7727 0906, www.caramel-shop.co.uk
UK-based brand selling sophisticated children's clothes in neutral colours and high-quality fabrics. Shoes and children's haircuts. Multiple locations.

Elias & Grace
158 Regent's Park Road, NW1
✆ 020 7449 0574, www.eliasandgrace.com
International brands, including Chloe, Marni, Quincy and Bonton. Excellent online shop including outfit styling.

Green Baby
345 Upper Street, N1
✆ 0800 023 4289, www.greenbaby.co.uk
Specialises in natural, environmentally friendly clothing and nappies. Mail order and online shop. Multiple locations.

Hop...like a bunny
12 Portland Road, W11
✆ 020 7221 6116
Delightful shop in Holland Park with international children's brands, including Miniature, Milibe and Elephantito clothing and shoes, and excellent selection of toys and decorative items.

Igloo
300 Upper Street, N1
✆ 020 7354 7303, www.iglookids.co.uk
Toys, clothes, shoes, children's haircuts. Multiple locations.

Mini Boden
✆ 0845 677 5000, www.boden.co.uk
Mail order catalogue or order online at their website. Fun, playful clothes, shoes and accessories for babies through to teens.

Rachel Riley

82 Marylebone High Street, W1

℗ 020 7935 8345, www.rachelriley.com

Traditional English clothes with a French influence. Multiple locations.

Sasti

281 Portobello Road, W10

℗ 020 8960 1125, www.sasti.co.uk

Funky, affordable children's wear all made in the UK.

Trotters

34 King's Road, SW3

℗ 020 7259 9620, www.trotters.co.uk

Wide range of clothing and shoes. Also children's haircuts.
Multiple locations.

### DID YOU KNOW?

When shopping for baby clothes, it's helpful to remember that generally, British sizes are spot on, European sizes are a tighter fit and American sizes tend to be cut generously. For example, an average-sized 3-month-old baby will usually fit British and American clothes marked as 3 months, but will fit European clothes marked as 6 months. It is therefore best to buy European baby clothes at least one size up.

## Costumes/fancy dress

Mystical Fairies

12 Flask Walk, NW3

℗ 020 7431 1888, www.mysticalfairies.co.uk

Will fulfil the dreams of any little princess. Carries every magical and mystifying fairy item imaginable (amongst other things).

Charlie Crow

℗ 01782 417 133, www.charliecrow.com

Online company offering a large collection of costumes for imaginative play. Equipment hire, nappy services and household goods delivery.

### Equipment hire, nappy services and household goods delivery

**Chelsea Baby Hire**

31 Osborne House, 414 Wimbledon Park Road, SW19

☏ 020 8789 9673, www.chelseababyhire.com

Equipment hire and delivery for long or short term, including cots, strollers, highchairs and car seats.

**Little Green Earthlets**

☏ 0845 072 4462, www.earthlets.co.uk

A full range of natural baby essentials, pregnancy products and other quality baby products. They are cloth nappy specialists and stock Mother-ease cloth nappies.

**Little Stars**

☏ 020 8621 4378, www.littlestars.co.uk

Offer a wide range of equipment and toys for hire as well as for purchase.

**Nappy Ever After**

96 Chalton Street, NW1

☏ 020 7383 5115, www.nappyeverafter.co.uk

Cotton nappy laundry service for central and north London.

**National Association of Nappy Services**

☏ 0121 693 4949, www.changeanappy.co.uk

A not-for-profit organisation that sets the standards and guidelines for the industry. Visit the website for nappy washing services closest to you.

**Go Real**

☏ 0845 850 0606, www.goreal.org.uk

Cloth nappy information service.

If you are looking to acquire gently used baby items, such as pushchairs, highchairs, furniture and clothing, check out **www.nappyvalley.co.uk**, an online baby equipment recycling centre. The NCT runs a series of 'Nearly New' sales throughout the country. For dates and schedules, contact the NCT on ☏ 0300 330 0770 or visit **www.nctpregnancyandbabycare.com**. The Hampstead Women's Club and Kensington Chelsea Women's Club also hold 'Nearly New' sales in the spring and autumn respectively. They specialise in gently used children's clothes, equipment and toys. Contact details for

8

CHILDREN

147

these clubs can be found in *Chapter 18: Organisations – Charitable, social and service organisations.*

## Haircutters

For stores that provide children's haircuts, see *Children's wear* above.

### Tantrum
398 King's Road, SW10
✆ 020 7376 3966, www.yourtantrum.com
The only dedicated children's hairdressers in London. Multiple locations.

## Nursery furniture

See also *All-rounders* above. Other stores that specialise in nursery items include:

### Aspace
140 Chiswick High Road, W4
✆ 0845 872 2400, www.aspace.co.uk
Children's furniture, bedding and room accessories. Multiple locations.

### Bobo Kids
29 Elystan Street, SW3
✆ 020 7838 1020, www.bobokids.co.uk
Luxury boutique for designer kids furniture and accessories, interior design service available.

### Dragons of Walton Street
23 Walton Street, SW3
✆ 020 7589 3795, www.dragonsofwaltonstreet.com
Specialising in hand-painted furniture, matching accessories, fabrics and wallpaper.

### Naturalmat
99 Talbot Road, W11
✆ 020 7985 0474, www.naturalmat.co.uk
Known for its all natural mattresses and bedding, contemporary nursery furniture.

The Nursery Window

83 Walton Street, SW3

✆ 020 7581 3358, www.nurserywindow.co.uk

Specialising in children's furniture and accessories made from the shop's own fabric. Especially notable are the beautiful Moses baskets and hooded towels.

Wigwam

✆ 02380 580 990, www.wigwamfurniture.co.uk

Contemporary children's furniture and accessories.

## Toys

Most major department stores have large toy departments and Hamleys has everything! See also *All-rounders*, as well as certain stores for *Children's wear* listed above.

Early Learning Centre

36 King's Road, SW3

✆ 0871 231 3511, www.elc.co.uk

Specialising in educational toys for young children. Multiple locations.

Great Little Trading Company

✆ 0844 848 6000, www.gltc.co.uk

Practical, innovative products for children and parents. Also offers children's furniture and clothes.

Hamleys

188-196 Regent Street, W1

✆ 0871 704 1977, www.hamleys.com

World's largest toy shop!

Honeyjam

267 Portobello Road, W11

✆ 020 7243 0449, www.honeyjam.co.uk

Traditional wooden toys, dolls, dressing up and more.

Mulberry Bush

✆ 014 0379 0796, www.mulberrybush.co.uk

Selling traditional and innovative toys and gifts for babies and young children up to age 12. Good selection of wooden toys.

Petit Chou

15 St. Christopher's Place, W1

✆ 020 7486 3637, www.petitchou.co.uk

Fantastic wooden toys, beautiful artisan soft toys and small selection of clothing.

# Entertaining your children

When planning any sort of outing in London, it is always a good idea to call ahead to verify operating hours and the schedule of events. Things have a tendency to change on short notice and there is nothing worse than an unhappy child after a long journey. If you're interested in venturing outside London, see the *Theme parks* section in *Chapter 14: Sports and leisure – Parks*.

## Aquariums

### The London Aquarium

County Hall, Westminster Bridge Road, SE1

✆ 0871 663 1678, www.sealife.co.uk/london

Home to over 350 species including sharks, sting rays, crabs and more. Next to the London Eye.

### The Tropical Forest

Syon Park, Brentford, TW8

✆ 020 8847 4730, www.tropicalforest.co.uk

A small centre with tropical birds, crocodiles, snakes, frogs and various fish (some which can be fed). The highlight is the animal talk – children can learn and touch some of the creatures.

## Art

### Art 4 Fun

172 West End Lane, NW6

✆ 020 7794 0800, www.art4fun.com

Themed art activity centre focusing on painted ceramics. Birthday parties and workshops.

### Creative Wiz Kids

☎ 020 7794 6797, www.creativewizkids.com

Playgroups, after-school programmes and parties for children aged 1 to 7; creative play through art (music, painting, crafts).

### London Brass Rubbing Centre

The Crypt, St. Martin-in-the-Fields, WC2

☎ 020 7930 9306, www.stmartins-in-the-fields.org

Brass rubbings of various historical figures.

### Messy Hands

Jakobs, 20 Gloucester Road, SW7

☎ 07951 329 447

Arts and crafts classes, workshops, creative cookery club and parties for 18 months to 8 years old.

## Baby gyms

### Gymboree

☎ 0800 092 0911, www.gymboree-uk.com

Activity and music classes from birth to 5 years old. Available for parties. Multiple locations.

### The Little Gym

Westfield Shopping Centre, W12

☎ 020 8735 0817, www.thelittlegym.co.uk

Developmental gymnastics programme for children for 4 months. Summer camps, weekly classes, birthday parties. Multiple locations.

### Tumble Tots

☎ 020 8381 6585, www.tumbletots.com

Active physical play programme for children 6 months to 7 years old. Multiple locations.

## Boat trips

### Canal Cruises

250 Camden High Street, NW1

☎ 020 7485 4433, www.walkersquay.com

Cruises on Regent's Canal between Camden Lock and Little Venice.

### Jason's Trip

Jason's Wharf, opposite 60 Blomfield Road, W9

☎ 020 7286 3428, www.jasons.co.uk

Cruises (one way 45 minutes, return 1½ hours) on 100-year-old boat from Little Venice to Camden Lock. Live commentary.

### London Duck Tours

Chicheley Street, SE1

☎ 020 7928 3132, www.londonducktours.co.uk

Sightseeing road and river adventure.

### London WaterBus Company

Camden Place, NW1

☎ 020 7482 2660, www.londonwaterbus.com

Boat trips (one way 45 minutes, return 1½ hours) on Regent's Canal leaving from either Camden Lock or Little Venice via the zoo.

### Westminster Passenger Services Association

Westminster Pier, Victoria Embankment, SW1

☎ 020 7930 2062, www.wpsa.co.uk

River boat trips on the Thames to Kew Gardens, Richmond and Hampton Court. Single or return journeys.

Also look at **www.royalparks.org.uk** for paddle boat rides in Regent's Park and Hyde Park.

## City farms

They may live in a city, but your kids can experience farmyard animals and learn about where their food comes from at these city farms (visit **www. farmgarden.org.uk** for others):

### Freightliners Farm

Sheringham Road, N7

☎ 020 7609 0467, www.freightlinersfarm.org.uk

Five bee hives, goats, rabbits, cattle, farmyard birds, garden and café.

### Hackney City Farm

1a Goldsmiths Row, E2

☎ 020 7729 6381, www.hackneycityfarm.co.uk

Pigs, donkey, goats, sheep, calves, chickens, as well as garden. Delicious café serving Italian dishes.

Kentish Town City Farm

1 Cressfield Close, NW5

☏ 020 7916 5421, www.ktcityfarm.org.uk

Horses, pigs, sheep, goats and farmyard birds. Riding program, garden, pond. Manure available for a donation.

## Cookery

Cookie Crumbles

☏ 020 8876 9912, www.cookiecrumbles.net

Cooking classes and parties for ages 4 to 16. Workshops held at Maggie & Rose (Kensington) and Eddie Catz (Putney).

Kids' Cookery School

107 Gunnersbury Lane, W3

☏ 020 8992 8882, www.thekidscookeryschool.co.uk

Offers school holiday and half-term classes and workshops for ages 3 and up.

Messy Hands

See above under *Art*. Creative cookery classes, parties and holiday workshops for ages 18 months to 3 years.

## Dance

Cherry Childe School of Dancing

Trinity Hall, Hodford Road, NW11

☏ 020 8458 6962

Ballet, modern and tap classes.

Creative Movements

☏ 020 7435 8217, www.creativemovements.co.uk

Combination of dance, music, drama and storytelling for children 6 months to 9 years. Parties, workshops and classes offered in north London. Multiple locations.

English National Ballet School

Carlyle Building, Hortensia Road, SW10

☏ 020 7376 7076, www.enbschool.org.uk

Three-year full-time classical ballet training for the serious student beginning at age 16. Audition required.

8

CHILDREN

The Marylebone Ballet School and Vacani Ballet
St Mary's Church Precinct, Wyndham Place, W1
© 07887 574 390, www.marylebonebal et.co.uk
Classical ballet for children aged 3 and up. Bayswater location as well.

Rona Hart School of Dance & Drama
Rosslyn Hall, Willoughby Road, NW3
© 020 7435 7073
Offers classical ballet, tap and jazz classes from age 2½.

Royal Academy of Dance
36 Battersea Square, SW11
© 020 7326 8000, www.rad.org.uk
Ballet, jazz, tap and contemporary dance for all ages and abilities.

## Drama/theatre
Many of the following listings offer excellent children's workshops
and/or performances.

Albert and Friends Instant Circus
Riverside Studios, Crisp Road, W6
© 020 8237 1170, www.albertandfriendsinstantcircus.co.uk
Workshops for circus skills, dance, drama and music. Runs the largest youth
circus in London.

Allsorts Drama
© 020 8969 3249, www.allsortsdrama.com
Drama classes and workshops for ages 4 to 8. Includes music and
movement, improvisation, mime, characterisation, costume and stage
makeup. Multiple locations.

Chickenshed
Chase Side, Southgate, N14
© 020 8292 9222, www.chickenshed.org.uk
Regular performances, special interactive theatrical productions for
pre-schoolers and theatre education workshops for those aged 5 to 24.

Colour House Children's Theatre
Merton Abbey Mills, SW19
© 020 8542 5511, www.colourhousetheatre.co.uk

Children's shows for ages 3 and up. Also offers a stage school for 7 to 16 year olds teaching musical theatre, singing, dance and drama.

### Little Angel Theatre
14 Dagmar Passage, N1
✆ 020 7226 1787, www.littleangeltheatre.com
High quality puppet theatre aimed at family audiences. Saturday Puppet Club and projects.

### Polka Theatre
240 The Broadway, Wimbledon, SW19
✆ 020 8543 4888, www.polkatheatre.com
Theatre and educational programmes for children up to age 13.

### Puppet Theatre Barge
Moored in Little Venice opposite 35 Blomfield Road, W9
✆ 020 7249 6876, www.puppetbarge.com
A floating theatre on a River Thames barge. Marionette and puppet shows for children aged 4 and up.

### Stagecoach
✆ 0193 225 4333, www.stagecoach.co.uk
Drama, dance and singing classes for ages 4 to 16. Multiple locations with no more than 15 per group.

### Tricycle Theatre
269 Kilburn High Road, NW6
✆ 020 7328 1000, www.tricycle.co.uk
Theatre productions and cinema screenings on Saturdays for children, plus regular and half-term workshops.

### Unicorn Theatre for Children
147 Tooley Street, SE1
✆ 020 7645 0560, www.unicorntheatre.com
Theatre for children ages 4 to 12 years; offers a Youth Theatre for ages 10 to 16 and a Young Company for ages 16 to 19. Family show at Christmas. Theatre location varies, call for details.

Warehouse Theatre

Dingwall Road, Croydon

℗020 8680 4060, www.warehousetheatre.co.uk

Plays and shows on weekends for young children.

Westminster School of Performing Arts

12 Old Pye Street, SW1

℗07768 310 521, www.westminsterperformingarts.co.uk

Drama, piano, gymnastics, singing and dance for ages 3 to 18.

---

**DID YOU KNOW?**

A Pantomime is a traditional British Christmas play performed at various theatres throughout the country over the holiday season. Pantomimes are great family entertainment; a mix of fairy stories, folk tales and much loved cartoons, which encourage audience participation. The male roles are often played by women and female roles by men.

---

## Libraries

Your local library in London is well worth an investigative trip. In addition to excellent collections of children's books, many have CD and DVD lending programmes and organised activities for children. Many libraries have story reading and rhyme times for younger children. The library is also a prime source of information on other local happenings for children, especially during the school holidays. Children receive their own lending cards by providing proof of local residence. Check with your local council website or information number for library information (see *Chapter 5: Utilities – Local councils* for contact information).

## Museums

There are countless museums in and around London of interest to children of all ages. The major museums in London have special activities, exhibits and quizzes during school holidays. Ring for information or consult weekly events magazines. The Science Museum on Exhibition Road and The Royal Air Force Museum in North London are excellent choices for entertaining young children on rainy days. See *Chapter 16: Culture – Museums and galleries* for a listing of museums and galleries that includes a designation for those recommended for children.

### Music

**Culture Kids**

✆ 020 8540 4203, www.culture-kids.com

Pre-school music classes in Chelsea, Hampstead, Kensington and Marylebone.

**Gymboree**

✆ 0800 092 0911, www.gymboree-uk.com

Activity and music classes from birth to 5 years old. Available for parties. Multiple locations.

**London Suzuki Group**

✆ 01372 720 088, www.londonsuzukigroup.co.uk

Suzuki method for violin, cello and piano.

**Monkey Music**

✆ 01582 766 464, www.monkeymusic.co.uk

Music and movement classes for children from 3 months to 5 years old. Multiple locations.

**Royal College of Music**

Prince Consort Road, SW7

✆ 020 589 3643, www.rcm.ac.uk

Offers Saturday school advanced training to musicians aged 8 to 18 (audition required).

### Parks/playgrounds

There are over 80 parks within a seven-mile radius of Hyde Park Corner. Most parks are open dawn until dusk. See *Chapter 14: Sports and leisure – Parks* for a full listing of parks and details. Also look at **www.royalparks.org. uk** for up-to-date activities and events being held in some of London's most popular parks.

Some parks that are especially good for children are:

**Battersea Park**

Albert Bridge Road, SW11

✆ 020 8871 7532, www.batterseapark.org

Children's zoo, toddlers' playground and an adventure playground.

### Coram's Fields
93 Guilford Street, WC1
This inner-city playground has an under-5s' sand and water themed play area (bring children a change of clothes), small animal enclosure, paddling pool and adventure play area for children aged 5 and up.

### Golders Hill Park
North End Road, NW11
Within Hampstead Heath. Playground and small zoo.

### Hampstead Heath
Parliament Hill, NW3
www.hampstead heath.net
Swimming pool (the Lido), adventure playground (ages 8+), wading pool and children's playground (near Parliament Hill). Visit the website for special events and a map.

### Holland Park
Ilchester Place, W8
www.rbkc.gov.uk
Lovely children's play area on the southwestern side of the park has sand, swings and other equipment for the under-8s. Adventure playground for older children.

### Primrose Hill
Prince Albert Road, NW8
Just north of Regent's Park. Has a gated children's play area at the southern end of the park, bordering Prince Albert Road.

### Diana, Princess of Wales Memorial Playground
Kensington Gardens, W8
℡ 020 7298 2141, www.royalparks.gov.uk
Large gated play area on the north side of Kensington Gardens for children up to 12 years old. Sand, swings, slides and lots of wooden play pieces, including a pirate ship for children to climb on.

### Regent's Park
NW1
℡ 020 7486 7905, www.royalparks.gov.uk
Has three gated children's play areas, paddling and row boats, and at the

northern end of the park you will find London Zoo (which also contains a playground).

### St. Luke's Gardens
Sydney Street, SW3
✆ 020 7361 3003, www.rbkc.gov.uk
Popular children's play area convenient for Chelsea and South Kensington.

## Parties
Many of the companies listed above in the *Arts*, *Baby gyms*, *Cookery*, *Dance*, *Drama/theatre* and *Music* sections will host parties at their venues or provide entertainment at your home or another location. Be sure to book popular entertainers well in advance (three to four months prior to the event) to avoid disappointment.

### AnimalMan
✆ 01992 469 693, www.animalman.co.uk
Will bring a variety of animals to your party! Best for ages 4 to 8 with full show of 1½ hours.

### Blueberry Playsongs
✆ 020 8677 6871, www.blueberryplaysongs.co.uk
Guitar, songs and puppets for children's parties.

### Mr. Marvel
✆ 08707 662 525, www.mrmarvel.co.uk
Magic and fun, Punch & Judy, disco with snow and bubble machine for 3 to 6-year-olds.

### Mystical Fairies
See above under *Costumes/fancy dress*. Caters children's parties (for fairies and pirates) on the premises.

### Non Stop Party Shop
214-216 Kensington High Street, W8
✆ 020 7937 7200, www.nonstopparty.co.uk
Tableware, balloons and party products under one roof and online. Multiple locations.

8

CHILDREN

### Smartie Artie

✆ 01582 600 529, www.smartieartie.com

Party entertainer that includes puppets, games, comedy, magic and balloon making.

### Stage Star

✆ 07751 713 685, www.stagestar.com

Themed entertainment from professional actors, dancers and singers. Extras include face painters, organic catering, hand painted invitations, goody boxes and more.

### Starbags

Semmalina, 225 Ebury Street, SW1

✆ 020 7730 9333, www.starbags.info

Bespoke hand-made party bags, suitable for children and adults alike.

### Twizzle Parties & Events

✆ 0208 392 0860, www.twizzle.co.uk

Plans themed parties, mini-discos, puppet shows and sing-alongs with musical instruments for all ages. Party entertainment can include clowns, games, competitions and magic.

## Restaurants

There are a surprising number of London restaurants that positively welcome children. Sunday lunch is a popular family meal, so children are usually expected anywhere. Here is a small selection of child-friendly restaurants where you will always find a highchair.

### Carluccio's

8 Market Place, W1

✆ 020 7636 2228, www.carluccios.com

Casual Italian restaurant with children's menu. Multiple locations.

### Giraffe

6-8 Blandford Street, W1

✆ 020 7935 2333, www.giraffe.net

Family friendly for breakfast, lunch and dinner; eclectic menu. Multiple locations.

La Famiglia
7 Langton St, SW10
✆ 020 7351 0761, www.lafamiglia.co.uk
Great local Italian.

Le Pain Quotidien
72-75 Marylebone High Street, W1
✆ 020 7486 6154, www.lepainquotidien.com
Communal tables, delicious organic breads and pastries.

Rainforest Café
20 Shaftesbury Avenue, W1
✆ 020 7434 3111, www.therainforestcafe.co.uk
Full of screeching monkeys, jungle plants and baboons, for the young,
or young at heart.

Rossopomodoro
50-52 Monmouth Street, WC2
✆ 020 7240 9095, www.rossopomodoro.co.uk
Traditional food and wine of Naples, especially yummy pizza.
Multiple locations.

Tate Modern Café: Level 2
Bankside, SE1
✆ 020 7887 5014, www.tate.org.uk/modern
Eating on premises of the art museum.

Wagamama
1 Tavistock Street, WC2
✆ 020 7836 3330, www.wagamama.com
Asian noodle restaurant where diners eat at communal tables.
Multiple locations.

## Scouting and girl guides
Scouting and Girl guiding are organisations that provide a variety of activities and outdoor challenges for boys and girls. Through non-formal education, they strive to instil teamwork, leadership, life lessons and life skills in their participants. Contact the organisation to identify local chapters.

### Girlguiding UK

*☎ 020 7834 6242, www.girlguiding.org.uk*

For girl guides in the UK: Rainbows (ages 5 to 7), Brownies (ages 7 to 10), Guides (ages 10 to 14) and Senior Section (ages 14 to 25).

### World Association of Girl Guides and Girl Scouts

World Bureau, 12c Lyndhurst Road, NW3

*☎ 020 7794 1181, www.wagggsworld.org*

Umbrella organisation for all Girl Guide and Girl Scout organisations in the world.

### The Scout Association

Gilwell Park, Chingford, E4

*☎ 0845 300 1818, www.scouts.org.uk*

Open to boys and girls aged 6 to 25.

## Sports

In addition to the sports choices below, several health clubs offer excellent children's programmes. See *Chapter 14: Sports and leisure* for more information about sporting activities, including *Horse riding*, *Ice skating*, *Martial arts* and *Tennis*.

### Baseball/softball

### LondonSports Baseball/Softball

www.londonsports.com

Offers several youth baseball and softball leagues for children aged 5 to 13. Practice sessions and games take place at Wormwood Scrubs, Hammersmith during the spring.

### Basketball

### LondonSports Basketball

www.londonsports.com

Winter basketball programme for girls and boys aged 7 to 14. Many of the games are played at the American School in St. Johns Wood, though other locations are also in use.

### Cricket

**MCC Indoor Cricket School**

Lord's Cricket Grounds, St. Johns Wood, NW8

✆ 020 7616 8616, www.lords.org

Children aged 8 to 18 can learn cricket at the renowned 'home of cricket'.

### Football

**Little Kickers**

✆ 01235 859 250, www.littlekickers.co.uk

Offers classes for ages 18 months through 7, year round in blocks of 12 weeks. Multiple locations.

**LondonSports Football**

www.londonsports.com

Provides football leagues for boys and girls aged 4 to 13 at Wormwood Scrubs, Hammersmith during the school year.

### Swimming

Swimming pools offer lessons and regular activities for children as well as special programmes during school holidays. Many facilities have a separate shallow teaching pool for very small children, separate diving areas and wave machines. See *Chapter 14: Sports and leisure – Swimming* for more information.

**Aquababies**

✆ 01273 833 101, www.aquababies-uk.com

Swimming classes for babies and toddlers up to 4 years old.
Multiple locations

**Little Dippers**

✆ 0844 482 0222, www.littledippers.co.uk

Infant water safety training classes for babies. Multiple locations.

**Swimming Nature**

✆ 0870 094 9597, www.swimmingnature.com

Classes offered for babies 6 months and older. Multiple locations.

### Zoos

Visit the Good Zoo Guide Online at **www.goodzoos.com**, which has a complete listing of all of the zoos and wildlife parks in the UK.

Battersea Park Children's Zoo

Battersea Park, SW11

✆ 020 7924 5826, www.batterseapark.org

ZSL London Zoo

Outer Circle, Regent's Park, NW1

✆ 020 7722 3333, www.zsl.org

ZSL Whipsnade Zoo

Dunstable, Bedfordshire

✆ 01582 872 171, www.zsl.org

Walk or drive over 600 acres. Tour bus and train also available. Animals are enclosed in very large spaces.

# Resources for parents

Angels & Urchins

✆ 020 8741 1035, www.angelsandurchins.co.uk

A stylish and helpful quarterly magazine for families living in London. Available in many children's stores, schools or by paid subscription.

Babyccino Kids

www.babyccinokids.com

Chic daily blog for mums in the city – recommends kids products, clothes, books, crafts projects, recipes and more. Check out the London city guide with tips for where to eat, go, shop and play.

Families

✆ 020 8696 9680, www.familiesonline.co.uk

Useful local magazine and website for families with young children in London areas. Publishes different editions specific to postcode. Available free in many children's stores, schools or by post on subscription. The website is a great resource, covering issues such as health, childcare, schools and birthday parties.

London Baby Directory

www.babydirectory.com

Useful resource book for under 5's for shopping, childcare, nurseries, activities, parties and more, available in various children's stores or online.

### London4Kidz

www.london4kidz.co.uk

Updated information on entertainment and attractions for children in and around London.

### Mini-et-moi

www.mini-et-moi.com

Information on places and activities in London available to new mums and under-2s.

### Mumsnet

www.mumsnet.com

Content driven by the community of parents, pooling knowledge, experience and support. Good reviews on baby products and excellent chat boards, as well as discounts to baby stores. Also publish Mumsnet Guides, a series of parenting and lifestyle books.

### Parents' Directory

℡ 020 7733 0088, www.parentsdirectories.com

Directories published twice a year in April and October with information on nurseries, schools, au pair and nanny agencies, nappy services, after school and holiday activities and more. Available for South West, South East, North West and Central London and distributed in ante-natal clinics, libraries, health centres, etc.

### Time Out London

www.timeout.com/london

Time Out offers a kids section on its website and its weekly magazine found at newsagents and available by subscription, as well as an information-packed annual guidebook, *London for Children*.

### Visit London

www.visitlondon.com

Good starting point for any London information. There is a special family section on their website that lists family-friendly attractions, events and activities.

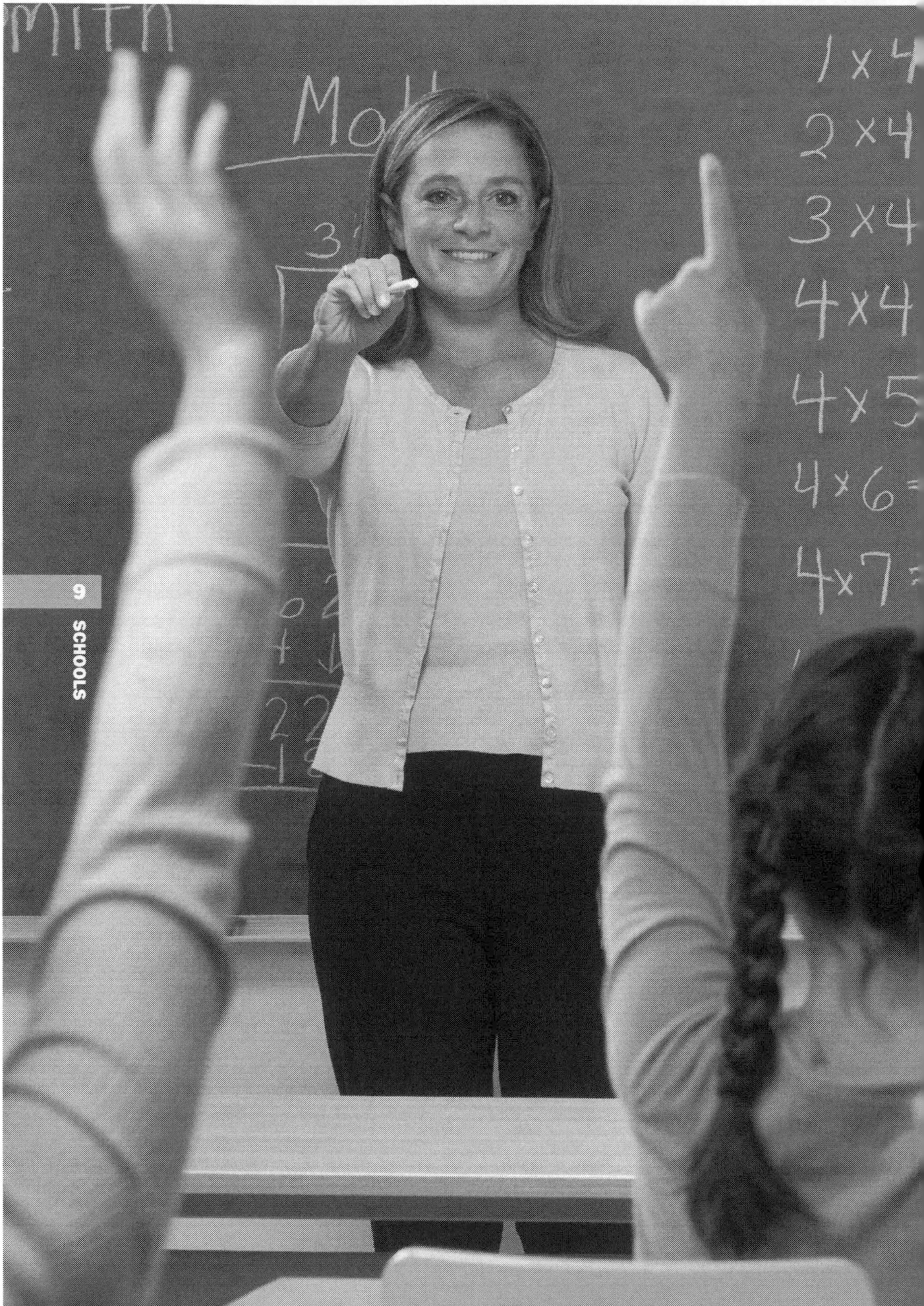
1x4
2x4
3x4
4x4
4x5
4x6
4x7

# Schools

The London area is full of excellent schools. Finding the school that best meets the needs of one's child and family can take considerable time due to the choice available. The decision should involve a number of considerations, including: your estimated length of time in England, your children's ages, adaptability of the children and the overall impact that a change to the English system might have on the children and family.

Before making a decision, families should talk to friends and colleagues with children of similar ages. Additionally, families should visit and speak to as many different schools as possible. Education consultants may also be a valuable resource in selecting the right school.

## IN THIS CHAPTER...

- The British school system
- Publications and resources
- Educational consultants
- Independent British schools: nursery, prep, senior and boarding

- International, foreign national and American schools
- Learning difficulties or special needs
- Applying to American universities
- British vs American school system

# The British school system

Children in the UK must be in full-time education the term after their fifth birthday. Many local authorities will accept children into school at the beginning of the term that they turn five. From September 2011, schools must accept children into primary school the September following the child's fourth birthday. However, parents may still choose that the child begin school later in the year or at the compulsory age. Parents may also request that their child attend part-time until the compulsory age. There may be some differences depending on school (state or independent, see below), so it is best to contact each school individually.

The system can be confusing to a newcomer and may differ from location to location. Within the British school system, schools are generally grouped into two categories: state schools, which are run by the Government, and independent schools, which are privately run and fee-paying. Confusingly, independent schools are also referred to as public schools in many areas. State schools may also include religious foundations schools (i.e., the Church of England and Roman Catholic schools).

## State schools

As in any country, some state schools outperform independent schools in the same area. Therefore, choosing a state school may be a very viable option. However, places in the top state schools are very competitive to obtain, as families move to the respective areas to register their children at a very early age. In many instances, matters are even more complicated for incoming families, as many state schools restrict registration until a family can prove residence in the relevant catchment area. This makes it very difficult to simultaneously co-ordinate housing and schooling.

State schools follow the National Curriculum and are subjected to periodic standardised testing called **SATs** (Standardized Assessment Tasks) up through the age of 13 or 14. At the age of 14, students commence their **GCSE** (General Certificate of Secondary Education), a two-year program ending in a standardised exam also known as the GCSE. Following GCSE, students will either move on to study a vocational trade or pursue **A levels** (Advanced Level), which are required for entrance to University. A student may take several A level courses, typically concentrating on the subjects he or she hopes to study at University (e.g., sciences or languages). Each A level course also concludes with a standardised test, and A level results are crucial to the British University admissions process. While independent schools are not obliged to comply with the A level curriculum, many do.

Each school (whether state or independent) has its GCSE and A Level exam results published annually as part of the National League Tables that are released in the major British newspapers. They can be useful but, as their critics point out, they represent only one measure of each school's success. In addition, certain independent schools offer the International GCSE (**IGCSE**), but this is not recognised for League Table purposes; as such, certain highly regarded schools may appear anomalously in this part of the League Table. The Good Schools Guide (**www.goodschoolsguide.co.uk**; see more information below) has a good discussion on their limitations. Additionally, the Office for Standards in Education (**Ofsted**), an independent organisation that objectively reports the standards and quality of each school, making recommendations where necessary, inspects all state schools. You can read each school's Ofsted report on the Ofsted website at **www.ofsted.gov.uk**. Nursery school reports are also available.

To enrol your child in a state school, you should contact the school directly as well as the Local Education Authority (**LEA**) of the borough in which you plan to live. Most boroughs provide guidance documents and contact information on-line.

In addition, the following organisations may also provide helpful advice:

The British Council
10 Spring Gardens, SW1
✆ 020 7389 4387, www.britishcouncil.org
An education information service.

The Department for Children, Schools and Families
Sanctuary Buildings, Great Smith Street, SW1
✆ 08700 002 288, www.dcsf.gov.uk
Overall policy setting government department; they supply the telephone number for your LEA.

Ofsted
Alexandra House, 125 Kingsway, WC2
✆ 08456 404 045, www.ofsted.gov.uk

## Independent schools

Independent schools vary in size, facilities and, most importantly, in philosophy towards education. For example, some schools adhere to sections of the National Curriculum, where others have abolished A levels and now offer the International Baccalaureate (covered in more detail below).

Entrance into most schools is determined by examination and/or personal interview. Due to the limited number of spaces and high demand, many schools require long advance notice for admission. As a result, many parents register their children at birth. However, incoming parents should not be put off, nor should news that there is no place for your child at a particular school discourage you. Gracious determination sometimes pays dividends.

Although only about 7 per cent of students in England attend independent schools, there are over 2,000 to choose from, including local day schools and boarding schools. The boarding school tradition is strong in the UK, and it is not uncommon for boys to be sent away at age eight and girls at age eleven. Many good schools, both primary and secondary, are single sex. A number of publications and consulting services are around to help you select a day or boarding school.

Examinations and interviews for entry into independent secondary schools should be expected. Boys and girls take entrance exams at different ages. Boys take an exam for Preparatory School at age 7 or 8 years and the Common Entrance Exam at age 13, while girls take the '11+' or Common Entrance Exam at age 11, 12 or 13. Many schools have organised open days when groups of prospective parents (and their children) are shown around the school, with opportunities to meet the staff.

All independent schools, including American and international schools, are inspected regularly by the Independent Schools Inspectorate (**ISI**), an independent body which reports on the standards and quality of Independent Schools. You can read a copy of each school's report on the ISI website at **www.isi.net**.

**DID YOU KNOW?**

Independent schools in England are often referred to as **public schools**. Until 1902, there were no publicly supported secondary schools in England. Public schools were supported by an endowment, with a governing body, and were available to all members of the public provided they could pay for tuition costs. Private schools were run for private profit. In recent years, all schools formerly called public schools now refer to themselves as independent schools, but the national press (and many individuals) still use the term public school when referring to independent schools. In particular, the older, more prestigious, fee-paying schools mentioned in the Public Schools Act of 1868 (Charterhouse, Eton, Harrow, Merchant Taylors', Rugby, Shrewsbury, St. Paul's, Westminster and Winchester) are typically still referred to as public schools.

# Publications and resources

*Gabbitas Guide to Independent Schools*
Gabbitas Educational Consultants
Carrington House, 126-130 Regent Street, W1
✆ 020 7734 0161, www.gabbitas.co.uk
A comprehensive directory of independent schools (pre-prep to senior) with a geographical directory and advertisements.

*The Good Schools Guide*
3 Craven Mews, SW11
✆ 020 7801 0191, www.goodschoolsguide.co.uk
Information on over 350 top private and state schools in the UK (junior and senior, day and boarding), including an online subscription option that offers a catchments area map based on your postcode.

*The Independent Schools Council*
St. Vincent House, 30 Orange Street, WC2
✆ 020 7766 7070, www.isc.co.uk
A wide variety of online resources, including a dedicated Parent Zone, with the opportunity to search for independent schools.

9

SCHOOLS

*Which London School? & the South East*
www.whichlondonschool.co.uk
Published annually. This guide lists details of independent day, boarding, nursery and international schools in London and South East area. The book is available through **www.johncattbookshop.com** or may be purchased from booksellers such as **www.amazon.co.uk**.

# Educational consultants

Educational consultants can prove extremely valuable and helpful as one looks for schools in the London area. As mentioned above, educational consultants are not only extremely knowledgeable about schools in the London area, but also often have good contacts at schools that may be helpful in obtaining a place. A good educational consultant will usually start by 'interviewing' you to better understand what schools might be a good match. The educational consultant will usually arrange for you to receive school prospectuses. Additionally, he or she will typically arrange for visits to the school, possibly accompanying you on the visits, and then assisting you through the admissions process. However, a good educational consultant will not tell you which school to choose – that is a very personal choice.

Below are some educational consultants that Junior League of London members have utilised.

### Humphrys' Education Limited
Erasmus House, Church Square, Shepperton, TW17
✆ 0193 2250 368, www.humphrys-education.com
Martin Humphrys, the Managing Director, has been a teacher, housemaster, athletics coach and the general manager for the University of Westminster Union in the UK. Additionally, he has advised the US State Department and various other associations and agencies on the position of schools within the UK.

### Bowker Consulting Ltd
Suite 38, 500 Avebury Boulevard, Milton Keynes, MK9
✆ 01908 547 950, www.bowker.org.uk
A variety of services for both domestic and expatriate families.

School Choice International, Inc.

1600 Harrison Avenue, Suite 208, Mamaroneck, NY 10543, USA

✆ +1 914 328 3000, www.schoolchoiceintl.com

Elizabeth Perelstein, the President, has been a teacher, a primary school administrator, a university administrator and a board of education trustee. She lived in England for three years, during which time she visited numerous British schools and guided many families through the school selection process.

The Good Schools Guide Advisory Service

3 Craven Mews, SW11

✆ 020 7801 0191, www.goodschoolsguide.co.uk

A consultancy run by The Good Schools Guide® to advise parents, on a one-to-one basis, on choosing the best schools for their children.

# Independent British schools: nursery, prep, senior and boarding

The school system in the UK can be confusing. The independent (i.e., privately run) school system in particular, has no standard age at which nursery, junior or senior schools begin and end.

In general, nursery schools take children between the ages of 2½ and 5 years; junior schools will take children from age 5 to 11 or 13 and senior school begins at age 11 for girls and age 13 for boys.

State schools are a bit more straightforward. There is pre-school (for the under 5's), primary school (aged 5 to 11 or 13) and secondary school (until graduation at age 18).

## Age and grade equivalents

The following chart may be helpful as you enquire about British schools.

| Age (in years) – Beginning of School Year | English Year | English Independent School System Level | English State School Level | American Grade | American School Level |
|---|---|---|---|---|---|
| 4 | Reception | Pre-Prep | Pre-School | Pre-Kindergarten | Pre-School |
| 5 | Year 1 | Pre-Prep | Primary or Infant's School | Kindergarten | Elementary |
| 6 | Year 2 | Pre-Prep | Primary or Infant's School | First Grade | Elementary |
| 7 | Year 3 | Pre-Prep or Prep Depending on School | Primary or Junior's School | Second Grade | Elementary |
| 8 | Year 4 | Pre-Prep or Prep Depending on School | Primary or Junior's School | Third Grade | Elementary |
| 9 | Year 5 | Prep | Primary or Junior's School | Fourth Grade | Elementary or Middle Depending on School |
| 10 | Year 6 | Prep | Primary or Junior's School | Fifth Grade | Elementary or Middle Depending on School |
| 11 | Year 7 | Prep for boys, Senior for girls | Secondary School | Sixth Grade | Elementary or Middle Depending on School |
| 12 | Year 8 | Prep for boys, Senior for girls | Secondary School | Seventh Grade | Elementary or Middle Depending on School |
| 13 | Year 9 | Senior | Secondary School | Eighth Grade | Elementary or Middle Depending on School |
| 14 | Year 10, First year of GCSE | Senior | Secondary School | Ninth Grade | High School |
| 15 | Year 11, Second year of GCSE | Senior | Secondary School | Tenth Grade | High School |
| 16 | Year 12, First year of A Levels | Senior | Sixth Form College | Eleventh Grade | High School |
| 17 | Year 13, Second Year of A Levels | Senior | Sixth Form College | Twelfth Grade | High School |

There is a also helpful chart comparing the differing English school systems on the Wikipedia website (**www.wikipedia.org**) entitled 'Education in England'.

### Independent schools in London

Junior League of London members know a number of private or independent English schools. The schools have been divided into the following groups: nursery, junior/pre-prep schools and senior/preparatory schools.

Our list is by no means exhaustive; there are many more good schools than are listed here. These are simply schools recommended by at least one of our members.

### Nursery (boys and girls)

Note that in many cases, it is wise to register a child for nursery school as soon as possible, even at birth. Unless otherwise noted, each school accepts children from the ages of 2½ to 5 years.

Acorn Nursery School
2 Lansdowne Crescent, W11
✆ 020 7727 2122
(Ages 2 years 6 months to 5 years 6 months).

Asquith Nurseries
West Hampstead Day Nursery, 11 Woodchurch Road, NW6
✆ 01753 201 122, www.asquithnurseries.co.uk
(Ages 3 months to 5 years).

The Boltons Nursery School
262 Fulham Road, SW10 9EL
✆ 020 7351 6993

Broadhurst School
19 Greencroft Gardens, NW6
✆ 020 7328 4280, www.broadhurstschool.com

The Chelsea Pre-prep & Nursery
St. Andrew's Church, Park Walk, SW10
✆ 020 7352 4856, www.chelseapreprepandnursery.co.uk

Chelsea Open Air Nursery School
51 Glebe Place, SW3
© 020 7352 8374, www.coans.rbkc.sch.uk
(Ages 3 to 5).

Eaton Square Nursery and Preparatory School
79 Eccleston Square, SW1
© 020 7931 9469, www.eatonsquareschool.com
(Ages 2½ to 13).

Falkner House
19 Brechin Place, SW7
© 020 7373 4501, www.falknerhouse.co.uk
(Girls, ages 3 to 11).

Garden House School
Turks Row, SW3
© 020 7730 1652 (Girls' School) or © 020 7730 6652 (Boys' School)
www.gardenhouseschool.co.uk
(Ages 3 to 11).

Great Beginnings Montessori Nursery School
37-39 Brendon Street, W1
© 020 7258 1066, www.greatbeginningsnursery.com
(Ages 2 to 6).

The Hampshire School
63 Ennismore Gardens, SW7
© 020 7584 3297, www.ths.westminster.sch.uk
(Ages 3 to 5).

Hampstead Hill School
St. Stephens Hall, Pond Street, NW3
© 020 7435 6262

Holland Park Nursery School
The Undercroft, St. John's Church, Landsdowne Crescent, W11
© 020 7221 2194

The Knightsbridge Kindergarten
St. Peter's Church, 119 Eaton Square, SW1
☎ 020 7371 2306
(Ages 2 to 5).

Ladbroke Square Montessori School
43 Ladbroke Square, W11
☎ 020 7229 0125
(Ages 2½ to 5½).

The Maria Montessori School
26 Lyndhurst Gardens, NW3
☎ 020 7435 3646, www.mariamontessorischools.co.uk
(Ages 2½ to 12). There are branches in Notting Hill, Bayswater, Holly Park, Hampstead and West Hampstead.

The Minors Nursery School
10 Pembridge Square, W2
☎ 020 7727 7253, www.minorsnursery.co.uk
(Ages 2½ to 4½).

Miss Daisy's Nursery
Fountain Court Club Room, Ebury Square, SW1
☎ 020 7730 5797, www.missdaisysnursery.com
(Ages 2 to 5).

The Willcocks Nursery School
Holy Trinity Church, Prince Consort Road, SW7
☎ 020 7937 2027, www.willcocksnurseryschool.com

North Bridge House Nursery School
33 Fitzjohn's Avenue, NW3
☎ 020 7435 9641, www.northbridgehouse.com
There is also an associated junior school.

The Oak Tree Nursery
6 Arkwright Rd, NW3
☎ 020 7435 1916, www.devonshirehouseschool.co.uk
(Starts at 2½). At pre-reception children join the Devonshire House Preparatory School, listed under Co-educational schools below.

9
SCHOOLS

Paint Pots Montessori Schools
London House, 266 Fulham Road, SW10
(Ages 18 months to 8 years). There are branches in Bayswater, Hyde Park and Chelsea.

The Phoenix School
36 College Crescent, NW3
✆ 020 7722 4433, www.ucs.org.uk
(Ages 3 to 7). Part of the University College School, with associated junior and senior schools.

Rainbow Montessori School
13 Woodchurch Road, NW6
✆ 020 7328 8986, www.rainbowmontessori.co.uk

Ravenstone House Queensbury Place
22 Queensbury Place, SW7
✆ 020 7584 7955
(Ages 1 to 3).

Ravenstone House
Hyde Park, Albion Street, St. Georges Fields, W2
✆ 020 7262 1190
(Ages 2 months to 7 years).

Ringrose Kindergarten
32 Lupus St, SW1
✆ 020 7976 6511

Ringrose Kindergarten (Chelsea)
St. Lukes Church Hall, St. Lukes Street, SW3
✆ 020 7352 8784

Rolfe's Nursery School
206-208 Kensington Park Road, W11
✆ 020 7727 8300, www.rolfesnurseryschool.co.uk

St. Marks Square Nursery School
St. Marks Church, Regents Park Road, NW1
✆ 020 7586 8383, www.stmarkssquarenurseryschool.org.uk

St. Christina's School
25 St. Edmund's Terrace, NW8
✆ 020 7722 8784, www.stchristinas.org.uk
(Boys, ages 3 to 7; Girls, ages 3 to 11).

St. Johns Wood Pre-Preparatory School
Lord's Roundabout, NW8
✆ 020 7722 7149, www.sjwpre-prep.org.uk
(Ages 3 to 7).

Thomas's Kindergarten
14 Ranelagh Grove, SW1
✆ 020 7730 3596
and The Crypt, St. Mary's Church, Battersea Church Road, SW11
✆ 020 7738 0400, www.thomas-s.co.uk

Strawberry Fields Nursery School
Notting Hill Community Church, Kensington Park Road, W11
✆ 020 7727 8363

Toddlers Inn
Cicely Davis Hall, Cochrane Street, NW8
✆ 020 7586 0520
(Ages 2 to 5).

Young England Kindergarten
St. Saviour's Hall, St. George's Square, SW1
✆ 020 7834 3171, www.youngenglandkindergarten.co.uk

**Boys' junior and preparatory schools**

Arnold House
1-3 Loudoun Road, NW8
✆ 020 7266 4840, www.arnoldhouse.co.uk
(Ages 5 to 13).

Colet Court (St. Paul's Preparatory School)
Lonsdale Road, SW13
✆ 020 8748 3461, www.stpaulsschool.org.uk
(Ages 7/8 to 13).

Dulwich College Junior School
Dulwich Common, SE21
℃ 020 8299 9248, www.dulwich.org.uk

Eaton House Belgravia
3-5 Eaton Gate, SW1W
℃ 020 7924 6000, www.eatonhouseschools.com
(Ages 4 to 8).

Eaton House The Manor
58 Clapham Common Northside, SW4
℃ 020 7924 6000, www.eatonhouseschools.com
(Boys, ages 8 to 13; also pre-prep for boys and girls, ages 4 to 8).

The Falcons Pre-Preparatory School
2 Burnaby Gardens, Chiswick, W4
℃ 020 8747 8393, www.falconschool.com
(Ages 3 to 8).

The Hall
23 Crossfield Road, NW3
℃ 020 7722 1700, www.hallschool.co.uk
(Ages 5 to 13).

Hawkesdown House School
27 Edge St, W8
℃ 020 7727 9090, www.hawkesdown.co.uk
(Ages 3 to 8).

Lyndhurst House School
24, Lyndhurst Gardens, NW3
℃ 020 7435 4936, www.lyndhursthouse.co.uk
(Ages 6 to 13).

St. Anthony's Preparatory School
90 Fitzjohn's Ave, NW3
℃ 020 7431 1066, www.stanthonysprep.org.uk
(Ages 5 to 13).

St. Philip's School
6 Wetherby Place, SW7
✆ 020 7373 3944, www.stphilipsschool.co.uk
(Ages 7 to 13).

University College School Junior School
11 Holly Hill, NW3
✆ 020 7435 3068, www.ucs.org.uk
(Ages 7 to 11).

Sussex House School
68 Cadogan Square, SW1
✆ 020 7584 1741
(Ages 8 to 13).

Tower House Preparatory School
188 Sheen Lane, SW14
✆ 020 8876 3323, www.thsboys.org.uk
(Ages 4 to 13).

Wimbledon College Prep School
33 Edge Hill, SW19
✆ 020 8946 7000, www.donhead.org.uk
(Ages 11 to 18).

Westminster Under School
Adrian House, 27 Vincent Square, SW1
✆ 020 7821 5788, www.westminsterunder.org.uk
(Ages 8 to 13).

Wetherby School
11 Pembridge Square, W2
✆ 020 7727 9581, www.wetherbyschool.co.uk
(Ages 4 to 8).

Wetherby Preparatory School
Bryanston Square, W1
✆ 020 7535 3520, www.wetherbyprep.co.uk
(Ages 7 to 13).

9

SCHOOLS

## Boys' senior schools

The following schools are for boys aged 13 to 18 unless noted otherwise.

City of London School
Queen Victoria Street, EC4
✆ 020 7489 0291, www.clsb.org
(Ages 10 to 18).

Dulwich College
Dulwich Common, SE21
✆ 020 8693 3601, www.dulwich.org.uk
(Ages 7 to 18).

King's College School (Wimbledon)
Southside, Wimbledon Common, SW19
✆ 020 8255 5300, www.kcs.org.uk

St. Paul's School
Lonsdale Road, SW13
✆ 020 8748 9162, www.stpaulsschool.org.uk

University College School (UCS)
Frognal, Hampstead, NW3
✆ 020 7435 2215, www.ucs.org.uk
(Ages 11 to 18).

Westminster School
Little Dean's Yard, SW1
✆ 020 7963 1000, www.westminster.org.uk

Wimbledon College
Edge Hill, SW19
✆ 020 8946 2533, www.wimbledoncollege.org.uk
(Ages 11 to 18).

## Boys' boarding schools

The following boarding schools are affiliated with the Church of England:

Charterhouse
Godalming, Surrey, GU7
✆ 01483 291 500, www.charterhouse.org.uk

Eton College
Windsor, Berkshire, SL4
℡ 01753 671 000, www.etoncollege.com

Harrow School
5 High Street, Harrow on the Hill, Middlesex, HA1
℡ 020 8872 8000, www.harrowschool.org.uk

Marlborough College
Wiltshire, SN8
℡ 01672 892 200, www.marlboroughcollege.org

Millfield
Edgarley Hall, Glastonbury, Somerset, BA6
℡ 01458 832 446, www.millfieldprep.com

Radley College
Abingdon, Oxford, OX14
℡ 01235 543 000, www.radley.org.uk

Winchester College
College Street, Winchester, Hampshire, SO23
℡ 01962 621 100, www.winchestercollege.org

For information on boys' boarding schools administered by the Roman Catholic Church, contact:

Catholic Education Service for England and Wales
39 Eccleston Square, SW1
℡ 0207 901 1900, www.cesew.org.uk

## Girls' junior and preparatory schools

Bute House Preparatory School for Girls
Bute House, Luxemburg Gardens, W6
℡ 020 7603 7381, www.butehouse.co.uk
(Ages 4 to 11).

Cavendish School
179 Arlington Road, NW1
℡ 020 7485 1958, www.cavendish-school.co.uk
(Ages 3 to 11).

Channing School
Fairseat, the Junior School, The Bank, Highgate, N6
© 020 8342 9862, www.channing.co.uk
(Ages 4 to 11).

City of London School for Girls
St. Gile's Terrace, Barbican, EC2
© 020 7847 5500, www.clsg.org.uk
(Ages 7 to 18).

Falkner House
19 Brechin Place, SW7
© 020 7373 4501, www.falknerhouse.co.uk
(Ages 4 to 11).

Francis Holland (Sloane Square)
39 Graham Terrace, SW1
© 020 7730 2971, www.francisholland.org.uk
(Ages 4 to 18).

Glendower Preparatory School
87 Queen's Gate, SW7
© 020 7370 1927, www.glendowerprep.org
(Ages 4 to 11).

James Allen's Girls' School (JAGS)
144 East Dulwich Grove, SE22
© 020 8693 1181, www.jags.org.uk
(Ages 4 to 19).

Kensington Preparatory School
596 Fulham Road, SW6
© 020 7731 9300, www.kensingtonprep.gdst.net
(Ages 4 to 11).

Notting Hill and Ealing High School
2 Cleveland Road, W13
© 020 8799 8400, www.nhehs.gdst.net
(Ages 5 to 18).

Pembridge Hall School
18 Pembridge Square, W2
☎ 020 7229 0121, www.pembridgehall.co.uk
(Ages 4½ to 11).

Putney High School
35 Putney Hill, SW15
☎ 020 8788 4886, www.putneyhigh.co.uk
(Ages 4 to 18).

Queen's College Preparatory School
61 Portland Place, W1
☎ 020 7291 0660, www.qcps.org.uk
(Ages 3½-11).

Queen's Gate School
131-133 Queen's Gate, SW7
☎ 020 7589 3587, www.queensgate.org.uk
(Ages 4 to 18).

The Royal School Hampstead
65 Rosslyn Hill, NW3
☎ 020 7794 7708, www.royalschoolhampstead.net
(Ages 3 to 18).

Sarum Hall
15 Eton Avenue, NW3
☎ 020 7794 2261, www.sarumhallschool.co.uk
(Ages 3 to 11).

South Hampstead High School
3 Maresfield Gardens, NW3
☎ 020 7435 2899, www.shhs.gdst.net
(Ages 4 to 18).

St. Christopher's School
2 Belsize Lane, NW3
☎ 020 7435 1521, www.st-christophers.hampstead.sch.uk
(Ages 4 to 11).

St. Margaret's School

18 Kidderpore Gardens, NW3

✆020 7435 2439, www.st-margarets.co.uk

(Ages 4 to 16).

The Study Preparatory School

Wilberforce House, Camp Road, Wimbledon Common, SW19

✆020 8947 6969, www.thestudyprep.co.uk

(Ages 4 to 11).

Ursuline Convent Preparatory School

18 The Downs, SW20

✆020 8947 0859, www.ursuline-prep.merton.sch.uk

(Ages 3 to 12).

Wimbledon High School

Mansel Road, SW19

✆020 8971 0900, www.wimbledonhigh.gdst.net

(Ages 4 to 19).

## Girls' senior schools

All schools accept girls from age 11 unless otherwise noted.

Channing School

The Bank, Highgate, N6

✆020 8340 2328, www.channing.co.uk

City of London School for Girls

St. Gile's Terrace, Barbican, EC2Y

✆020 7847 5500, www.clsg.org.uk

Francis Holland (Regents Park)

Clarence Gate, Ivor Place, NW1

✆020 7723 0176, www.francisholland.org.uk

(Ages 11 to 18).

The Godolphin and Latymer School

Iffley Road, W6

✆020 8741 1936, www.godolphinandlatymer.com

James Allen's Girls' School (JAGS)
144 East Dulwich Grove, SE22
✆ 020 8693 1181, www.jags.org.uk
(Ages 4 to 19).

More House School
22-24 Pont Street, SW1X
✆ 020 7235 2855, www.morehouse.org.uk

North London Collegiate School
Canons, Canons Drive, Edgware, HA8
✆ 020 8952 0912, www.nlcs.org.uk
(Ages 4 to 18).

Putney High School
35 Putney Hill, SW15
✆ 020 8788 4886, www.putneyhigh.co.uk

The Royal School Hampstead
65 Rosslyn Hill, NW3
✆ 020 7794 7708, www.royalschoolhampstead.net
(Ages 3 to 18).

Queen's Gate School
131-133 Queen's Gate, SW7
✆ 020 7589 3587, www.queensgate.org.uk

South Hampstead High School
3 Maresfield Gardens, NW3
✆ 020 7435 2899, www.shhs.gdst.net

St. Paul's Girls' School
Brook Green, W6
✆ 020 7603 2288, www.spgs.org
(Ages 11 to 18).

Westminster School
Little Dean's Yard, SW1
✆ 020 7963 1003, www.westminster.org.uk
(Girls accepted age 16+).

Wimbledon High School
Mansel Road, SW19
✆ 020 8971 0900, www.wimbledonhigh.gdst.net
(Ages 4 to 19).

## Girls' boarding schools
The following boarding schools are affiliated with the Church of England:

Benenden School
Cranbrook, Kent, TN17
✆ 01580 240 592, www.benenden.kent.sch.uk

Cheltenham Ladies College
Bayshill Road, Cheltenham, Gloucestershire, GL50
✆ 01242 520 691, www.cheltladiescollege.org

Heathfield St. Mary's School
London Road, Ascot, Berkshire, SL5
✆ 01344 898 343, www.heathfieldstmarys.com

Roedean School
Roedean Way, Brighton, BN2
✆ 01273 667 500, www.roedean.co.uk

St. Mary's School (Calne)
Calne, Wiltshire, SN11
✆ 01249 857 200, www.stmaryscalne.org

Wycombe Abbey School
High Wycombe, Buckinghamshire, HP11
✆ 01494 520 381, www.wycombeabbey.com

The following boarding schools are administered by the Roman Catholic Church:

Marymount International School
George Road, Kingston-upon-Thames, KT2
✆ 020 8949 0571, www,marymountlondon.com

St. Mary's School (Ascot)
Ascot, St. Mary's Road, Berkshire, SL5
✆ 01344 623 721, www.st-marys-ascot.co.uk

Woldingham School
Marden Park, Woldingham, Surrey, CR3
✆ 01883 349 431, www.woldinghamschool.co.uk

For additional information on girls' boarding schools administered by the Roman Catholic Church, contact:

Catholic Education Service for England and Wales
39 Eccleston Square, SW1
✆ 020 7901 9100, www.cesew.org.uk

## Co-educational schools

Abercorn School
28 Abercorn Place, NW8
✆ 020 7286 4785, www.abercornschool.com
(Ages 2 to 13).

Belmont School
The Ridgeway, Mill Hill Village, NW7
✆ 020 8906 7270, www.belmonstschool.com
(Ages 7 to 13).

Cameron House
4 The Vale, SW3
✆ 020 7352 4040, www.cameronhouseschool.org
(Ages 4½ to 11).

Devonshire House Preparatory School
2 Arkwright Road, NW3
✆ 020 7435 1916, www.devonshirehouseschool.co.uk
(Ages 2 to 13).

Finton House School
171 Trinity Road, SW17
✆ 020 8682 0921, www.fintonhouse.org.uk
(Ages 4 to 11).

Eaton Square School

79 Eccleston Square, SW1

✆ 020 7931 9469, www.eatonsquareschool.com

(Ages 2 to 13).

Eridge House School

1 Fulham Park Road, SW6

✆ 020 7371 9009, www.eridgehouse.co.uk

(Ages 2 to 11).

Emanuel School

Battersea Rise, SW11

✆ 020 8870 4171, www.emanuel.org.uk

(Ages 10 to 18).

Garden House School

Turks Row, SW3

✆ 020 7730 1652, www.gardenhouseschool.co.uk

(Ages 3 to 11).

The Hampshire Schools

Knightsbridge Upper School, 63 Ennismore Gardens, SW7

✆ 020 7584 3297, www.ths.westminster.sch.uk

(Ages 4 to 13).

Hampstead Hill School

St. Stephen's Hall, Pond Street, NW3

✆ 020 7435 6262

(Ages 2 to 9).

The Hall School Wimbledon

17 The Downs, SW20

✆ 020 8879 9200, www.hsw.co.uk

(Ages 11 to 16).

The Harrodian School

Lonsdale Road, SW13

✆ 020 8748 6117, www.harrodian.com

(Ages 4 to 18).

Highgate School
3 Bishopswood Road, N6
✆ 020 8340 9193, www.highgateschool.org.uk
(Ages 3 to 18).

Hill House International Junior School
Hill House, Hans Place, SW1
✆ 020 7584 1331, www.hillhouseschool.co.uk
(Ages 3 to 13).

Hurlingham School
122 Putney Bridge Road, SW15
✆ 020 8874 7186, www.hurlinghamschool.co.uk
(Ages 4 to 11).

Ibstock Place School
Clarence Lane, SW15
✆ 020 8876 9991, www.ibstockplaceschool.co.uk
(Ages 3 to 18).

Knightsbridge School
67 Pont Street, SW1
✆ 020 7590 9000, www.knightbridgeschool.com
(Ages 3 to 13).

Lion House School
The Old Methodist Hall, Gwendolen Avenue, SW15
✆ 020 8780 9446, www.lionhouseschool.co.uk
(Ages 2 to 18).

Newton Preparatory School
149 Battersea Park Road, SW8
✆ 020 7720 4091, www.newtonprep.com
(Ages 3 to 13).

Norland Place School
162-166 Holland Park Avenue, W11
✆ 020 7603 9103, www.norlandplace.com
(Ages 4 to 11).

9

SCHOOLS

North Bridge House Preparatory School
1 Gloucester Avenue, NW1
✆ 020 7267 2542, www.northbridgehouse.com
(Ages 4 to 18).

Notting Hill Preparatory School
95 Lancaster Road, W11
✆ 020 7221 0727, www.nottinghillprep.com
(Ages 5 to 13).

Portland Place School
56-58 Portland Place, W1
✆ 020 7307 8700, www.portland-place.co.uk
(Ages 11 to 18).

Prospect House School
75 Putney Hill, SW15
✆ 020 8780 0456, www.prospecths.org.uk
(Ages 3 to 11).

Ravenscourt Park Preparatory School
16 Ravenscourt Avenue, Ravenscourt Park, W6
✆ 020 8846 9153, www.rpps.co.uk
(Ages 4 to 11).

Redcliffe School
47 Redcliffe Gardens, SW10
✆ 020 7352 9247, www.redcliffeschool.com
(Ages 3 to 11).

The Roche School
11 Frogmore, SW18
✆ 020 8877 0823, www.therocheschool.co.uk
(Ages 2 to 11).

St. Christina's School
25 St. Edmund's Terrace, NW8
✆ 020 7722 8784, www.st-christinas.org.uk
(Boys, ages 3 to 7; girls, ages 3 to 11).

St. Joseph's Roman Catholic Primary School
Highgate Hill, N19
✆ 020 7272 1270

Thomas's Preparatory School
28–40 Battersea High Street, SW11
✆ 020 7978 0900, www.thomas-s.co.uk
(Ages 4½ to 13). Also locations in Kensington, Clapham and Fulham.

Eaton House The Vale
2 Elvaston Place, SW7
✆ 020 7924 6000
(Ages 4 to 11).

In addition, more and more boys' schools are taking in girls at sixth form and lower. Please consult the publications listed earlier in this chapter for up-to-date information.

# International, foreign national and American schools

A number of international schools in the London area cater specifically to expatriate children. These schools are experienced in working with students and families making an international transition. While they all class themselves as international schools, some do specialise in a national curriculum, while others offer a much more international curriculum; many are increasingly adopting the International Baccalaureate (**IB**) standards. Some of the schools provide education for students of specific nationalities with classes taught in their native tongue.

For information on all schools part of the London International Schools Association (**LISA**), visit their website at **www.lisa.org.uk**.

### The International Baccalaureate (IB)

The IB programme is a recognised leader in the field of international education, known for its Diploma Programme. The IB Diploma Programme for 16- to 19-year olds (or the last two years of American high school) is the only such certification recognised by universities internationally; in fact, it is not only accepted, but also highly regarded as a rigorous programme by universities in over 120 countries, including the US, Canada and the UK. Often universities will offer university credit for competent completion of specific IB courses. The IB Diploma is increasingly offered in many top-performing high schools in the US and Canada, with students taking IB courses to fulfil requirements for their high school diploma. A number of International and American Schools in London offer the IB Diploma alongside the American High School Diploma.

The IB Programme also includes the less well-known Middle Years Programme (**MYP**), for students in grades six through ten, and Primary Years Programme (**PYP**), for students in grades pre-kindergarten through five. Like the Diploma Programme, the MYP and PYP are increasingly offered in American, Canadian and International Schools around the world, making it very easy for children to transition from one IB school to another. For more information on the IB, visit their website at **www.ibo.org**.

**International schools (boarding and day)**
The following schools offer an international environment for students from all over the world:

The American School in London
1 Waverley Place, NW8
℡ 020 7449 1200, www.asl.org
Co-educational day school, 1,200 pupils. The oldest American School in London with a large modern campus. High percentage of American students. (Ages 4 to 18).

ACS International Schools
www.acs-england.co.uk
Three campuses in London (see below). The schools are approximately 50 per cent American. The other 50 per cent represent more than 60 different nationalities.

ACS Cobham
Heywood, Portsmouth Road, Surrey, KT11
℡ 01932 867 251
Co-educational boarding and day school, 1,350 pupils. A 120-acre campus offering state of the art sports facilities. The IB Diploma is offered in 11th and 12th grade. Limited EAL support is offered in 8th grade through 12th grade. (Ages 4 to 19).

ACS Egham

Woodlee, London Road (A30), Surrey TW20

✆ 01784 430 800

Offers the IB Diploma, MYP and PYP.

ACS Hillingdon

Hillingdon Court, 108 Vine Lane, Middlesex, UB10

✆ 01895 259 771

Co-educational day school, 600 pupils. Set on an elegant country
estate with modern facilities, offers bus service from Central London.
(Ages 4 to 19).

International Community School

4 York Terrace East, NW1

✆ 020 7935 1206, www.skola.co.uk

A small school with over 65 nationalities that has a strong English Language
and Special Needs department. (Ages 4 to 18).

International School of London

139 Gunnersbury Avenue W3

✆ 020 8992 5823, www.islondon.com

Co-educational day school, 220 pupils. Offers the IB Diploma, MYP and
PYP. (Ages 4 to 18).

Marymount International School

George Road, Kingston upon Thames, Surrey, KT2

✆ 020 8949 0571, www.marymountlondon.com

Girls only, day and boarding, 340 girls. Offers IB in addition to American
curriculum. (Ages 11 to 18).

Southbank International School

✆ 020 7229 8230, www.southbank.org

Three campuses in London (see below). Co-educational day school, 250
pupils. Approximately 30 per cent of the pupils are American. Offers the IB
Diploma, MYP and PYP. (Ages 3 to 18).

Southbank Hampstead

16 Netherhall Gardens, NW3

✆ 020 7431 1200

(Ages 3 to 14).

Southbank Kensington

36-38 Kensington Park Rd, W11

✆ 020 7229 8230

(Ages 3 to 11).

Southbank Westminster

63-65 Portland Place, W1B

✆ 020 7436 9699

(Ages 11 to 18).

TASIS The American School in England

Coldharbour Lane, Thorpe, Surrey, TW20

✆ 01932 565 252, www.tasis.com

Co-educational boarding and day, 880 pupils. Large percentage of the students are American. Offers the IB Diploma. (Ages 4 to 18).

Woodside Park International School

88 Woodside Park Rd, N12

✆ 020 8920 0600, www.wpis.org

Small school offering the IB Diploma, MYP and PYP.

## French

Ecole Francaise Jacques Prevert

59 Brook Green, W6

✆ 020 7602 6871, www.ecoleprevert.org.uk

Co-educational school. (Ages 4 to 10).

Lycée Francais Charles de Gaulle

35 Cromwell Road, SW7

✆ 020 7584 6322, www.lyceefrancais.org.uk

Co-educational day school. (Ages 4 to 18).

## German

The German School

Douglas House, Petersham Road, Richmond, Surrey, TW10

✆ 020 8940 2510

Co-educational day school. German curriculum. (Ages 5 to 19).

### Japanese

The Japanese School
87 Creffield Road, Acton, W3
✆ 020 8993 7145
Co-educational day school. (Ages 6 to 15).

### Norwegian

The Norwegian School
28 Arterberry Road, Wimbledon, SW20
✆ 020 8947 6617
Co-educational kindergarden, primary and lower secondary school.
(Ages 2 to 16).

### Swedish

Swedish School in London
82 Lonsdale Road, SW13
✆ 020 8741 1751, www.swedishschool-london.org.uk
Co-educational day school. (Ages 3½ to 16).

# Learning difficulties or special needs

UK law requires that all state schools must do their best to meet a student's special education needs (**SEN**), sometimes with the help of outside specialists. There are various guides available to parents on this process, obtainable from your local education authority (**LEA**).

The UK recognises that children can have different levels or kinds of SEN. The most basic level of extra help is known as School Action and can range from a different way of teaching certain things, to extra help from an adult, to using particular equipment like a special desk.

If the School Action does not yield sufficient progress, the teacher or SEN coordinator (SENCO) will talk to the parents about asking for advice from additional persons such as a specialist teacher or speech therapist. This level of help is called School Action Plus.

If School Action or School Action Plus does not yield sufficient results, then the parents or school can ask for a statutory assessment for the student – an analysis to identify the student's SEN and what special help is required for the student to learn effectively. (If the school requests the assessment, the parents should always be consulted first.)

The LEA conducts the statutory assessment and produces a draft of a statement of SEN, which will describe the child's SEN and the special help in education they should receive. The parents will receive a copy of the statement for comment before it is finalised for their input and comment.

The parents of a student with a statement of SEN have a right to say which state school they want their child to attend, either mainstream or special. The LEA must agree to send the student to the school of choice as long as the school is suitable for the child's age, ability, skills and SEN; the student meets any academic selection criteria the school might have (though most state schools do not select pupils this way); the child's presence will not have a negative impact on the education of the other children; and the placement will be an efficient use of the LEA's resources.

Special schools usually take children with particular types of special needs.

Additional information on this process is available at **www.direct.gov.uk**, **www.education.gov.uk** or through your LEA.

It is advisable to phone any potential independent schools before visiting and sending in an application, to discuss the school's curriculum and your child's needs. It is often helpful to speak with the Registrar and Head at a British school or the Director of Admissions at American or international schools.

An educational consultant may be useful to contact, particularly to discuss approaching independent schools, as most are experienced in finding placements for students requiring additional support, have contacts at the various schools and a good knowledge of the level of support each can offer, whether an independent, state, American or international school.

Whether speaking to a school or an educational consultant, it is essential you share all information about your child and the type of support the child currently receives. Withholding information can easily result in a student either not being accepted or, even worse, being asked to leave a school. Both are very difficult situations for families.

## Publications

John Catt's, *Which School? for Special Needs* is published and updated annually. It can be purchased from the John Catt's website: at **www.johncatt bookshop.com**.

**Some schools offering Specialised Learning Support are:**

Blossom House

8A The Drive, Wimbledon, SW20

℡ 020 8946 7348, www.blossomhouseschool.co.uk

Specialises in speech and language problems and associated difficulties such as fine motor problems or poor organisational skills. (Ages 3 to 11 years).

Centre Academy

92 St. John's Hill, Battersea, SW11

℡ 020 7738 2344

Provides both British and American Curriculum. Full evaluation, testing and counselling services. Additional programmes held after school and on Saturday mornings. Over 23 years of expertise of working with dyslexia and ADD in the UK. (Ages 8 to 18 years).

The Dominie

55 Warriner Gardens, SW11

℡ 020 7720 8783, www.thedominie.co.uk

A co-educational day school for dyslexic and dyspraxic children for children. (Ages 6 to 13).

Fairley House School

30 Causton Street, SW1

℡ 020 7976 5456, www.fairleyhouse.org.uk

Caters for special learning difficulties (dyslexia and dyspraxia). This can include problems with receptive and expressive language, with information processing, with auditory and visual recall and with fine and gross motor control. (Ages 6 to 12).

Dyslexia Action

London Centre, 2 Grosvenor Gardens, SW1

℡ 020 730 8890, www.dyslexiaaction.org.uk

Also lectures, workshops and seminars.

The Moat School

Bishop's Avenue, SW6

℡ 020 7610 9018, www.moatschool.org.uk

Whole-school approach for pupils with specific learning difficulties. Structured and individual programmes. (Ages 11 to 16).

Swiss Cottage School

80 Avenue Road, NW8

℡ 020 7681 8080, www.swisscottage.camden.sch.uk

State-maintained school for physically disabled children. (Ages 2 to 16).

For additional information on other dyslexia centres:

The British Dyslexia Association

Unit 8, Bracknell Beeches, Old Bracknell Lane, Bracknell, RG12

℡ 0845 251 9002, www.bdadyslexia.org.uk

## Applying to American universities

If your child has attended English schools through A level exams and wishes to attend an American university, few English schools will have prepared him or her for the required SAT exams or be able to help select the best university for his or her needs. A service available in London that might be of help is the:

US-UK Fulbright Commission

Educational Advisory Service, Fulbright House, 62 Doughty Street, WC1

℡ 020 7404 6834, www.fulbright.co.uk/study-in-the-us

This organisation principally advises students concerning university study in the US. They hold an annual university day and have a comprehensive reference library of information on US colleges. Additionally, they supply information concerning American colleges in the UK and a comprehensive library of US college catalogues is also available.

## British vs American school system

What school system is right for you? After much debate, we decided that the best way to convey the differences was to ask two parents to express their own, personal feelings on the subject; one whose children are in an American school and one whose children are in an English school. We hope that their views will prove helpful.

### The American school system

For those living in London, there are some fine American schools in the area. If your children have started in the American system, or if they plan to return to it, it may be preferable for them to continue in the American tradition. There are major curriculum differences between the American and English systems resulting in adjustments for the children when they come to London and again when they leave. The American schools eliminate this problem since they strictly adhere to the school programme in the US as well as the calendar year.

The turnover in the American schools is about one-third each year, about the same as the turnover of Americans living in London. The advantage of this is that a child entering the school for the first time does not feel 'new' as there are many others in the same situation. A disadvantage is that a child may have to say goodbye to some of his or her friends each year. American schools are very aware of the adjustments the children are required to make and the social programmes provided at the schools reflect an understanding of this issue.

As is the case in public schools in the US, self expression and creativity are encouraged in American schools overseas.

A high school student who is planning to return to the US for college will be able to take the necessary tests and receive college guidance.

American schools have a high percentage of Americans attending, but many nationalities are represented. Consequently, there is a deeper learning adventure through shared experiences of classmates who have lived all over the world.

## The British school system

The British school system is a traditional one and justifiably famous for its strong discipline and emphasis on the basics of education: reading, writing and maths. Proper education begins at an early age, children begin reading at four and learning French, and sometimes Latin, well before secondary school. A highly structured approach is standard, which might strike some as a bit stifling, but one can be assured that the child will be well equipped for handling work that is more complex later.

In and around London, there are numerous fine British schools; some large, some small, and each has its own philosophy. One can choose a school that is predominantly English or one that caters to the needs of the international community. Some are emphatically academic; some offer a well-rounded curriculum with excellent programmes in sports and/or music. Some schools are co-educational, but many of the finest schools remain single sex schools.

Most British schools require students to wear a uniform. While this may seem costly initially, the outfits are usually sturdy and practical. Uniforms also ensure that your child will be reasonably well 'turned out' and eliminate all competition to be 'best dressed'. Most mothers love uniforms.

Perhaps the most intangible advantage of sending your child to a British school is that of having a decidedly British experience. Your child will participate in British life and have British friends. You, as parents, will have greater exposure to British families and to 'local' life. Your child may develop exemplary manners, learn to keep a stiff upper lip in difficult situations and speak with a British accent, but most importantly, your child (and you) will gain invaluable experience of the life and culture of the community in which you live.

# 10

# Cooking, food and drink

The best way to approach cooking in a foreign country is to focus on all the marvellous new tastes and new ingredients available and not to focus on the few ingredients that cannot be easily or inexpensively obtained. The British weigh their ingredients, so purchasing an inexpensive kitchen scale will simplify cooking with British recipes.

The British are well known for many things, but food has traditionally not been high on the list. Modern British cooking, however, is changing that perception as it reflects the diversity of the people who have settled in Britain. Purchase any one of the excellent cookbooks by modern British cooks, such as Nigella Lawson, Jamie Oliver or Nigel Slater, and you will be pleasantly surprised. Reliable classics include *Delia Smith's Cookery Course* or *Mary Berry's Complete Cookbook*.

Many British recipes list ingredients in both imperial and metric measurements. If you are not used to these measurements, the conversion tables in this chapter and a calculator may be among your most important cooking tools. British ovens are often smaller than those you may be used to so make sure that your pans fit in the oven before you start!

## IN THIS CHAPTER...

- Measurement conversions
- Cooking temperatures
- Drinking water
- Baking products
- Dairy products
- To market, to market
- International foods and specialities
- Pubs and off-licenses
- Food glossary

# Measurement conversions

## Liquid measures

| Description | UK imperial/metric | US imperial |
|---|---|---|
| Teaspoon | 5 ml | 1/6 oz |
| Dessertspoon | 10 ml | 1/3 oz |
| Tablespoon | 15 ml | 1/2 oz |
| Gill | 150 ml | 5 oz |
| Cup | 10 oz/290 ml | 8 oz/250 ml |
| Pint | 20 oz/585 ml | 16 oz/470 ml |

## Dry measures

| Ingredient | UK imperial | UK metric | US imperial |
|---|---|---|---|
| Flour | 5 oz | 140 g | 1 cup |
| Sugar | 1 oz | 25 g | 2 tbsp |
| | 8 oz | 225 g | 1 cup |
| Brown sugar | 6 oz | 170 g | 1 cup |
| Breadcrumbs or nuts | 4 oz | 115 g | 1 cup |
| Yeast | 1/4 oz | 7 g | 2 1/2 tsp |
| Butter | 1 oz | 30 g | 2 tbsp |
| | 8 oz | 230 g | 1 cup |
| | 4 oz | 113 g | 1 stick (8 tbsp) |

When measuring dry ingredients such as flour or sugar for a British recipe, remember to weigh the items as the ingredients will be listed in ounces or grams. (Remember, eight ounces of two different ingredients may have distinctly different volumes.)

Once you start saving British recipes from magazines and newspapers, having a set of British measuring utensils and a scale on hand will make cooking much less time consuming.

## Further conversions

| Ounces to grams | Multiply by 28 |
|---|---|
| Quarts to litres | Multiply quarts by 0.95 |
| Pounds to grams | Multiply pounds by 450 |
| Pounds to kilograms | Multiply pounds by 0.450 |
| Kilograms to pounds | Multiply kilograms by 2.2 |
| Stones to pounds | Multiply by 14 |
| Centigrade to fahrenheit | Multiply C by 1.8 and add 32 |
| Fahrenheit to centigrade | Multiply F by 5, subtract 32 and then divide by 9 |

# Cooking temperatures

| Celsius | Fahrenheit | Gas mark | Description |
|---|---|---|---|
| 110 | 225 | $\frac{1}{4}$ | Very slow |
| 125 | 250 | $\frac{1}{2}$ | Very slow |
| 140 | 275 | 1 | Slow |
| 150 | 300 | 2 | Slow |
| 165 | 325 | 3 | Moderate |
| 180 | 350 | 4 | Moderate |
| 190 | 375 | 5 | Moderate/hot |
| 200 | 400 | 6 | Moderate/hot |
| 220 | 425 | 7 | Hot |
| 230 | 450 | 8 | Hot |
| 240 | 475 | 9 | Very hot |

For fan-assisted ovens you should either turn the heat down slightly or decrease the cooking time.

# Drinking water

The quality of tap water is regulated by EC and UK legislation. Bottled mineral water is not required to be as thoroughly and regularly tested as tap water, and is more likely to contain higher levels of bacteria. London tap water is very hard and some people may find it unpalatable. Water purifiers are a popular alternative to buying bottled water and range from small activated carbon filters attached to a jug to plumbed-in filter systems.

The evidence of hard water may be seen on the inside of your kettle, on showerheads and on other household appliances in the form of limescale. Limescale should be removed periodically with a commercial limescale remover (available at supermarkets) or by using a boiled mixture of one-half cup white vinegar and one-half cup water. Remember to rinse appliances well after they have been cleaned. It is always a good idea to empty a kettle after each use to avoid re-boiling water, which can concentrate the hardness. This practice is especially important when using boiled water to make baby formula.

For more information on the quality of your drinking water contact your local water authority (the contact details will be on your water bill). In central London contact *Thames Water* on © 0845 9200 800 or **www.thameswater.co.uk**.

If you are interested in using bottled water from a company that rents water coolers and provides reusable bottles, look for a company that is a member of the *British Water Cooler Association* (**www.bwca.org.uk**). One good option is:

Culligan International (UK) Ltd
The Gateway Centre, Coronation Road, High Wycombe,
Buckinghamshire HP12 3SU
© 01376 334 200, www.culligan.co.uk

# Baking products

### Flour
There are many types of flour available in the UK and below are some of the most common:

| | |
|---|---|
| Plain flour | A soft wheat flour. Used as a pastry flour and for thickening sauces and gravies. |
| Superfine plain flour | Light white flour used in British recipes for cakes with a delicate texture. |

| Self-raising flour | Raising agent already included, requiring no additional baking powder. |
| Strong flour | White flour of high gluten content for breads and puff pastry. |
| Malted wheat flour | Brown flour with malted wheat grains for a distinctive texture and nutty flavour. |
| Wholemeal flour | Whole wheat flour for baking and breads. |

## Baking powder

British baking powder is half the strength of that used in North America. If you are using an American recipe, remember to double the amount.

## Bicarbonate of soda

Baking soda is known as bicarbonate of soda in the UK.

## Yeast

Dry yeast in the UK is sold in 7 gram/¼ ounce sachets. To substitute dry yeast in a North American recipe, use only half the amount required.

## Sugar

The British have several varieties of sugar, some of which are better to cook with than others. Here is a description of the most common types of sugar found in supermarkets:

| Caster sugar | A finer granulated sugar that dissolves easily and is ideal for baking or desserts. |
| Demerara sugar | A coarse, crunchy, brown sugar. It is good in coffee or over cereals but is not a substitute for brown sugar in baking. |
| Icing sugar | Also known as confectioner's or powdered sugar. |
| Muscovado sugar | A soft, dark sugar used in cooking fruit cakes, baked bean casseroles and barbeque sauces. |
| Soft light and dark brown sugars | Used mainly in baking. |
| Vanilla sugar | A white sugar flavoured with vanilla; primarily used in custards/puddings. |

### Gelatine

Gelatine (or gelatin) comes powdered and in packets called sachets. Some speciality shops also sell gelatine in leaves which need to be dissolved in hot water. The amount of gelatine in sachets varies from brand to brand. As a guideline, 15 grams (1 tablespoon) should set 480ml (16oz) of liquid. The contents of one package of *Knox Unflavoured Gelatine* is the equivalent of 15 grams, 1 tablespoon or ½ ounce.

Flavoured gelatine called *Quick Jel* comes in sachets and is perfect for adding to fruit flans. It saves having to make a full quantity of jelly and sets much quicker.

**DID YOU KNOW?**

The American generic term derived from the brand name *Jello* is called **jelly** in the UK because it comes in a concentrated gel. It may not work as a substitute in North American recipes and other baking.

### Chocolate

Most cooking chocolate comes in one of three basic forms:

| | |
|---|---|
| Bitter | A dark bittersweet chocolate used for rich icings and cakes and as a covering for sweets. |
| Plain | Similar to semi-sweet chocolate. |
| Cake covering chocolate | Chocolate icing or frosting. |

**DID YOU KNOW?**

It is difficult to locate unsweetened chocolate in the UK. Speciality shops such as *Selfridges, Harrods, Partridges, Whole Foods* or *Fortnum & Mason* may carry it, but it will be expensive.

For recipes requiring unsweetened chocolate, substitute 3½ tablespoons of unsweetened cocoa plus 1 tablespoon of butter or margarine to equal a one-ounce square of unsweetened chocolate.

# Dairy products

## Milk

Milk can be purchased in supermarkets and grocers' shops or it can be delivered to your door in plastic containers or returnable glass bottles that are all one size: an Imperial pint (20 ounces). To arrange milk delivery in your area, check **www.delivermilk.co.uk** or see *Chapter 11: Services – Food* under *Food deliveries – groceries*. All milk in the UK is pasteurised but not all types are homogenised, so check the label if that is a concern.

## Cream

Cream in the UK has a higher fat content than in some other countries.

| | |
|---|---|
| Half cream | Used like American half and half. |
| Single cream | 18% butterfat, slightly thicker than half cream. |
| Double cream | 48% butterfat. Poured over fruits and desserts. If whipped too much, double cream turns to butter. |
| Sour cream | 18% butterfat. |
| Crème fraiche | 39% butterfat. Also comes in a half-fat version. Similar to sour cream but slightly thicker and less acidic. |
| Spooning cream | 30% butterfat. Not suitable for coffee or whipping. Spoon over fruit and desserts. |
| Whipping cream | 40% butter fat. Suitable for recipes that call for heavy or whipping cream. |
| Clotted cream | A speciality from the West of England. Very thick; used on fruits and desserts and on scones for cream teas. |
| Fromage frais | A lightly whipped, lower-fat equivalent of double cream that can be used when cooking. Fruit flavoured fromage frais is a good source of calcium and is often given as a snack to children. |

## Cheese

English cheeses range from Gloucester (pronounced GLOS-ter), which is mild, to Blue Stilton, which is blue-veined and has a strong, sharp flavour.

In between those extremes, there is Lancashire (LANK-a-sheer) which grates easily and is good in cooking, and Leicester (LES-ter) which is similar to Cheddar. English, Scottish and Irish Cheddars are wonderful all-purpose cheeses that range from mild to mature. Danish Havarti can be substituted for Monterey Jack.

Most international cheeses can be found in a good grocery store or speciality cheese shop.

### Butter and margarine

Butter and margarine are widely available in several different varieties.

Butter is supplied by different dairy regions in the UK, Ireland and Europe and the difference in taste is a matter of personal preference. Margarine made from 100 per cent polyunsaturated fats is sold in grocery stores along with butter/margarine blends.

### Eggs

Most eggs are brown and are not refrigerated in supermarkets. They do not need refrigeration because they are so fresh; the 'use by' date stamped on each individual egg is the 21st day after the egg was laid. Both free-range and organic eggs are readily available.

## To market, to market

### Fruits and vegetables

There is a wide and wonderful assortment of fresh fruits and vegetables available year round in Britain. You are likely to find a good selection at your local grocery store and market. With the increase in popularity of organic produce, you will find areas within larger stores dedicated to these products.

### Beef

Most beef is English but **Scotch beef** is available at most butchers and supermarkets for a higher price and is considered to be of better quality.

A roast, on or off the bone, is called a **joint**. Ground beef is called **mince**. Minced steak is the leanest. If you are accustomed to beef from corn-fed cattle, UK beef may taste slightly different as most UK cattle are grass-fed rather than corn-fed. Steaks for grilling are available in several different cuts, the most common being **sirloin**, **fillet** (FILL-it), **rib eye** and **rump**. For a pot roast, look for **topside**, **silverside** or **brisket** cuts.

## Lamb

British spring lamb is a real treat and unsurpassed for taste. A less expensive alternative is frozen New Zealand lamb. Lamb is available in chops, racks, cutlets, leg roasts and shoulders.

## Pork

Pork roast as well as chops, tenderloin and spareribs (called American or Chinese spareribs) are all cuts that are easily found in supermarkets.

**Gammon** is one of the best and most expensive of hams. It is uncooked when purchased. York ham is also of high quality. A wide variety of bacon is available smoked or unsmoked. The most common bacon in the UK is **back bacon**. Similar to Canadian bacon, it is larger and meatier than **streaky/crispy bacon**, which is usually thinner and streaked with fat (similar to American bacon). UK sausages (especially breakfast sausages), tend to have a high cereal content, and come in many different flavours and varieties.

## Poultry

A wide variety of poultry is available, including free-range chicken, local corn-fed chicken and French corn-fed chicken, (of which the most famous is from Bresse). In larger supermarkets, you can find turkey, duck and game birds (such as grouse and pheasant in season). If you prefer, ask for grain-fed, free-range or organic chickens.

## Fish

Fish (usually cod, haddock or halibut) and chips is one meal that the British made famous. The availability of fresh local fish is never far away; plaice, skate, brill, flounder, sea bass, sea bream, haddock and cod are readily available!

The best quality of lemon sole and Dover sole can be purchased after April. Salmon, from Scotland and Ireland, is best in June, July and August.

There is a large range of shellfish available from local fishmongers and specialist food halls, whilst more and more supermarkets now have their own fish and shellfish counters. Look for prawns, crabs, mussels, scallops, lobsters, oysters (in season), langoustines, cockles, whelks and winkles. You may find that most prawns are sold cooked because they are imported; raw prawns can be very expensive.

For a list of recommended butchers and fishmongers, see *Chapter 11: Services – Food.*

**DID YOU KNOW?**

When buying fresh fish, look for brightness, prominent eyes and red gills. The fishmonger will scale, clean and fillet a fish if asked.

### Department and speciality stores

Department stores offer a large range of foods and products in their food halls. An international assortment can be found at Harrods, Selfridges, Partridges, Whole Foods, Fortnum & Mason and Harvey Nichols. Marks & Spencer Simply Food is unique in that it only carries its own brand of products, including ready-prepared food and meals. Although the food is more expensive in these department store halls, they are wonderful for speciality items, prepared meals, and foreign products. Several offer home delivery and online orders.

### Farmers' markets

Farmers' markets provide an opportunity to purchase locally produced food at its freshest, seasonal peak. Almost all of the produce and goods you will find at a farmers' market has been produced, grown, baked or prepared by the individual stallholder, so you are always assured of the quality and freshness of the items. The selection of items available at a farmers' market will vary depending on season and location, but you can usually expect to find a good assortment of fruits, vegetables, meat, eggs, dairy products, and speciality products such as homemade preserves, breads and cakes that are not typically found in your local supermarket.

The popularity of farmers' markets in this country continues to grow as a means of encouraging consumers to buy local food and thus help support British farmers. There are markets in many different areas of London. Some of the more popular ones, such as Borough Market (**www.boroughmarket. org**) are listed in *Chapter 12: Shopping – Markets*. For more information or a complete list of locations and schedules, visit the London Farmers' Markets website **www.lfm.org.uk**. You can also contact the National Farmers' Retail and Markets Association on ℂ 0845 458 8420 or visit **www.farmers markets.net**.

10

COOKING, FOOD AND DRINK

## Farms

For the freshest fruit, pick your own. There are several 'pick-your-own' farms around the M25 motorway. It is advisable to ring each farm for directions, opening times and available crops. Additional items like farm fresh eggs, bread and honey may also be available. A day of picking your own fruit and vegetables is a great family outing. You can go to **www.pickyourown.org** for a full listing, but below are some of our local favourites:

Aldborough Hall Farm
Aldborough Road North, Ilford, IG2
℡ 020 8599 1338, www.aldboroughrealale.co.uk

Garson Farm
Winterdown Road, West End, Esher, KT10
℡ 01372 464 389, www.garsons.co.uk

Hewitts Farm
Court Road, Chelsfield Orpington, BR6
℡ 01959 534 666, www.hewittsfarm.co.uk

Parkside Farm
Hadley Road, Enfield, EN2
℡ 020 8367 2035, www.parksidefarmpyo.co.uk
Easily accessible from the M25; 20 different types of crops – all for picking.

Peterley Manor Farm
Prestwood, Great Missenden, HP16
℡ 01494 863 566, www.peterleymanorfarm.co.uk

## Local purveyors

Do try your local butcher, fishmonger, baker and greengrocer to find more personal service and begin to feel a part of your neighbourhood. See *Chapter 11: Services – Food* for a selection of local purveyors.

## Organic and health food

The Soil Association is the UK's leading campaigning and certification organisation for organic food and farming. They have an excellent website (**www.soilassociation.org**) that contains detailed information on all aspects of organic food and farming. The site also includes a complete list of retail outlets in London and throughout the UK that sell organic food products.

The Soil Association

South Plaza, Marlborough Street, Bristol, BS1

© 01173 145 000, www.soilassociation.org

See *Chapter 11: Services – Food* under *Food deliveries – organic groceries* for recommendations.

### Supermarkets

Asda, Sainsbury's, Tesco, Somerfield, Morrison's, Whole Foods, Marks & Spencer and Waitrose all have a large choice of competitively priced supermarkets in Britain, especially London. They offer a wide range of international products and many remain open for long hours or 24 hours a day, to meet busy consumer lifestyles.

Stores can be incredibly crowded and run out of items late in the day, before a holiday, or on the Saturday before a bank holiday. Few shops have packers or personnel to take your groceries to your car. Most stores provide plastic carrier bags, and you will often have to bag your own groceries. However, many stores now charge for bags, so you are encouraged to bring your own. Most chains have reward cards designed to give frequent shoppers special offerings and discounts.

Many local purveyors and larger supermarkets like *Sainsbury's* (**www. sainsburys.co.uk/groceries**), *Tesco* (**www.tesco.com**) and *Waitrose* (**www. ocado.com**), also offer online shopping and home delivery. In addition to the range of standard grocery items, several also offer a broad selection of wine, flowers, music, books, recipes and gift items. Delivery procedures vary, but in most cases, you will be able to specify a one- or two-hour prearranged time slot.

### Meal delivery

On the nights you are too tired to cook, it helps to have some restaurant delivery options on hand. Many restaurants do take-away, but most do not offer delivery. It is generally best to check online or call your restaurant of choice and ask. See *Chapter 11: Services – Food* under *Meal delivery* for services delivering a choice of meal cuisines within Central London.

# International foods and specialities

There are several books available (including *The Essential Guide to London's Best Food Shops* by Antonio Carluccio and *Food Lovers' London* by Jenny Linford) that provide detailed listings of markets and speciality food stores located in many areas of London. It may be worth purchasing one to become acquainted with your neighbourhood's offerings, or to locate specific ingredients.

The following list contains a very small selection of these shops.

## American

Harvey Nichols
5th Floor, 109-125 Knightsbridge, SW1
© 020 7235 5000, www.harveynichols.com

Fortnum & Mason
181 Piccadilly, W1
© 020 7734 8040, www.fortnumandmason.com
Delivery available.

Panzer's Delicatessen
13-19 Circus Road, NW8
© 020 7722 8596, www.panzers.co.uk
Delivery available.

Partridges
2-5 Duke of York Square, SW3
© 020 7730 0651
and 17-21 Gloucester Road, SW7
© 020 7581 0535, www.partridges.co.uk
Free local delivery.

Rosslyn Deli
56 Rosslyn Hill, Hampstead, NW3
© 020 7794 9210, www.rosslyndeli.net

Shepard Foods
59-61 Regent's Park Road, NW1
© 020 7586 4592

## Chinese

Loon Fung Supermarket
42-44 Gerrard Street, W1
✆ 020 7437 7332, www.loonfung.com

WingYip
395 Edgeware Road, NW2
✆ 020 8450 0422
and 544 Purley Way, Croydon, CR0
✆ 020 8688 4880, www.wingyip.com

## French

Bagatelle
44 Harrington Road, SW7
✆ 020 7581 1551, www.bagatelle-boutique.co.uk

Fileric
12 Queenstown Road, SW8
✆ 020 7584 2967

Villandry
170 Great Portland Street, W1
✆ 020 7631 3131, www.villandry.com
Multiple locations.

## Greek

Athenian Grocery
16A Moscow Road, W2
✆ 020 7229 6280

## Italian

Carluccio's
Garrick Street, Covent Garden, WC2
✆ 020 7836 0990, www.carluccios.com
Multiple locations, check for the one nearest to you.

Giacobazzi's Delicatessen
150 Fleet Road, NW3
© 020 7267 7222, www.giacobazzis.co.uk
Freshly made tortellini, lasagna, pizza and other Italian specialities.

La Picena
5 Walton Street, SW3, © 020 7584 6573

Luigi's Delicatessen
349 Fulham Road, SW10
© 020 7352 7739, www.luigismailorder.com
Great deli and online mail order service for pasta, sauces, oils, cheese and other Italian products.

Speck
2 Holland Park Terrace, Portland Road, W11
© 020 7229 7005
and 6 Thayer Street, W1
© 020 7486 4872, www.speck-deli.co.uk
Freshly made sauces and pasta, good selection of cheeses, meats, wines and other Italian specialities.

## Japanese

Japan Centre Food Hall
14-16 Regent Street, SW1Y
© 020 3405 1151, www.japancentre.com
Japanese foods with a special interest in fresh and organic foods, delivery available.

## Korean

Centre Point Food Store
20-21 St. Giles High Street, WC2
© 020 7240 6147, www.cpfs.co.uk

## Kosher
Golders Green in north London has a wide range of stores offering Kosher fare.

Menachem Butcher Shop
15 Russell Parade, NW11
℗ 020 8201 8629

Panzer's Delicatessen
13-19 Circus Road, NW8
℗ 020 7722 8596, www.panzers.co.uk
Delivery available.

La Boucherie Kosher Ltd.
145 High Street, Barkingside, IG6
℗ 020 8551 9977

## Gourmet

Mortimer & Bennett
33 Turnham Green Terrace, W4
℗ 020 8995 4145, www.mortimerandbennett.co.uk

The Pie Man
16 Cale Street, SW3
℗ 020 7225 0587, www.thepieman.co.uk

Villandry
170 Great Portland Street, W1
℗ 020 7631 3131, www.villandry.com
Multiple locations.

Also try department store food halls such as Harrods, Harvey Nichols,
Fortnum & Mason and Selfridges.

## Warehouse Club

Costco
Hartspring Lane, Watford, WD25
℗ 0192 369 9805, www.costco.co.uk
Sells high-quality, nationally branded and selected private-label merchandise
at low prices to businesses purchasing for commercial use or resale, and
also to individuals who are members of selected employment groups.
Multiple locations.

# Pubs and off-licences

### Pubs

A pub is short for public house and is a building with a bar and one or more public rooms licensed for the sale and consumption of alcoholic drink, often also providing light meals. Pubs and licensed restaurants are entitled to serve drinks 'on' the premises to individuals over the age of eighteen. Pubs actually fulfil both requirements – you can stay for a drink or buy a bottle to take away with you – a useful thing to know if you are travelling and/or picnicking. London pub hours vary, although most pubs are open all day. Traditional hours are 11:00 to 23:00, however, licensed pubs may be open later as permitted by their local council. Beware of shorter hours in the countryside and on Sundays in London.

### Children

Pubs must have a special permit to allow children on-site. Only pubs that have a separate dining area or room that doesn't contain a bar counter serving drinks, are entitled for such a permit. The permit may also specify hours when children are allowed. Children are not allowed in pubs after 21:00. Therefore, if accompanied by children, it is appropriate to ask whether or not they are welcome.

### Off-licences

Liquor stores or wine shops are known as off-licences. These shops are licensed to sell beer, wine and spirits for consumption 'off' the premises. Most supermarkets also sell alcoholic beverages. Additionally, almost every neighbourhood has its own local off-licence incorporated within a small convenience store that sells everything from crisps to deodorant.

# Food glossary

| American | British |
| --- | --- |
| Almond paste | Marzipan |
| Arugula | Rocket |
| Bacon | Streaky bacon, or rasher |
| Baking soda | Bicarbonate of soda |
| Beer, dark with bitter taste | Bitter |

| | |
|---|---|
| Beer, golden in colour | Lager |
| Beet | Beetroot |
| Bread | Bread, split tin, bloomer |
| Broil | Grill |
| Cake | Cake, gateau |
| Can | Tin |
| Candy | Sweets |
| Celery root | Celeriac |
| Cheesecloth | Muslin |
| Chicory | Endive |
| Chips | Crisps |
| Chocolate chips | Chocolate buttons |
| Cilantro | Coriander |
| Confectioner's sugar | Icing sugar |
| Cookie | Biscuit |
| Cornstarch | Cornflour |
| Corn syrup | Golden syrup (similar to corn syrup) |
| Cart, grocery | Trolley |
| Cupcake | Fairy cake |
| Dessert | Pudding |
| Dishwashing liquid | Washing-up liquid |
| Drugstore | Chemist |
| Eggplant | Aubergine |
| English muffin | Muffin, crumpet |
| Fish stick | Fish finger |
| Flank steak | Skirt of beef |
| French fries | Chips |
| Frosting | Icing |
| Fruit pie | Fruit tart |
| Gelatin, unflavoured | Aspic power or gelatine |
| Green bean | Haricot or green bean |
| Green onion or scallion | Salad or spring onion |
| Ground beef | Ground or minced beef |
| Ham | Ham or gammon |
| Hamburger bun | Bap |
| Hominy grits | Maize meal |
| Hot dog | Frankfurter |

| | |
|---|---|
| Kool-Aid | Squash (a concentrate) |
| Jello | Jelly |
| Lemonade | Lemon squash |
| Liquor | Spirits |
| Liquor store | Off-licence |
| Molasses | Black treacle |
| Napkin | Serviette or table napkin |
| Peanut oil | Groundnut oil |
| Peapod | Mange tout |
| Pie, open, single crust, fruit | Flan or tart |
| Piecrust | Pastry case or flan case |
| Pits (cherry, peach) | Stones |
| Popsicle | Ice lolly |
| Potatoes, baked | Jacket potatoes |
| Potato chips | Crisps |
| Pound cake | Madeira cake |
| Raisins, golden | Sultanas |
| Roast (meat) | Joint or roast |
| Roll | Roulade |
| Sandwich (with lettuce, tomato) | Sandwich (with salad) |
| Seeds (fruit) | Pips |
| Seven-up/Sprite | Lemonade |
| Shrimp | Prawn |
| Sponge cake | Sponge cake/fingers/pudding |
| Tea biscuit | Scone |
| Turnip, yellow | Swede |
| Zucchini, small | Courgette |
| Zucchini, large | Marrow |

## Other helpful British terminology

### Food

| Term or Phrase | Interpretation |
|---|---|
| Bangers and mash | Sausages and mashed potatoes. |
| Branston or ploughman's pickle | A sweet and sour vegetable chutney. |

| | |
|---|---|
| Bubble and squeak | A patty made from swede and mashed potatoes. Other leftover vegetables may be added. |
| Children's tea | Children's evening meal. |
| Puddings (such as spotted dick or plum pudding) | Old-fashioned steamed or boiled cake-like desserts. |
| Toad in the hole | Sausage baked in a Yorkshire pudding. |
| Top and tail | Snipping the top and bottom off a fruit or vegetable. |
| Welsh rarebit | A fancy grilled cheese or 'cheese on toast' |

## Kitchen items

| American | British |
|---|---|
| Faucets | Taps |
| Garbage bags | Dustbin liners |
| Oven | Cooker |
| Plastic wrap | Cling film |
| Stove-top burners | Hobs |
| Wax paper | Greaseproof paper |

COOKING, FOOD AND DRINK

# Services

For many of our readers, this chapter is the most well-thumbed: the one they come back to again and again (even after living in London many, many years)! When you arrive somewhere new, ideally you'd have lots of friends to ask where to get reliable help and this is what the Junior League of London members have tried to do for you here.

While there are numerous agencies that provide a wide variety of services in London, our members have used all the service providers listed below. Please note that in some cases, membership, engagement or booking fees can apply.

This chapter is divided into four sections of service providers: *Beauty and health*, *Food*, *General* and *Home*. We hope you find what you're looking for in these pages, but you don't, local newspapers, shops and libraries can provide useful local information. In addition, *Time Out* publishes an annual *Shop and Services Guide* for London and the following are useful sources for general services information.

## IN THIS CHAPTER...

- **Beauty and health**
- **Food**
- **General**
- **Home**

FOCUS

13 Prince of Wales Terrace, W8

© 020 7937 7799, www.focus-info.org

FOCUS is a not-for-profit, membership-based organisation providing services and resources for internationals in the UK. Among its services, FOCUS offers resource lists and service recommendations. FOCUS membership is £100 for one year and includes full access to their website.

Yellow Pages

© 118 247, www.yell.com

Telephone and online directory with addresses and phone numbers for businesses and services throughout the UK.

# Beauty and health

For more information about healthcare in the UK, see *Chapter 7: Healthcare*.

## Alternative and complementary treatments

See *Chapter 7: Healthcare – Complimentary medicine*.

## At home

### Return to Glory

© 0845 337 4933, www.returntoglory.co.uk

Home visit health and beauty service. Face, nails, massage, fitness and more all at home.

### Unlisted London

1 Berkeley Street, W1

© 0845 225 5505, www.unlistedlondon.com

Beautiful salon near Harrods, but specialises in providing beauty services in your home.

## Barbers

### Adams of London

12 St. George Street, W1

© 020 7499 9779

'Enry 'Iggins

7 Flask Walk, NW3

℗ 020 7435 6007

and 69 Chalk Farm, NW1

℗ 020 7482 4481, www.enryiggins.co.uk

George F. Trumper

20 Jermyn Street, SW1

℗ 020 7734 1370

and 9 Curzon Street, W1

℗ 020 7499 1850, www.trumpers.com

Traditional barber since 1875, fragrances and grooming products, ties and cufflinks. Very professional service.

Truefitt & Hill Gentlemen's Grooming

71 St. James Street, SW1

℗ 020 7493 8496, www.truefittandhill.co.uk

## Children's haircutters

See *Chapter 8: Children – Shopping and services.*

## Counsellors

See *Chapter 7: Healthcare – Counselling.*

## Dentists

See *Chapter 7: Healthcare – Dental care.*

## Hair salons

Most hair salons offer services to men, women and children.

Aveda

174 High Holborn, WC1

℗ 020 7759 7355, www.aveda.co.uk

Great services and a café. Multiple locations.

Charles Worthington

34 Great Queen Street, WC2

℗ 020 7831 5303, www.charlesworthington.com

Multiple locations.

Daniel Galvin
58-60 George Street, W1
© 020 7486 8601, www.danielgalvin.com
Colour specialists with range of other beauty services.

Jo Hansford
19 Mount Street, W1
© 020 7495 7774, www.johansford.com
Colour specialists.

John Frieda
75 New Cavendish Street, W1
© 020 7636 1401, www.johnfrieda.com
Multiple locations.

## Nails

Nail Girls
50 Cross Street, N1
© 020 7359 2772, www.nailgirls.co.uk

Nails Inc.
41 South Molton Street, W1
© 020 7499 8333, www.nailsinc.com
Multiple locations, most of which are located in London department stores.

Margaret Dabbs
7 New Cavendish Street, W1
© 020 7487 5510, www.margaretdabbs.co.uk
Offers medical pedicures.

Prim Nail Beauty
2 Erskine Road, NW3
© 020 7586 6366, www.primuk.com
Nails and other services, including spray tanning.

Most of the *Spas* listed below also offer nail services.

## Personal trainers
See *Chapter 14: Sports and leisure – Personal training*.

## Spas

Bliss
60 Sloane Avenue, SW3
℗ 020 7590 6146, www.blisslondon.co.uk
Fabulous pampering.

Cowshed
119 Portland Road, W11
℗ 020 7078 1944, www.cowshedonline.com
Their first stand alone spa. Multiple locations.

Hydrohealing
216a Kensington Park Road, W11
℗ 020 7727 2570, www.hydrohealing.com
Spa and wellness centre offering massage, facials and other treatments.

The Sanctuary
12 Floral Street, WC2
℗ 014 423 0330, www.thesanctuary.co.uk
Aromatherapy, facials, massage and treatments.

SPACE.NK
127-131 Westbourne Grove, W2
℗ 020 7727 8063, www.spacenk.co.uk
A wide selection of facials, aromatherapy, massage and treatments.
Multiple locations.

Urban Retreat at Harrods
5th Floor, 87 Brompton Road, SW1
℗ 020 7893 8333, www.urbanretreat.co.uk
Crème de la Mer treatments and more.

## Waxing

Ministry of Waxing
17 South Molton Street, W1
℗ 020 7409 7343, www.ministryofwaxing.com
International chain started in Singapore, they know what they're doing.
The mantra here is HSQ (hygiene, speed, quality). Multiple locations.

Strip Soho

69 Berwick Street, W1

✆ 020 7434 4222, www.stripwaxbar.com

Unique brand of virtually pain-free warm waxing. Paraben-free spray tanning at Soho store. Multiple locations.

# Food

For more information about food in the UK, see *Chapter 10: Cooking, food and drink*, in particular the *International foods and specialities* section may be of interest.

## Bakeries

### Baker & Spice

47 Denyer Street, SW3

✆ 020 7589 4734, www.bakerandspice.uk.com

Wide selection of breads baked in an old brick oven. A selection of prepared foods and catering services are also available. Multiple locations.

### Beverly Hills Bakery

77 E. King Henry's Road, SW3

✆ 020 7586 0070, www.beverlyhillsbakery.com

Wide selection of American baked goods, including muffins, cookies and pies. Gift basket delivery service available.

### The Chelsea Cake Shop

66 Lower Sloane Street, SW1

✆ 020 7730 6277, www.chelseacakeshop.co.uk

Custom-designed cakes for special occasions.

### Clarke's

122 Kensington Church Street, W8

✆ 020 7229 2190, www.sallyclarke.com

Wonderful breads, cakes and tarts. Clarke's also has a well-regarded restaurant at the same address.

Gail's Bread

64 Hampstead High Street, NW3

☎ 020 7794 5700, www.gailsbread.co.uk

Great for bread and pastries. Organic and chemical-free. Multiple locations.

Jane Asher Party Cakes & Sugarcraft

22-24 Cale Street, SW3

☎ 020 7584 6177, www.jane-asher.co.uk

This is the cake shop to end all cake shops. You can specify your design or pick from a vast portfolio of ideas and you don't even have to visit the store since they offer a mail order service. They also use GM-free and organic produce whenever possible.

Konditor & Cook

10 Stoney Street, SE1

☎ 020 7407 5100, www.konditorandcook.com

This bakery features fancy fondant-covered cakes in vibrant hues of fuschia, violet and lime. A unique and personalised cake service. Full menu of gourmet takeaway available. Multiple locations.

Primrose Bakery

69 Gloucester Avenue, NW1

☎ 020 7483 4222, www.primrosebaker.org.uk

Specialises in cupcakes and layer cakes. Lovely seating area and great cookbook. Covent Garden location also.

## Butchers

Kent & Sons

59 St. John's Wood High Street, NW8

☎ 020 7722 2258, www.kents-butchers.co.uk

Offers a wide range of convenient, ready-to-cook items such as breaded veal escalopes and chicken or lamb kebabs. Excellent service and an outstanding selection of the highest quality.

**DID YOU KNOW?**

Selfridge's Food Hall sells great meat at supermarket prices.

11

SERVICES

Organic butchers

C. Lidgate

110 Holland Park Avenue, W11

© 020 7727 8243, www.lidgates.com

Delivers throughout London. Founded in 1850, the shop specialises in naturally reared meat, including organic meat from Prince Charles' Highgrove estate. Also sells a wide variety of homemade sausages, quiches and award-winning pies. Supplies turkey and all the fixings at Thanksgiving to American expats.

The Ginger Pig

10 Moxon Street, W1

© 020 7935 7788, www.thegingerpig.co.uk

Superbly organic hung beef, lamb, mutton and great cuts of fine pork. They make pork pies and hamburgers, cure and smoke their own bacon and produce a huge range of their own punchy sausages. Free-range turkeys may be ordered at Christmas time or other holidays. Also at Borough Market.

Randall's Butchers

113 Wandsworth Bridge Road, SW6

© 020 7736 3426

Outstanding selection and excellent service. Offers first-quality organic and free-range beef, lamb and poultry. A wide variety of game is offered in season, as well as haggis, homemade sausages, venison and wild boar. Kelly Bronze turkeys are available at Christmas. A cheese counter at the back offers British and continental cheeses.

Sheepdrove Organic Farm Family Butcher

5 Clifton Road, Maida Vale, W9

© 020 7266 3838, www.sheepdrove.com

Top quality organic meat. Also delivers through online shop.

W. J. Miller

14 Stratford Road, W8

© 020 7937 1777

A fine selection of first-class organic meats. Also offers Middle Eastern specialities such as baklava, cow's milk feta cheese and marinated olives.

A festive offering is Victorian Royal Roast – a goose stuffed with duck stuffed with pheasant, then chicken, partridge and quail, all boned!

## Wyndham House Poultry

2 Stoney Street, SE1

© 020 7403 4788

Family butcher specialising in poultry in Borough Market. The home-bred chickens are especially fine.

## Caterers

### Clare's Kitchen

41 Chalcot Road, NW1

© 020 7586 8433, www.clareskitchen.co.uk

Prepared meals made daily. Catering for lunch, dinner, teas, picnic, canapés menus and more. Small wine list.

### Delectable Feasts/David Deavis

23 Crimscott Street, SW11

© 020 7232 3063, www.delectablefeasts.co.uk

Provides professional catering and party planning for brunches, lunches, hampers, afternoon teas, parties and banquets.

### Finns

4 Elystan Street, SW3

© 020 7225 0733, www.finnsfchelseagreen.com

Prepared meals made daily; caters for dinner parties.

### Melrose and Morgan

42 Gloucester Avenue, NW1

© 020 7722 0011, www.melroseandmorgan.com

Delicious ready-made meals and store cupboard essentials. Catering includes every day menus, sharing menus, picnic menus and afternoon tea. Hampstead location as well.

### New Quebec Quisine

17 Enterprise Way, Triangle Business Centre, NW10

© 020 8960 8654, www.newquebecquisine.co.uk

Innovative, healthy cuisine specialising in outdoor dining and catering.

Ottolenghi
287 Upper Street, N1
© 020 7288 1454, www.ottolenghi.co.uk
Excellent catering, although even better known for its restaurants with
glorious salads, quiches and pastries. Multiple locations.

The Pie Man Catering Company
16 Cale Street, SW3
© 020 7225 0587, www.thepieman.co.uk
Shop and catering for large or small events.

## Cheese shops

La Fromagerie
2-4 Moxon Street, London W1
© 020 7935 0341, www.lafromagerie.co.uk
Amazing walk-in cheese closet, delicious restaurant and fresh produce.
Highbury location as well.

Neal's Yard Dairy
17 Shorts Gardens, WC2
© 020 7240 5700, www.nealsyarddairy.co.uk
The dairy has a selection of its own cheeses and also offers a decadent
cheese selection from various cheese makers throughout the UK.
Often carried by other delis supermarkets, including Selfridges Food Hall.

Paxton & Whitfield Ltd.
93 Jermyn Street, SW1
© 020 7930 0259, www.paxtonandwhitfield.co.uk
Since 1797, this shop continues to specialise in sourcing and maturing
exceptional cheese, and complementing wine.

## Fishmongers

You can purchase very fresh fish and seafood at the food halls in Selfridges,
Harrods and Harvey Nichols.

James Knight of Mayfair
67 Notting Hill Gate, W11
© 020 7221 6177, www.james-knight.com

Cope's Seafood Company
700 Fulham Road, SW6
© 020 7371 7300

Fishworks
89 Marylebone High Street, W1
© 020 7935 9796, www.fishworks.co.uk
Multiple locations

La Petite Poissonnerie
75 Gloucester Avenue, NW1
© 020 7483 4435, www.lapetitepoissonnerie.com

## Food deliveries

Groceries

Marks & Spencer
© 020 7935 4422, www.marksandspencer.com
Non-food items can be ordered online and food items can be ordered online and picked up in-store. They will also deliver in-store food purchases to your home (selection and order form is on their website). Multiple locations.

Milk & More (part of Dairy Crest Group)
© 0845 606 3606, www.milkdeliveries.co.uk
Delivery of milk and dairy products. Multiple locations.

Nappy Express
128 High Road, N11
© 020 8361 4040, www.nappyexpress.co.uk
Next-day delivery of nappies, baby products, toiletries, food, cleaning products, laundry products, etc.

Sainsbury's
www.sainsburys.co.uk
Full-service grocery store. Multiple locations.

Skyco
The Mayford Centre, Woking, GU22
© 01483 776 4444, www.skyco.uk.com
International food club with an emphasis on North American products.

Tesco

www.tesco.com

Full-service grocery store, wine, flowers, music, books and gift items. Multiple locations.

Waitrose

www.ocado.com

Full-service grocery store that focuses on premium-quality products and outstanding customer service. Large selection of organic products.

Organic groceries

Abel & Cole

16 Waterside Way, Plough Lane, SW17

℡ 0845 262 6262, www.abelandcole.co.uk

Cartons of organic foods delivered weekly.

Daylesford Organic

44B Pimlico Road, SW1

℡ 020 7881 8060, www.daylesfordorganic.com

Sells its own organic products, including meats, produce, jams, baked items, soups, cleaning supplies and more. Online shop and some products carried by **www.ocado.com**. Multiple locations.

Farmaround

Mercury Road, Richmond, DL10

℡ 020 7627 8066, www.farmaround.co.uk

Organic seasonal produce by the box from farms in Kent and Sussex delivered to your door.

Organic Delivery Company

70 Rivington Street, EC2A

℡ 020 7739 8181, www.organicdelivery.co.uk

Specialises in organic and gourmet products.

Planet Organic

42 Westbourne Grove, W2

℡ 020 7727 2227, www.planetorganic.com

One-stop supermarket selling a complete range of organic produce, environmentally friendly household cleaners, body care products and cosmetics. Deli, cheese and bakery counter, coffee and juice bar and fresh fish counter. Multiple locations.

### Pomona
179 Haverstock Hill, NW3
℡ 020 7916 2676
Excellent fresh organic fruits and vegetables. Delivers in-store purchases or pre-arranged orders within a three-mile radius.

### Riverford Organic
Buckfastleigh, Devon, TQ11
℡ 0845 600 2311, www.riverford.co.uk
Free delivery of organic seasonal vegetables and fruit, meat, dairy, soup and juices fresh from the farm.

### Whole Foods Market
The Barkers Building, 63-97 Kensington High Street, W8
℡ 020 7368 4500, www.wholefoodsmarket.com
Three-storey organic supermarket offering a wide array of products with a café/food court area on the top floor. Delivers in-store purchases. Additional smaller stores located in Soho, Camden and Clapham Junction.

## Meal delivery

### Deliverance
℡ 08448 750 400, www.deliverance.co.uk
Ten menus, including sushi, salads, Chinese, Italian, Indian and much more, delivered to most areas of Central London.

### Room Service Deliveries
℡ 020 7644 6666, www.roomservice.co.uk
Offers a choice of over 50 restaurants with varied cuisines and delivers to most areas of central London.

# General

## Car cleaning and servicing

**DID YOU KNOW?**

Many larger supermarkets and shopping centres offer quick and inexpensive car washes in the car park while you shop?

American Carwash Company
35 Great Eastern Street, EC2
℃020 7278 0600, www.americancarwash.co.uk
Car cleaning and valet service. Multiple locations.

Andrew Brock Automobile Engineer
31a Shawbury Road, SE22
℃020 8299 0299
Efficient and trustworthy car servicing.

Q-Park Fly Away Car Storage
Heathrow Airport
℃020 8759 1567 or ℃08700 134786
A unique service for travellers using the car park at Heathrow Airport. The company will collect, store and return your car for your return. They will also wash and service your vehicle while you are away.

Whitney's
5 Steele Road, Park Royal, NW10
℃020 8965-2095
Body work for cars. Ask for Phil. Turns around the car in one week and is exceptionally fairly priced.

## Chartered accountants

Buzzacott LLP
12 New Fetter Lane, EC4
℃020 7556 1200, www.buzzacott.co.uk

11

SERVICES

Grashoff & Co.
35 Whellock Road, W4
✆ 020 8995 4748, www.taxandmoney.co.uk

Summers & Co.
6 Jacob's Well Mews, W1
✆ 020 7935 0123, www.sumco.co.uk

## Clothes hire

Costumes (fancy dress)

Angels Fancy Dress
119 Shaftsbury Avenue, WC2
✆ 020 7836 5678, www.fancydress.com
All types of costumes for both children and adults. Delivery available.

The Carnival Store
95 Hammersmith Road, W14
✆ 020 7603 2918, www.carnivalstore.co.uk
All types of costumes for both children and adults; also carries
period costumes.

Hats

Hectic Hat Hire
236 Munster Road, SW6
✆ 020 7381 5127, www.hectichathire.co.uk

Wedding and formal attire

Moss Bros.
88 Regent Street, W1
✆ 020 7494 0665, www.mossbros.co.uk
Gentlemen's formal wear for sale or hire. Multiple locations.

One Night Stand
8 Chelsea Manor Studios, Flood Street, SW3
✆ 020 7352 4848, www.onenightstand.co.uk
Evening dress hire for women. Appointment required.

## Florists

Most of the shops listed below offer Interflora services. There are also flower markets around London, see *Chapter 12: Shopping – Markets.*

### Angel Flowers
60 Upper Street, N1
✆ 020 7704 6312, www.angel-flowers.co.uk

### The Flower Van
Michelin Building
81 Fulham Road, SW3
✆ 020 7589 1852
Sells simple, seasonal quality flowers. Delivery available.

### Jane Packer Flowers
32-34 New Cavendish Street
✆ 020 7935 2673, www.jane-packer.co.uk
Offers same-day delivery within a five-mile radius of the store.

### Moyses Steven
Sloane Square, SW1
✆ 020 8772 0094, www.moysesflowers.co.uk
Located inside Peter Jones. Florists since 1876, online service available.

### Paula Pryke
The Flower House, Cynthia Street, N1
✆ 020 7837 7336, www.paula-pryke-flowers.com
Also at Liberty store in Soho. Online service available.

### Wild at Heart
54 Pimlico Road, SW1
✆ 020 7229 1174, www.wildatheart.com
Multiple locations.

## Insurance

**DID YOU KNOW?**

British Gas offers insurance coverage for major appliances whether or not you have a gas contract with them. They will repair major appliances (i.e., dishwasher, oven, freezer, microwave). Monthly insurance packages are available for as many or as few appliances as you like. Contact ℂ 0845 950 0400.

### Direct Line
ℂ 0845 246 8701 (car) or ℂ 0845 246 8703 (home), www.directline.com
Comprehensive insurance company that offers policies for travel, home, car and other areas.

### Ellis David Limited
ℂ 020 7354 3881, www.ellisdavid.com
Insurance brokers with an American accent, they offer the added benefit of car coverage in North America at no extra cost.

### Francis Townsend and Hayward
ℂ 0845 345 9000, www.francistownsend.co.uk
Insurance brokers who can handle most requirements, including contents insurance for rented accommodations.

### Norwich Union
ℂ 0800 068 5637 (car) or ℂ 0800 068 5598 (home), www.norwichunion.com
Comprehensive insurance company offering policies for car, home, health and travel.

## Kennels and catteries (quarantine and boarding)
The regulations governing animal quarantine are evolving and easing with the arrival of pet passports. Please see in *Chapter 1: Moving – Bringing your pet to the UK* for information regarding quarantine kennels and quarantine requirements.

### The Animal Inn
Dover Road, Ringwould, Near Deal, CT14
ℂ 01304 373 597, www.quarantine.co.uk
Cats and dogs. Five minutes from the white cliffs of Dover, this facility is considered state of the art as far as quarantines and boarding kennels go.

The Granary Kennels

Hawkridge Wood, Frilsham, Hermitage, Thatcham, RG18

© 01635 201 489, www.thegranarykennels.co.uk

Boarding for cats and dogs.

Kents Farm

Kents Lane, North Weald, Essex, CM16

© 01992 522 183, www.lekf.co.uk

Boarding and quarantine for cats, dogs and other animals. Located 19 miles from London in the Essex countryside. Offers collection and delivery from London and other counties.

Leander International Kennels Ltd

Arden Grange, London Road, Albourne, West Sussex, BN6

© 01273 833 390, www.ardengrange.com

Arden Grange has very impressive credentials in the pet food industry and an excellent reputation in caring for and feeding other people's pets at their beautifully appointed kennels and cattery set in the rolling Sussex Downs.

## Monogramming and engraving

Harrods

87-135 Brompton Road, SW1

© 0845 605 1234, www.harrods.com

The linen department has a monogramming service for items purchased at the store.

Monogrammed Linen Shop

168- 170 Walton Street, SW3

© 020 7589 4033, www.monogrammedlinenshop.com

Leading linen shop in London with a monogramming service department.

Bennett & Thorogood

Unit 109, Grays Antique Market, 58 Davies Street, W1

© 020 7408 1880

Engravers of precious metals and glass.

## Party planners and supplies

For children's parties, see the *Parties* section in *Chapter 8: Children – Entertaining your children.*

### Fait Accompli
212 The Plaza, 535 Kings Road, SW10
ⓒ 020 7352 2777, www.faitaccompli.co.uk
Specialises in organising parties and events.

### Gorgeous Gourmets
Unit D, Gresham Way, Wimbledon, SW19
ⓒ 020 8944 7771, www.gorgeousgourmets.co.uk
Catering equipment for banqueting or small parties. Their Gourmet Foods division offers catering services for dinner parties, cocktail parties and buffets.

### HSS Hire
ⓒ 0845 602 196, www.hss.com
Very comprehensive list of items for professional or personal hire, including party supplies (china, glassware, linen, furniture, etc.).

### Non Stop Party Shop
214-216 Kensington High Street, W8
ⓒ 020 7937 7200, www.nonstopparty.co.uk
A retail store that offers balloon decoration, party accessories and costumes. Multiple locations.

### Party Party
3 & 11 Southampton Road, NW5
ⓒ 020 7267 9084, www.partypartyuk.com
Two retail stores; one offering balloon services (including delivery) and the other offering various party supplies, accessories, gifts and costumes.

### Party Planners (Lady Elizabeth Anson)
56 Ladbroke Grove, W11
ⓒ 020 7229 9666, www.party-planners.co.uk
Will arrange everything for any social function.

## Pet groomers and supplies
See *Veterinarians* below for a list of pet clinics.

### Animal Crackers
94 Fleet Road, NW3
ⓒ 020 7485 1476
Comprehensive selection of pet food and accessories.

K9 Capers

Rutherford Way, Crawley, West Sussex, RH10

℗ 0845 259 0284, www.k9capers.com

Store and online retailer. Professional pet care products and services.
Products can be delivered free anywhere in the UK.

Pet Pavilion

Chelsea Farmers Market, 125 Sydney Street, SW3

℗ 020 7376 8800, www.petpavilion.co.uk

Highly recommended for pet grooming. Also sells pet accessories.
Multiple locations.

Primrose Hill Pets

132 Regent's Park Road, NW1

℗ 020 7483 2023, www.primrosehillpets.co.uk

Sells a wide range of pet food and accessories and includes a small
grooming salon.

## Pet sitting

Animal Aunts

Smugglers Cottage, Green Lane, Petersfield, GU31

℗ 01730 821 529, www.animalaunts.co.uk

They care for your pets in your home. Pet sitting service covers London,
Surrey and other areas.

Animal Concierge

℗ 07799 005 558, www.animalconcierge.co.uk

Works with clients and pets for a very personal and tailored service.
Regular services include pet sitting, dog walking, puppy training and
small animal care. Also run a VIP Concierge Membership and luxury
services such as 'Doggie's Day Out', personal shopping and pet parties.

## Photographers and artists

Contre-Jour

40 Martell Road, West Dulwich, SE21

℗ 020 8670 1234, www.contre-jour.co.uk

Families, children and weddings. Will travel throughout Europe and the UK.

Lamar Raine

140 Abbeville Road, SW4

☎ 020 7622 6520, www.lamarraine.com

Artist who does portraits of both people and homes in watercolour and crayons and hand-cut silhouettes.

Martin Oliver Photography

1 Hoxton Square, N1

☎ 020 7033 0054, www.martinoliver.com

Gorgeous family photos. Will do birthday parties and special occasions.

Parklife Contemporary Portrait Photography

19 Astell Street, SW3

☎ 020 3069 0144, www.parklifephotography.co.uk

Family photography in the great outdoors.

## Problem solvers and lifestyle management

Buy:Time UK

94 New Bond Street, W1

☎ 0870 486 2624, www.buy-time.co.uk

Claire Brynteson is a lifestyle manager. She'll swoop in and organise closets or do whatever needs doing. You buy blocks of time.

Clear of Clutter

☎ 07930 983 452, www.clearofclutter.com

A joy to work with. Professional organising, intuitive Feng Shui, before/after moving, bereavement/separation decluttering.

Coathanger

☎ 0870 460 6194, www.coathanger.net

Personal fashion stylist and wardrobe coordinator. Will sort your clothing at home, as well as shopping.

Ministry of Time

1a Kingsford Street, NW5

☎ 07717 568376, www.ministryoftime.co.uk

Tailored lifestyle management services to help you to take control of your life and leave all the time-consuming jobs to someone else.

11

SERVICES

MoveMinder

© 020 7101 9796, www.moveminder.co.uk

Management, help, support and advice for moving house. Packing, moving, unpacking, finding movers, change of addresses, any help you need.

Personal Time Saver

809 Howard House, Dolphin Square, SW1

© 020 7828 2977, www.personaltimesaver.co.uk

Problem solving for busy people. Can provide a wide range of services from running errands, party organisation and access for deliveries in your absence.

Quintessentially

© 0845 388 4329, www.quintessentially.com

Private members' club well-known for its 24-hour concierge service for travel, events, entertainment, clubs, spas and restaurants.

## Shoe repair

D Cobbler

44 Queensway, W2

© 07752 812 084

Timpson

© 0161 946 6200, www.timpson.co.uk

Shoe repair and other services, such as key cutting. Multiple locations.

## Tailors/alterations

In addition to those listed below, many dry-cleaning shops offer an alteration service.

Designer Alterations

220a Queenstown Road, SW11

© 020 7498 4360, www.designeralterations.com

First Tailored Alterations

85 Lower Sloane Street, SW1

© 020 7730 1400

K.S. Tailoring Services
13 Saville Row, W1
✆ 020 7437 9345
Open Saturdays for fittings.

Thimble Alterations and Repairs
24 Thackeray Street, W8
✆ 020 7938 1161

## Taxis and minicabs

Unlike black cabs, which are licensed, minicabs cannot be hailed from the street and must be booked by phone. Since they are not regulated and most minicab firms are local, standards may vary. Transport for London has a service where you can text CAB to 60TFL (60835) to get the numbers of one taxi and two licensed minicab firms in the area from which you are texting. See also *Chapter 6: Transportation – Minicabs*.

Addison Lee
35-37 William Road, NW1
✆ 0844 800 6677, www.addisonlee.com
The market leader for moving people and parcels throughout London. Can provide cars with child safety seats upon request. Can book by telephone, online or with iPhone app.

Airport Cars
✆ 020 8877 3000, www.jetcars.co.uk
Can be paid in advance with a credit card.

Computer Cab
✆ 020 8901 4444, www.computercab.co.uk
Computer Cab is London's largest supplier of licensed radio taxis covering the entire London area with five fleets: ComCab London, DataCab, Zingo, Call a Cab (suburban) and local taxis (local black taxi cabs). Online booking available.

Meadway Radio Cars
1019-1021 Finchley Road, NW11
✆ 020 7328 5555, www.meadway.com
Online booking available.

TA Chauffeurs
23 Conway Road, Hounslow, TW4
© 08450 179 779, www.ta-chauffeurs.co.uk
Excellent service. Great with helping families with children.

## Veterinarians

### Abingdon Veterinary Clinic
85 Earls Court Road, W8
© 020 7937 8215, www.abingdonclinic.co.uk

### Brompton Veterinary Clinic
96 Fulham Road, SW3
© 020 7225 2915
24-hour emergency cover at clinic. In addition to regular veterinary services for dogs and cats, has a grooming service for long-haired cats.

### Elizabeth Street Veterinary Clinic
55 Elizabeth Street, SW1
© 020 7730 9102, www.esvc.co.uk
Offers emergency veterinary service 24 hours a day, 365 days a year to members of specific clinics. The regular day clinic is very good as well. Appointment required.

### Primrose Hill Pet Clinic
138 Gloucester Avenue, NW1
© 020 7586 8806

### The Village Vet Practice
11 Belsize Terrace, NW3
© 020 779 4948, www.villagevet.co.uk
Emergency service 24 hours a day, 365 days a year. Multiple locations.

# Home

## Antique and fine furniture repairers and restorers

### G.A. Keefe Restorations
84 Woodford Crescent, Pinner, HA5
© 020 8868 2095

Antique and modern furniture repair and restoration. Also specialises in French polishing.

Hornsby Interiors
35 Thurloe Place, SW7
✆ 020 7225 2888, www.hornsbyinteriors.co.uk
Repairs and restoration of both modern and antique furniture, including reupholstery. Also offers services such as French polishing, gilding and re-caning.

## Burglar alarms and locksmiths

Banham Security
235 Kensington High Street, W8
✆ 0844 482 9122, www.banham.com

Central Monitoring Services (CMS)
✆ 020 7627 0344, www.cmskeyholding.com
For alarm activation and monitoring.

Chubb Electronic Security
✆ 0800 282 494, www.chubb.co.uk

Tara Alarms
Pascal Street, SW8
✆ 020 7819 3720, www.tarasecurity.com
Central London only.

Timpson
✆ 0161 946 6200, www.timpson.co.uk
Locksmiths and other services, such as key cutting. Multiple locations.

## Carpenters and painters
Also see *Handymen* below.

Tom Baker
✆ 07751 596 952
Internal and external decorator. Particularly good with wallpaper and paint effects.

John Gilgan
✆ 020 8883 8496
Fantastic carpenter.

Mark Skrzypczak
✆ 07950 049 168
A wonderful builder; particularly skilful in carpentry. Absolutely reliable and reasonably priced.

**DID YOU KNOW?**

In the UK, a **decorator** means a painter, plasterer and/or wallpaper hanger, not an interior designer.

## Carpet and upholstery cleaners

Designcare
94 Mount Pleasant, St Albans, AL2
✆ 020 8964 2266
Carpet and sofa cleaning; extremely professional and there is not a stain that they cannot remove. Ask for Nigel.

Homebirds
✆ 0845 373 4352, www.home-birds.co.uk
Upholstery and carpet cleans with eco-friendly solutions available.

Look New
12 Market Place, NW11
✆ 020 7431 2298, www.looknewdrycleaners.com
Blind, carpet, curtain care and leather restoration with collection and delivery depending on your location.

Pilgrim Payne & Co. Ltd.
Rosemount Road, HA0
✆ 020 8453 5350, www.pilgrimpayne.co.uk
Carpet, upholstery and curtain cleaning with great care and attention.

Safeclean
✆ 0800 585 693, www.safeclean.co.uk
Uses only environmentally friendly products to clean carpets and upholstery.

## Christmas trees

Cut Christmas trees can be bought at nurseries, flower shops and many local open air markets, including the Columbia Flower Market (see *Chapter 12: Shopping – Markets*). See *Garden Centres and nurseries* below for more recommendations.

### British Christmas Tree Growers Association
© 0131 644 1100, www.bctga.co.uk
This is the trade association for those who grow specialist Christmas trees in Great Britain and Northern Ireland. Visit the website for a number of locations where you can chop down your own Christmas tree. Many sites have attractions for children and refreshment facilities.

### The Christmas Forest
© 020 7348 9080, www.christmasforest.co.uk
Various locations throughout London.

### Clifton Nurseries, Ltd
5A Clifton Villas, W9
© 020 7289 6851, www.clifton.co.uk
Delivery and removal of Christmas trees.

### Down to Earth
87 Kentish Town Road, NW1
© 07956 176 482, www.pauldowntoearth.com
Leading gardener and landscape specialist.

### Pedlars
© 01330 850 400, www.pedlars.co.uk
Sells Christmas trees and decorations at Selfridges.

### Santa Fir Christmas Tree Farm
Guildford Road, Cranleigh, Surrey GU5
© 01483 268 296, www.santafir.com

## Computers and repairs

For basic computer supplies check the *Yellow Pages* at **www.yell.com**. Alternatively, visit Tottenham Court Road in WC2, where there are a number of electronics and computer shops. For computer use by the hour and printing facilities, check with your local library.

Apple Store
235 Regent Street, W1
℃ 020 7153 9000, www.apple.com/uk

Gerry Beggs
℃ 07985 113 295, ww.gerrybeggs.com
Independent IT solutions for PC and Mac, including data back-up and
system restoration, software installation and configuration and file repair
and disaster recovery.

Honeylight Computers
54 Moreton Street, SW1
℃ 020 782 10670, www.honeylight.co.uk
Computer services and repairs.

Netural (Yaron Samuel)
5 Accommodation Road, NW11
℃ 08704 410 046
Computer network repairs, upgrades and sales. Yaron is terrific at analysing
your computer needs and determining how best to improve your system.
He has a can-do attitude, is very knowledgeable, professional, and stands
by his product.

PC World
℃ 0844 561 0000, www.pcworld.co.uk
A chain of computer stores that can satisfy almost every computer need.
Some have in-store technicians to answer questions regarding computer
problems. Multiple locations.

## DIY and tools hire

There are many local DIY stores. We have only listed the large chains
that can be found throughout London. Check the Yellow Pages at
**www.yell.com** for a complete listing.

B&Q
℃ 084 5609 6688, www.diy.com
A wide selection of DIY and garden needs. Open seven days a week;
delivery available. Multiple locations.

Homebase

℃ 0845 077 8888, www.homebase.co.uk

All your DIY household needs, including a gardening centre. Open seven days a week. Delivery available. Multiple locations.

HSS Hire

℃ 0845 602 1961, www.hss.com

Tools of every kind, catering and event equipment for hire.
Multiple locations.

## Domestic help and house cleaners

If you are looking for information about childcare, see the *Agencies for childcare* section in *Chapter 8: Children – Childcare*.

The Clean Team

116 Boundary Road, NW8

℃ 020 7625 5999

Professional team of cleaners who use their own cleaning products and equipment.

Hampstead Helpers

7B Heath Street, NW3

℃ 020 7435 3637

Regular housework, one-off cleans (spring cleaning, moving), after-party cleans and professional ironing service. Fully insured.

Homebirds

℃ 0845 373 4352, www.home-birds.co.uk

Regular and spring cleans, after builders cleans, with eco-friendly solutions available. An ethical cleaning agency.

Workbusters

202 New Kings Road, SW6

℃ 020 7751 2345, www.workbustersltd.free-online.co.uk

Domestic cleaners.

## Garden centres and nurseries

From the most elaborate garden to the simplest flower box, London is in bloom most of the year. The following are a few suggestions for putting some colour into your life.

Camden Garden Centre
2 Barker Drive, St. Pancreas Way, NW1
✆ 020 7387 7080, www.camdengardencentre.co.uk
A full-service garden centre with a large selection of outdoor and indoor plants, as well as books, grills and patio furniture. Knowledgeable and helpful staff. Delivery available.

The Chelsea Gardener
125 Sydney Street, SW3
✆ 020 7352 5656, www.chelseagardener.com
Comprehensive garden centre selling everything from shrubs and plants to gardening furniture and books. Also has excellent selection of houseplants and a florist department.

Clifton Nurseries
5A Clifton Villas, W9
✆ 020 7289 6851, www.clifton.co.uk
An excellent all-purpose garden centre. Services also include garden design and delivery.

Diana Milner Garden Design
13 Princess Road, NW1
✆ 020 7586 5715, www.dianamilnergardendesigns.com
Garden shop and garden design and maintenance services available.

Fulham Palace Garden Centre
Bishop's Avenue, SW6
✆ 020 7736 2640/9820, www.fulhamgardencentre.com
Good selection of plants, pots and shrubs. Garden landscaping and delivery available.

Hampstead Garden Centre
163 Iverson Road, NW6
✆ 020 7328 3208
Full-service garden centre. Large selection of outdoor plants with smaller offerings of garden furniture and indoor plants.

Petersham Nurseries
Church Lane, Richmond, TW10
✆ 020 8940 5230, www.petershamnurseries.com

A short drive outside of London near Richmond Park. Well stocked nursery, garden supplies and vintage garden furniture. Lovely café and restaurant. A great day out.

### Handymen

#### EZ Builders
☎ 020 8740 8187, www.ezbuilders.co.uk
Plumbers, builders, decorators, carpenters and electricians for all household jobs.

#### The Handy Squad
☎ 0800 012 1212
Professional handyman service. Small odd jobs, such as hanging blinds or curtains, assembling flat-pack furniture, changing light bulbs, sealing and re-grouting bath and shower rooms.

#### Pimlico Plumbers
Pimlico House, 1 Sail Street, SE11
☎ 020 7928 8888, www.pimlicoplumbers.com
24-hour service. Plumbing, heating, electrics, appliances, carpentry, locksmiths and more.

#### Red Box
15 Young Street, W8
☎ 020 7381 1539, www.redboxlondon.com
Various home maintenance and repair services. Certified for plumbing, heating and electrical jobs. Primarily works in West London postcode area to provide a high level of service response.

### Interior designers
Most major department stores carrying decorating materials will advise and assist you with draperies, upholstery and other work. Fabric and wallpaper are sold by the metre. Liberty's fabrics are world famous and of a consistently high quality. John Lewis and Peter Jones also carry quality fabrics and are known for their superior haberdashery.

**Metric Equivalents:**

| Metric | Imperial |
|---|---|
| 1 centimetre (1cm) | 0.33 inches |
| 2.5cm | 1 inch |
| 30cm | 1 foot |
| 90cm | 1 yard |
| 1 metre (1m) | 39.4 inches |

Colefax and Fowler
39 Brook Street, W1
℗ 020 7493 2231, www.colefax.com
Best known for fabrics and wallpapers, yet it is a renowned decorating firm that also sells antiques. Also stocks Jane Churchill fabric, wallpaper and paint.

Conran Shop
Michelin House, 81 Fulham Road, SW3
℗ 020 7589 7401, www.conran.com
Made to measure blinds, curtains, rugs and furniture. Multiple locations.

Fiona Campbell
259 New King's Road, SW6
℗ 020 7731 3681, www.fionacampbelldesign.co.uk
Specialises in curtain making.

Fox Linton
Chelsea Harbour Design Centre, Lots Road, SW10
℗ 020 7368 7700, www.foxlinton.com
This collaboration between Mary Fox Linton and Philip Cadle encompasses some of the best names in fabric exclusive to Fox Linton in the UK.

Mint
2 North Terrace, SW3
℗ 020 7225 2228, www.mintshop.co.uk
Looking for something eclectic or cutting edge? Look no further than Mint. Internationally regarded. Design services available.

Nina Campbell
9 Walton Street, SW3
℗ 020 7225 1011, www.ninacampbell.com
Sells her own fabric and wallpaper.

Paint & Paper Library
5 Elystan Street, SW3
℗ 020 7823 7755, www.paintlibrary.co.uk
Wallpaper and paint specialists; complete online service (request samples,
buy products, communicate with designers).

Percy Bass Ltd.
184 Walton Street, SW3
℗ 020 7589 4853, www.percybass.com
Total interior design service, building work, odd jobs, such as hanging
pictures, refilling cushions and putting up shelves, restoration and repairs
of furniture and paintings.

Skandium
86 Marylebone High Street, W1
℗ 020 7935 2077, www.skandium.com
Scandinavian designed furniture, lighting, fabrics and accessories.
Interior design services available. Multiple locations.

## Movers

Aussie Man & Van
℗ 020 8870 4003, www.mandandvan.biz
Friendly full-service packing and removals, including storage.

Cadogan Tate
℗ 0800 988 6010, www.cadogantate.com
Encompasses everything from residential and business moves to worldwide
moves and the moving and storage of fine art. Also offers secure storage
facilities and bespoke storage services in the UK, Paris and New York.

The Collectors
℗ 0800 542 5747, www.collectors-london.co.uk
Reliable and efficient removal service. Specialists in small removals,
from one box to a flat or a complete office removal.

Moves

*℗* 020 8267 6000, www.moves.co.uk

A high-quality moving service. They also offer reasonably priced interim storage at their own warehouse.

Portobello Car & Van Rental

3 Bramley Road, W10

*℗* 020 7792 1133, www.portobello-vans.co.uk

If you want to move yourself, car and van hire.

## Pest Control

Safeguard Pest Control

Churchill Business Park, Westerham, TN16

*℗* 0800 195 7776, www.safeguardpestcontrol.co.uk

Elimination and prevention of mice, rats, wasps, fleas, flies, ants, squirrels, and cockroaches.

## Piano tuner

11

SERVICES

Jacque Samuel Pianos

142 Edgware Road, W2

*℗* 020 7723 8818, www.jspianos.com

## Picture framing

Campbell's of Walton Street

1a Stronsa Road, W12

*℗* 020 8743 3666

Exceptional service. Picture restoration, cleaning and framing.

John Jones

4 Morris Place, N4

*℗* 020 7281 5439, www.johnjones.co.uk

Arguably the best (and most expensive) in London. Museum standard framing.

Railings Gallery

5 New Cavendish Street, W1

*℗* 020 7935 1114, www.railings-gallery.com

Expert framing services with a variety of choices.

## Recycling

Most communities offer recycling for some or all of the following: glass, cans, plastics, newspapers, magazines, rags, food and Christmas trees, with many now providing door-side pick up on designated days (for more information, see *Chapter 5: Utilities – Recycling & waste*). For information about facilities or door-side pick up in your area, contact your local council, town hall or public library (see *Chapter 5: Utilities – Local councils* for a listing of local councils). You can also visit **www.wasteonline.org.uk** for more general information on recycling and waste in London.

---

**DID YOU KNOW?**

You can earn cash by recycling your old mobile phones, cameras, MP3 players and ink cartridges. Visit **www.simplydrop.co.uk** to request a freepost envelope and drop in the nearest post box. The Recycling Appeal also collects mobile phones and printer cartridges for re-use and recycling and donates to charities. Visit **www.recyclingappeal.com** to select a charity and request freepost envelopes.

---

Second-hand goods and clothing can be donated to local charity shops, which will resell them to raise funds. These stores also offer shoppers the opportunity to find name-brand clothing and bric-a-brac for bargain prices. Consult **www.charityshops.org.uk** or the *Yellow Pages* for the shops convenient to you. You can also give and get things at **www.freecycle.org**.

## Self-storage

Some removals companies also offer storage facilities, see *Movers* above.

The Big Yellow Self Storage
✆ 0800 783 4949, www.bigyellow.co.uk
Multiple locations.

LockAway Self Storage
48A Boundary Road, NW8
✆ 020 7372 0100, www.lockaway.co.uk
Located just around the corner from the American School in London.

Safestore
✆ 0800 524 4738, www.safestore.co.uk
Multiple locations.

# Shopping

London offers an incredible selection of stores and shopping experiences. With centuries-old traditional British shops, newly-built shopping centres, street markets, chic boutiques and the bustling high streets, shopping in London will satisfy nearly every shopper's desires.

This chapter is meant to be a general guide to shopping in London. For a more comprehensive list, the annual *Time Out Shop and Services Guide* is a useful resource for shops and services in London. For those interested in some of the more traditional speciality shops in London, we recommend The Little Bookroom's guide by Eugenia Bell, *The Traditional Shops & Restaurants of London*.

## IN THIS CHAPTER...

- Department stores
- Shopping centres
- Markets
- Art and antiques
- Books
- Outlet shopping
- Clothing size charts

Virtually every town has its own **high street** (a main shopping street that fulfils most shopping needs). In addition to apparel, you will usually find chemists, grocery stores, mobile phone stores, newsagents, bookstores, electronics stores and restaurants. The biggest high street shopping areas in central London are Oxford Street and Regent Street. There you'll find the flagship stores of most major UK and many international retailers.

Other great shopping areas include Neal Street and the Piazza in Covent Garden, Marylebone High Street (just north of Oxford Street), Bond Street (just south of Oxford Street), Kensington High Street, Westbourne Grove (Notting Hill), the King's Road (Chelsea) and Knightsbridge, which boasts two of London's best department stores, Harrods and Harvey Nichols. A good website that lists all the shops and restaurants for London's most popular streets is **www.streetsensation.co.uk**. If you can't find what you are looking for in this chapter, you may want to review *Chapter 8: Children* for shopping relating to children and maternity, *Chapter 10: Cooking, food and drink* for food related shopping, *Chapter 11: Services – Food* for bakeries, butchers, groceries and more or *Chapter 11: Services – General* or *– Home* for items such as pet and garden supplies.

**DID YOU KNOW?**

The vast majority of London's shops have two large sales each year: one in January (starting late December) and one in July (starting late June). It is becoming more common for shops to hold mid-season sales as well.

# Department stores

The list below contains a mixture of large department stores with multiple branches and smaller, speciality department stores.

Argos

80-110 New Oxford Street, WC1

℗ 0845 640 2020, www.argos.co.uk

A catalogue store stocking a wide range of consumer products, including furniture, kitchen appliances, children's toys, sports equipment and electronics. Delivery available. Multiple locations.

**Bhs**

252-258 Oxford Street, W1

📞 0845 841 0246, www.bhs.co.uk

Offers relatively inexpensive clothing and home goods. Multiple locations.

**Debenhams**

334-348 Oxford Street, W1

📞 0844 561 6161, www.debenhams.com

General purpose department store. Multiple locations.

**Fenwick**

63 New Bond Street, W1

📞 020 7629 9161, www.fenwick.co.uk

Up-market clothes and accessories. Multiple locations.

**Fortnum & Mason**

181 Piccadilly, W1

📞 020 7734 8040, www.fortnumandmason.com

Offers old world charm and atmosphere. The ground floor houses a formal food hall stocked with gourmet goods including speciality teas and jams, fabulous pre-made & made to order hampers and a genteel setting for an afternoon tea. Goods sold on other floors include up-market kitchenware, home goods, leather and luggage and men's and women's accessories.

**Harrods**

87-135 Brompton Road, SW1

📞 020 7730 1234, www.harrods.com

London's most famous emporium and the UK's largest shop. Unequalled grandeur fills their food halls. Known for their twice yearly sales and amazing range of goods (exotic animals to medieval instruments), Harrods offers over 60 fashion departments, including an excellent selection of designer shoes.

**Harvey Nichols**

109-125 Knightsbridge, SW1

📞 020 7235 5000, www.harveynichols.com

Offers a fabulous array of designer collections and exquisite home furnishings. Don't miss the drinks bar and café on the fifth floor, which sits alongside the food hall. The window displays are legendary.

### John Lewis

300 Oxford Street, W1

✆ 020 7629 7711, www.johnlewis.com

Known for their curtain department and household items selection.
Also boasts an electronics section (with excellent guarantee policies) and a
range of stylish, functional clothing. Its famed 'never knowingly undersold'
policy means prices, as a rule, are very reasonable. Online shop and
delivery available. Multiple locations.

### House of Fraser

318 Oxford Street, W1

✆ 0844 800 3752, www.houseoffraser.co.uk

A wide range of services is available in many of the stores, including hair
salons, beauty treatment rooms, nail bars, restaurants, coffee bars and a
complimentary personal shopping service for both men and women.
Multiple locations.

### Liberty

210-220 Regent Street, W1

✆ 020 7734 1234, www.liberty.co.uk

Housed in two adjoining Tudor-style buildings, Liberty is famous for its
eponymous print fabrics, Art Deco period furniture and a unique selection
of home goods and designer fashions.

### Marks & Spencer

458 Oxford Street, W1

✆ 020 7935 7954, www.marksandspencer.com

Not only a department store carrying women's, men's and children's
fashions focusing on good value at the right price, M&S (or Marks and
Sparks, as it's commonly called) also has a popular grocery store as well
as pre-made food hall known as *Simply Food*. Multiple locations.

### Peter Jones

Sloane Square, SW1

✆ 020 7730 3434, www.peterjones.co.uk

Affiliated with the John Lewis Partnership. Carries many of the same lines
as John Lewis.

Selfridges

400 Oxford Street, W1

© 0800 123 400, www.selfridges.co.uk

Large and varied selection of cutting-edge fashion for men, women and children. The UK's second largest shop (after Harrods) boasts London's largest cosmetics hall, a spectacular toy department and a gourmet food hall. Offers a number of in-store restaurants that range from sprawling family-oriented affairs to hip coffee bars.

# Shopping centres

If you are seeking the convenience of a one-stop shopping mall, go no further than Shepherd's Bush for the Westfield London shopping centre. For the others, you'll need to head a bit outside of Central London.

Bluewater

Kent, DA9

© 0870 777 0252, www.bluewater.co.uk

Just off Junction 2 of the M25 at Greenhithe in Kent. Bluewater has over 300 stores, including a vast number of up-market shops, more than 40 restaurants and a 13-screen cinema.

Brent Cross

Hendon, NW4

© 020 8202 8095, www.brentcross-london.com

London's second largest shopping centre (after Westfield London). Located at the junction of the A406 (North Circular) and the A41. 150 shops including John Lewis and Fenwick.

Westfield London

Ariel Way, W12

© 020 3371 2300, www.westfield.com/london

Westfield London is Europe's largest urban shopping centre and boasts an entire wing dedicated to up-market international brands such as Prada, Chanel and Valentino in addition to high street stores. The mall is located right next to the Shepherd's Bush tube stop on the Central Line.

**DID YOU KNOW?**

A Value Added Tax (**VAT**) of 17.5 per cent, which is due to rise to 20 per cent in 2011, is added to most goods purchased in the UK. You are only eligible for a **VAT refund** if you are visiting the UK and you intend to take the purchased goods out of the UK within three months after purchase. To reclaim the VAT on items purchased, you must have the retailer fill out the export documentation. If you live in the UK or in any country within the EU, you do not qualify for a VAT refund.

# Markets

With over 70 markets in London, it is not uncommon to stumble upon one whilst taking a stroll. The markets vary greatly in size, the variety of goods on offer and the overall feel. And, in a city as expensive as London, you can find some true gems and save a significant amount of money by market shopping. Below are some of the most popular markets in London. If you're interested in a more comprehensive list of markets, a very good resource guide is Andrew Kershman's *The London Market Guide*. For a list of antique markets, see the section in this chapter entitled *Art and antiques* below.

Berwick Street Market

Berwick Street and Rupert Street, W1

Offers the best and cheapest selection of fruit and vegetables in central London. There are also good cheese, fish, bread, herb and spice stalls and inexpensive household goods. Open 09:00-17:00 Monday to Saturday.

Borough Market

8 Southwark Street, SE1

www.boroughmarket.org.uk

This superb farmers' market, nicknamed London's Larder, has been trading here since 1756. There are some good cut flowers, as well as quality coffee, fruit, vegetables, fishmongers and butchers. A number of traders offer organic produce and gourmet food selections. Open 11:00-17:00 Thursday; 12.00-18.00 Friday; 09:00-16:00 Saturday.

Brick Lane Market

Brick Lane, E1

www.visitbricklane.org

Furniture, old books, jewellery, watches, food, bicycles, handbags, this market offers something for everyone. The market itself changes from week to week so look for new stalls on adjacent streets. Open 06:00-13:00 Sundays.

## Brixton Market
Electric Avenue, SW9
www.brixtonmarket.net
All kinds of wonderful Afro-Caribbean food from goat's meat to plantains. Open 08:00-17:30 Monday to Saturday; 08:00-15:00 Wednesday.

## Camden Market
Buck Street, Camden High Street and Camden Lock, NW1
www.camdenlock.net
Camden Market is really made up of six markets selling everything, including antiques, furniture, health food, retro clothing, jewellery, arts and crafts. Saturday is the busiest day since the entire market is open. Many shops and stalls are open every day. Teens and those who like to re-live the '70s punk lifestyle will be at home here. Open 10:00-18:00 Tuesday to Friday and 09:00-18:00 Saturday and Sunday.

## Columbia Road Flower Market
4 Columbia Road, E2
www.columbiaroad.info
Without question this is the prettiest street market in town. Flowers, shrubs, bedding plants and other horticultural delights are spread in all directions, while the shops stock flowers, garden accessories, and even gifts and furniture. Visit in December to pick up a Christmas tree, poinsettia and a wreath. Open 08:00-14:00 Sundays.

## Greenwich Market
Greenwich High Road, SE10
www.greenwichmarket.net
Antiques and collectibles are Thursday and Friday only. Most shops, cafes and restaurants are open seven days a week. Open 10.00-17:30 Wednesday to Sunday and Bank Holiday Mondays.

## Leadenhall Market
Gracechurch Street, EC3
It's not a traditional London market, but Leadenhall Market, whose retailers

include upscale clothing shops and foodie paradises, is worth visiting for the beautiful Victorian arcade in which it's situated. Open 11:00-16:00 Monday to Friday.

### New Covent Garden Market
Nine Elms Lane, SW8
© 020 7720 2211, www.cgma.gov.uk
Largest fresh produce wholesale market in the country. Individuals may buy flowers and produce at vendors' discretion. Free entry for anyone on foot, £4 for any vehicle. Open 03:00-11:00 Monday to Friday and 04:00-11:00 Saturday.

### Portobello Road Market
Portobello Road, W10
www.portobelloroad.co.uk
Over 2,000 stalls of hip new and vintage clothes, jewellery, old medals, paintings, silver, objects d'art, great food, flowers and ambience. Saturday is by far the busiest day (and the only day for antiques); so if you go, arrive early and be prepared to face the crowds. Shops are open six days a week. Open 08:00-18:30 Monday to Wednesday, Friday and Saturday and 09:00-13:00 Thursday.

### Spitalfields Market
65 Brushfield Street, E1
www.visitspitalfields.com
Crafts and antiques stalls are set up through the week, but on Friday and Sunday, the market comes alive with a dozen or so organic producers selling relishes, pickles, herbs and spices, breads and cakes, and fruit and vegetables. Open 10:00-16:00 Monday to Friday and 09:00-17:00 Sunday.

### Walthamstow Market
Walthamstow High Street, E17
Claims to be Britain's longest daily street market, with 450 stalls selling cheap clothing, fruit and vegetables, as well as household items. Open 08:00-17:00 Tuesday through Saturday.

# Art and antiques

Antique hunting in London is a joy. No matter how elegant or humble the establishment, gracious haggling is always permitted. Dealers are often prepared to come down 10 per cent, which they say is a trade discount. If they do not come down, do not persist, as the price may genuinely be the best they can give.

## Antique fairs

There are too many antique fairs in and around London to list them all. For complete listings of regularly scheduled Sunday fairs in London and throughout the UK, check the weekly newspaper *The Antiques Trade Gazette*, the weekly magazine *Time Out: London* or the monthly magazines *The Antique Collector* and *The Antique Dealer and Collector's Guide*. All are available at larger newsstands.

Some of the Junior League of London members' favourites are:

### The Association of Art and Antiques Dealers
✆ 020 7823 3511, www.lapada.co.uk
Hosts several fairs a year.

### The British Antique Dealers' Association
✆ 020 7589 4128, www.bada.org
Holds antiques & fine art fairs.

### The Chelsea Antiques Fair
✆ 01825 744 074, www.penman-fairs.co.uk
Boutique style fair held in the Chelsea Old Town Hall in both the autumn and spring.

### The Decorative Antiques and Textiles Fair
✆ 020 7616 9327, www.decorativefair.com
Held in Battersea Park generally in January, April and September.

### The Fine Arts & Antiques Fair
www.olympia-antiques.co.uk
Held in Olympia in February, June and November.

## Antique markets

There are antique markets all over London where groups of dealers, specialising in a variety of antiques or collectibles at all different price levels, display their goods. The following indoor markets contain numerous permanent stalls that deal in smaller items such as silver, prints and ceramics.

Admiral Vernon

141-149 Portobello Road, W11

✆ 020 7727 5240, www.portobelloroad.co.uk

The busiest arcade on Portobello Road, with over 200 private dealers. It features 17th-19th century porcelain, advertising art and antique textiles. Open Saturday only.

Alfie's Antique Market

13-25 Church Street, NW8

✆ 020 7723 6066, www.alfiesantiques.com

London's largest antique market. A fabulous maze of treasures in a historical street market and a source of some real bargains. The basement is packed with antique textiles, 19th century furniture, jewellery and accessories, while on the upper levels you might find French country furniture or 1960s furniture and lighting. Closed Sunday and Monday.

Bond Street Antiques Centre

124 New Bond Street, W1

✆ 020 7493 1854

Internationally renowned for silver and jewellery, vintage watches and objects d'art. Closed Sunday.

Camden Passage

Camden Passage, N1

www.camdenpassageislington.co.uk

Around 200 antiques dealers in the mall, arcade, shop and market stalls. Open Wednesday and Saturday.

Chelsea Antique Market

245-253 King's Road, SW3

✆ 020 7352 5689

A great place for finding unusual antiques. Prices tend to be higher than in other markets in London, although more-modestly priced pieces can be found. Closed Sunday.

Gray's Antique Market & Grays in the Mews

58 Davies Street and 1-7 Davies Mews, W1

✆ 020 7629 7034, www.graysantiques.com

The front hall has an enormous collection of antique jewellery and silverware dealers. The Mews is a bit cheaper but offers no less desirable collectibles, particularly, tinplate toys. Closed Saturday and Sunday.

## London Silver Vaults

Chancery House, Chancery Lane, WC2

✆ 020 7242 3844, www.thesilvervaults.com

World's largest collection of antique silver. These subterranean vaults are home to over 40 dealers offering every imaginable kind of silver item, from antique to modern. They also offer a wealth of knowledge (many are second- and third-generation dealers). Prices range from £10 to £100,000+, so you should find something to suit you. Closed Sunday.

## Antique shops

If you are looking for a specialist dealer, The British Antique Dealers Association (✆ 020 7589 4128, **www.bada.org**) will send a list of members on request.

A wide selection of high-end antiques can be found on Bond Street, the King's Road, the South Kensington end of Fulham Road and Kensington Church Street, which also has shops specialising in china and glass. Pimlico Road is interesting for unusual and decorative pieces. Specific Junior League of London members' recommendations include:

## Angus Adams Antiques

8 Newlands Place, Hartfield Road, East Sussex RH18

✆ 013 4282 2294, www.chevertons.co.uk

Great prices and friendly service.

## The Millinery Works

87 Southgate Road, N1

✆ 020 7359 2019, www.millineryworks.co.uk

Specialises in arts & crafts and furniture.

## Auction houses

Dealers or agents purchase the majority of their stock from auction houses. Therefore, auction houses are a good and fun alternative for antique hunting if you have the time and you remember to view the items carefully (during the preview, which is usually a few days before the sale).

Auction houses offer services to assist their customers. They can provide a detailed summary of a specific piece or they can arrange to have a specialist

12

SHOPPING

273

work with you during the preview. At the viewing, you can purchase a catalogue, which includes descriptions and estimates for each lot. Bidding is easy. First, you register and receive a paddle with a number. When the lot you are interested in comes up, raise your hand. The auctioneer will take your bid. If you are successful, he or she will note your number. It's that simple!

The main auction houses are Christie's and Sotheby's. Visit their websites (listed below) or look at listings in the newspaper or magazines for specific auctions.

Bonhams
101 New Bond Street, W1
✆ 020 7447 7447, www.bonhams.com

Christie's
85 Old Brompton Road, SW7
✆ 020 7930 6074, www.christies.com

Lots Road Auctions
71-73 Lots Road, SW10
✆ 020 7376 6800, www.lotsroad.com
Two sales every Sunday. The lots can be viewed online. The full catalogue is available from 19:30 on Thursdays.

Rosebery's
74-76 Knight's Hill, SE27
✆ 020 8761 2522, www.roseberys.co.uk
Twelve catalogued sales a year.

Sotheby's
34-35 New Bond Street, W1
✆ 020 7293 5000, www.sothebys.com

## Art fairs and galleries
There are several art fairs held in London. Two major contemporary art fairs are listed below.

The Affordable Art Fair
Battersea Park
www.affordableartfair
Numerous galleries throughout London and other parts of the UK display

their various collections of contemporary art from just £50 up to £3,000. A great place to browse, buy and learn about art all under one roof. The event is held bi-annually generally in March and October.

Frieze Art Fair
www.friezeartfair.com
Held in mid-October at Regent's Park, the Frieze Art Fair features over 150 of the most exciting contemporary art galleries in the world. The fair also includes specially commissioned artists' projects, a prestigious talks programme and an artist-led education schedule.

Whether your taste is for Old Masters or young contemporary artists, London has many fine art galleries. The more expensive dealers are concentrated in St. James and Mayfair; others are scattered throughout the city. The Society of London Art Dealers website at **www.slad.org.uk** has a list of various galleries throughout London as well as upcoming exhibitions and art fairs.

# Books

Chain bookstores like Waterstone's, Books Etc. and WH Smith are ubiquitous in London. These offer a good general selection of standard books in print.

If you're looking for speciality books, maybe something old, out of print or an art book, you're in luck because London is still peppered with small, independent bookstores. Many sell a mix of new and used books, often devoted to specialist themes to differentiate themselves from the chains. Others are devoted exclusively to dusty and dog-eared, second-hand books or rare first editions and leather-bound gems. The heart of London's book trade is found in the Bloomsbury area, where a number of fine bookshops are clustered around the British Museum. You also might want to wander around Cecil Court and Charing Cross Road, where book lovers will find a number of second-hand and specialist book, poster and print shops devoted to many subjects. Here's a short list of some of our favourite independent and speciality bookshops in London. (For children's bookstores see *Chapter 8: Children – Shopping*.)

Biblion
17 Davies Mews, W1
Ⓒ 020 7629 1374, www.biblion.co.uk
A must see for any book lover with a vast collection of antiquarian

booksellers located under one roof. You can spend hours here sampling the merchandise. Visit their website, where nearly three million books are listed by more than 500 dealers. This is the UK's largest website by far for rare, antiquarian and second-hand books.

### Books for Cooks
4 Blenheim Crescent, W11
© 020 7221 1992, www.booksforcooks.com
A vast array of cookbooks is stacked floor to ceiling. The knowledgeable staff will help with suggestions or special orders. There is a small kitchen where they test recipes and offer courses, but you'll need to book early.

### Daunt Books
83 Marylebone High Street, W1
© 020 7224 2295, www.dauntbooks.co.uk
Unique arrangement of travel guides, novels and non-fiction arranged by country. Also includes good general selection. Multiple locations.

### Foyle's
113-119 Charing Cross Road, WC2
© 020 7437 5660, www.foyles.co.uk
A massive one-of-a-kind store. If you are looking for that hard to find book, this is the place.

### Gay's the Word
66 Marchmont Street, WC1
© 020 7278 7654, www.gaystheword.co.uk
The UK's first lesbian and gay bookshop.

### Gekoski
13 Bathurst mews, London, W2
© 020 7706 2735, www.gekoski.co.uk
Sells rare and first editions of 19th century and modern literature.

### Hatchard's
187 Piccadilly, W1
© 020 7439 9921, www.hatchards.co.uk
Excellent selection; bookseller since 1797.

### Henry Sotheran
2 Sackville Street, W1

© 020 7439 6151, www.sotherans.co.uk

The longest established antiquarian booksellers in the world (York, 1761). Has a handsome ground floor room lined with glass-fronted cabinets packed with antiquarian books, supplemented by a downstairs print gallery.

### Keith Fawkes
1-3 Flask Walk, NW3

© 020 7435 0614

Hampstead's oldest antiquarian bookshop.

### Maggs Brothers
50 Berkeley Square, W1

© 020 7493 7160, www.maggs.com

Arguably the most prestigious antiquarian bookseller in London, selling pre-20th century manuscripts and first editions, with an outstanding selection in literature and travel.

### Persephone Books
59 Lamb's Conduit Street, WC1

© 020 7242 9292, www.persephonebooks.co.uk

Prints mainly neglected fiction and non-fiction by women, for women and about women. Titles include novels, short stories, diaries and cookery books, all of which are designed with a clear typeface, dove-grey jacket and 'fabric' endpaper and bookmark.

### The Travel Bookshop
13-15 Blenheim Crescent, W11

© 020 7229 5260, www.thetravelbookshop.com

Guidebooks, travelogues, literature, history and biography on countries around the world. Also has photographic titles, maps, atlases and an eclectic range of second-hand, rare and antiquarian books.

### Ulysses
40 Museum Street, WC1

© 020 7831 1600

Collection of modern first editions and 20th century classics. This shop is full of rare and second-hand books.

# Outlet shopping

There are many shopping outlets throughout the UK, and every one has a variety of shops offering discounts up to 70 per cent off the retail price of the products they sell. Visit **www.shoppingvillages.com** for a complete listing of outlet locations, opening hours, and new shops or special offerings.

Bicester Village
50 Pingle Drive, Bicester, OX26
✆ 0186 932 3200, www.bicestervillage.com
Top-quality merchandise from over 60 designer and famous brand-named shops.

Clarks Village Factory Shopping
Farm Road Street, Somerset, BA16
✆ 0145 884 0064, www.clarksvillage.co.uk
Nearly 60 shops.

Costco
Hartspring Lane, Watford, WD25
✆ 0192 369 9805, www.costco.co.uk
Sells high-quality, nationally branded and selected private-label merchandise at low prices to businesses purchasing for commercial use or resale, and also to individuals who are members of selected employment groups.

# Clothing size charts

There is no dearth of bespoke tailors in London, many of whom are to be found in Savile Row or Jermyn Street, for handmade shirts. If you are clothes shopping at department or high street stores, the following clothing size charts may come in handy. The tables below should be used as an approximate guide, as the actual sizes may vary according to the manufacturer, as well as the country of origin. Small sizes are generally difficult to obtain. It is advisable to try the clothing on to ensure the correct size. Children's clothes in the UK are usually based on the child's age using a calculated average weight and height. (*See Chapter 8: Children* for details on shops for children's clothing and maternity wear.)

## Women's Clothing

| UK | 8 | 10 | 12 | 14 | 16 | 18 | 20 | 22 | 24 |
|---|---|---|---|---|---|---|---|---|---|
| France | 36 | 38 | 40 | 42 | 44 | 46 | 48 | 50 | 52 |
| Germany | 34 | 36 | 38 | 40 | 42 | 44 | 46 | 48 | 50 |
| Italy | 40 | 42 | 44 | 46 | 48 | 50 | 52 | 54 | 56 |
| Australia | 10 | 12 | 14 | 16 | 18 | 20 | 22 | 24 | 26 |
| Japan | 9 | 11 | 13 | 15 | 17 | 19 | 21 | 23 | 25 |
| US | 6 | 8 | 10 | 12 | 14 | 16 | 18 | 20 | 22 |

## Women's Shoes

| UK | 3 | 3½ | 4 | 4½ | 5 | 5½ | 6 | 6½ | 7 | 7½ |
|---|---|---|---|---|---|---|---|---|---|---|
| Continental Europe | 35½ | 36 | 37 | 37½ | 38 | 38½ | 39 | 40 | 41 | 42 |
| Australia | 4 | 4½ | 5 | 5½ | 6 | 6½ | 7 | 7½ | 8 | 8½ |
| Japan | 21½ | 22 | 22½ | 23 | 23½ | 24 | 24½ | 25 | 25½ | 26 |
| US | 5½ | 6 | 6½ | 7 | 7½ | 8 | 8½ | 9 | 9½ | 10 |

## Men's Clothing

| UK | 32 | 34 | 36 | 38 | 40 | 42 | 44 | 46 |
|---|---|---|---|---|---|---|---|---|
| Continental Europe | 42 | 44 | 46 | 48 | 50 | 52 | 54 | 56 |
| Australia | 42 | 44 | 36 | 37 | 38 | 39 | 41 | 42 |
| Japan | – | S | – | M | L | – | LL | – |
| US | 32 | 34 | 36 | 38 | 40 | 42 | 44 | 46 |

## Men's Shirts or Collar Sizes

| UK | 14 | 14½ | 15 | 15½ | 16 | 16½ | 17 | 17½ |
|---|---|---|---|---|---|---|---|---|
| Continental Europe | 36 | 37 | 38 | 39 | 41 | 42 | 43 | 44 |
| Australia | 36 | 37 | 38 | 39 | 41 | 42 | 43 | 44 |
| Japan | 36 | 37 | 38 | 39 | 41 | 42 | 43 | 44 |
| US | 14 | 14½ | 15 | 15½ | 16 | 16½ | 17 | 17½ |

## Men's Shoes

| UK | 7½ | 8 | 8½ | 9 | 9½ | 10 | 10½ | 11 |
|---|---|---|---|---|---|---|---|---|
| Continental Europe | 41 | 42 | 43 | 43½ | 44 | 44½ | 45 | 45½ |
| Australia | 7½ | 8 | 8½ | 9 | 9½ | 10 | 10½ | 11 |
| Japan | 26 | 26½ | 27 | 27½ | 28 | 28½ | 29 | 29½ |
| US | 8 | 8½ | 9 | 9½ | 10 | 10½ | 11 | 11½ |

## Socks

| UK | 9½ | 10 | 10½ | 11 | 11½ | 12 | 12½ |
|---|---|---|---|---|---|---|---|
| Continental Europe | 39 | 40 | 41 | 42 | 43 | 44 | 45 |
| US | 9½ | 10 | 10½ | 11 | 11½ | 12 | 12½ |

# 13

# Continuing education

In London the opportunities for continuing education, whether it's academic, vocational or for fun, are immense. There are thousands of programmes offered in London every year and this chapter does not attempt to list all of them, but rather focuses on those courses that are well known and repeatedly attended by members of the Junior League of London. Please note that the cost of courses varies greatly and some mentioned here are quite costly, so do ask about the cost of a course while enquiring about dates and availability.

While this chapter focuses on certain areas of learning, don't let this listing of courses limit you. *Floodlight* (**www.floodlight.co.uk**) and *Hotcourses* (**www.hotcourses.co.uk**) are the standard online references for courses offered in London. Among its various publications, *Hotcourses* publishes *Hotcourses Magazine: London's Essential Course Guide* which can be found at most bookshops and newsagents as well as online.

## IN THIS CHAPTER...

- Art history
- Cookery
- Flower arranging
- Gardening and interior design
- Languages
- Museum and gallery lectures
- University and college courses
- Wine

Consider contacting your local council for information on hundreds of adult education classes, ranging from pottery, car mechanics and language courses to degrees in social work. The fees are usually very reasonable because they are government subsidised and classes are held at various locations in your neighbourhood.

# Art history

Prices vary depending on the duration of the course and the institution. Many courses follow a semester or school-year schedule; therefore it is advisable to book well in advance to secure a place. Additionally, many course offerings change based on current interest. For the most current curriculum content and schedule, call the school and ask for a brochure.

Christie's Education
153 Great Titchfield Street, W1
℗ 020 7665 4350, www.christies.edu
Christie's Education London is validated by the University of Glasgow to run a range of undergraduate and postgraduate courses.

The following one-year postgraduate study courses (three terms of 10 weeks each) can be taken as a Graduate Diplomas or a Master's degree (except the Arts of China which can only be taken as a Master's degree):

* Arts of Europe – Antiquity to Renaissance

* Art, Style and Design – Renaissance to Modernism

* Modern and Contemporary Art – late 19th century to the present

* Arts of China – Neolithic period to the present

Evening and short courses are also offered. These classes meet once a week for a specified number of weeks and cover a variety of specialised subjects.

Sotheby's Institute of Art
30 Bedford Square, WC1
℗ 020 7462 3232, www.sothebysinstitute.com
The Institute runs over 30 courses in all aspects of fine and decorative art at both undergraduate and postgraduate levels.

The following one-year postgraduate study courses (two semesters of full-time study and a third semester of independent study) can be taken as a Master's degree:

- Art Business
- Contemporary Art
- Photography
- Fine & Decorative Art
- East Asian Art
- Contemporary Design

Internationally recognised courses offer unique first-hand examination of works of art with privileged access to auction rooms. Acceptance is by application and interview.

Sotheby's also offers a variety of evening, daytime and short courses to the public covering various topics including the art market, design and the history of art.

The Art Study Circle
✆ 020 8788 6910, (Sara Hebblethwaite)
Art history lectures given weekly on Mondays in an informal setting by experts in their fields. Some lectures tie-in with current exhibitions in London and include visits. Half-day art lectures offered both in the morning and afternoon.

# Cookery

Books for Cooks
4 Blenheim Crescent, W11
✆ 020 7221 1992, www.booksforcooks.com
Special 3-hour workshops focusing on various topics, tips and cuisines. Imperative to book in advance since workshops fill up quickly.

Divertimenti
33/34 Marylebone High Street, W1
✆ 020 7846 8020, www.divertimenti.co.uk
Cookery school offers a range of one-off classes generally lasting two hours as well as courses and food tours. In each class, students receive

copies of the recipes, tastings of the dishes and a 10 per cent discount for shopping afterwards. Brompton Road location as well.

### Le Cordon Bleu Cookery School
114 Marylebone Lane, W1
📞 020 7935 3503, www.cordonbleu.edu
Offers career training, short and part-time courses, practical and demonstration classes. Because this school is world famous, there is often a waiting list for its diploma and certificate courses.

### Leith's School of Food and Wine
16-20 Wendell Road, W12
📞 020 8749 6400, www.leiths.com
The school offers diploma and certificate courses in food and wine for all levels, and a variety of short cookery courses.

### Tante Marie School of Cookery
Woodham House, Carlton Road, Woking, Surrey, GU21
📞 014 8372 6957, www.tantemarie.co.uk
Offers both certificate and diploma courses as well as occasional short-course demonstrations. A wide range of cuisine is covered.

# Flower arranging

### Jane Packer Flower School
32-34 New Cavendish Street, W1
📞 020 7486 1300, www.jane-packer.co.uk
Offers a four-week career course and a three-day introductory course in flower arranging. Also offers evening, one-day and half-day courses in a variety of subjects including dried flowers, Christmas decorations and wedding flowers.

### Paula Pryke Flowers
The Flower House, Cynthia Street, N1
📞 020 7837 7336, www.paula-pryke-flowers.com
One-day, half-day and multi-day courses are available on a variety of themes.

# Gardening and interior design

The British take great pride in their gardens and the following courses are very comprehensive.

The English Gardening School
Chelsea Wharf, 15 Lots Road, SW10
✆ 020 7352 4347, www.englishgardeningschool.co.uk
Offers one-year diploma courses in garden design, practical horticulture, botanical painting, plants and plantsmanship. Also offers short courses of varying length, on a wide range of topics such as garden design, Christmas wreaths and flower arranging. There are also distance-learning courses in design and horticulture available.

The Inchbald School of Design: Garden Design
32 Eccleston Square, SW1
✆ 020 7630 9011, www.inchbald.co.uk

The Inchbald School of Design: Interior Design
7 Eaton Gate, SW1
✆ 020 7730 5508, www.inchbald.co.uk
Offers a one-year diploma course, a 10-week certificate course and a Master's degree course in garden design (basic principles of design, plant knowledge, the role of fine art in design, garden architecture and business skills) or in interior design and decoration. Part-time and Saturday classes are also offered in garden design and interior decoration.

KLC School of Design
503 The Chambers, Chelsea Harbour, SW10
✆ 020 7376 3377, www.klc.co.uk
Offers a variety of full-time, part-time, short and open learning courses are available in interior design and garden design.

# Languages

Institut Francais
14 Cromwell Place, SW7
✆ 020 7581 2701, www.institut-francais.org.uk
The official French government centre of language and culture in London

offers courses at all levels; part-time or full-time, weekdays or weekends. Enrolment in a course provides access to the Institute's cultural centre, multimedia library and the children's library.

University of Westminster
309 Regent Street, W1
© 020 7911 5000, www.westminster.ac.uk
Offers courses in most European languages one evening a week from late September through May.

Oxford House College
30 Oxford St, W1
© 020 7580 9785, www.oxfordhousecollege.co.uk
Offers many language courses ranging from general English (to improve speaking, reading, writing and listening) to business-oriented skills to improve career prospects.

United International College Language House
76-78 Mortimer Street W1
© 020 7079 3334, www.uiclondon.com
Offers language courses in English, Spanish, Chinese, French, German, Italian and Japanese at a range of different levels.

# Museum and gallery lectures

Most museums and galleries offer regular free lectures and tours. Call or review individual websites for a schedule of events (see *Chapter 16: Culture* for museum listings). Many also offer the opportunity to receive e-mails of upcoming events. Information on talks and lectures, as well as new exhibits, can be found in the weekly magazine *Time Out: London*.

# University and college courses

There are numerous courses available: undergraduate, graduate, part-time and full-time. Check to see whether the course might be credited to any degree you are planning to complete. Tuition fees vary and if you have lived in the UK for a minimum of four years, or hold certain other residency equivalencies, you will qualify for home student tuition, which is generally half the price of the overseas student fee. For more information, visit the UK Council for International Student Affairs website at **www.ukcisa.org.uk**, as well as check with the school.

### The Open University
Walton Hall, Milton Keynes, MK7

✆ 0845 300 6090, www.open.ac.uk

Offers distant learning university courses to any resident of the European Union and Switzerland over 18 years of age. Methods of instruction include television courses, tutorials and correspondence work.

### The University of London
Birkbeck College, Malet Street, WC1

✆ 020 7631 6000, www.bbk.ac.uk

Offers certificate and diploma courses, as well as one and two- term courses to anyone over 18 years of age. Classes usually meet two hours a week for 24 weeks.

# Wine

### Christie's Education
153 Great Titchfield Street, W1

✆ 020 7665 4350, www.christies.edu

The Wine Course introduces wines from all over the world using French wines as the benchmark. One evening a week on Tuesdays for five weeks; available six times per year. Occasional one-off master classes on fine and rare wines, wines of the New World and seminars abroad.

### Berry Brothers
3 St. James Street, SW1

✆ 020 7396 9685, www.bbr.com

Berry's wine school offers a wide range of courses for both novices and wine connoisseurs. Courses range from one-day courses to certificate-program evening classes.

# 14

# Sports and leisure

Sports and games are a huge part of British life. Many sports were invented, developed or unified by the British, including golf, skiing, tennis and football to name a few. Just about every sport is enjoyed somewhere, from the most popular sport of angling (a fishing sport with over 2.2 million participants), to the more arcane sports of lawnmower racing and curling. Team sports traditionally have a higher profile. Association football, rugby football and cricket are the most popular. Golf, racing and motor sports also have large followings. For a description of some of the more popular British sports and sporting events, see the *British sporting glossary* at the end of this chapter.

In addition to watching sport, there are many ways to participate in sport as well. The sections at the end of this chapter list sports facilities and various fitness activities, as well as London's many parks where locals engage in a bit of recreational sport and leisure.

**14**

**SPORTS AND LEISURE**

## IN THIS CHAPTER...

- Spectator sports
- Fitness and sports facilities
- Cycling
- Dance and fitness classes
- Golf
- Horse riding
- Ice hockey
- Ice skating
- Martial arts
- Personal training
- Rowing
- Rugby
- Running
- Sailing
- Swimming
- Tennis
- Walking and hiking
- Yoga and Pilates
- Parks
- British sporting glossary

# Spectator sports

Tickets to see the biggest sporting events are quite difficult to obtain, with the most sought after being Wimbledon (tennis), the FA Cup Final (football), Six Nations fixtures (rugby union), Test cricket matches (cricket) and the Formula One British Grand Prix (car racing). Unless you are affiliated with a club, have very good connections or you are prepared to pay vastly inflated prices on the black market, the best way to attend one of these events may be through your employer purchasing a corporate hospitality package, or to somehow acquire an invitation to another corporate box or tent. Try The Sporting Traveller (✆0173 724 4398, **www.thesportingtraveller.com**) or Matchpoint (✆020 8332 7384, **www.matchpoint.co.uk**), which both offer deals for all these popular sporting events. Ticketmaster (✆0870 4000 700, **www.ticketmaster.co.uk**) is another option. Regardless of where tickets are found, the best advice is to purchase them early.

## Football

Association football (the word soccer is rarely used) is the national game and every visitor should experience at least one match. The English football league system is a pyramid of leagues interconnected by rules of promotion and regulation. There are two top national leagues – the Premier League (Level 1), which consists of the top 20 clubs, and the Football League (Levels 2-4), the original football association for England and Wales and which currently represents more than 70 clubs. More information on levels, leagues, and ranking systems for both men's and women's football can be found through the Football Association website at **www.thefa.com**.

The official football season runs from August until April, ending with the drama and passion of the FA Cup Final in May. Among other events, FA Cup Finals are normally played at Wembley Stadium. Sixty-five per cent of tickets are allocated to season ticket holders of the two clubs contesting the Final. The remainder of the tickets are for the football league, its members and hospitality packages. These are always available for a price – expect to pay at least £500 per ticket.

## Premier League

Several of the FA Premier League teams are located in London (visit **www. premierleague.com** for a current listing). Tickets to see habitual premiership teams like Arsenal, Chelsea and Tottenham Hotspur are hard to obtain, particularly for high-profile matches. Other teams' tickets may be easier to get hold of, such as Charlton, Fulham and West Ham United. Most football clubs allow for bookings via the telephone or online. If you cannot find tickets to a Premier League match, try one of the London clubs in Nationwide Division One (just below the Premier League). It is usually easier to acquire tickets and many times offers a more representative taste of the national game. Crystal Palace Football Club (**www.cpfc.co.uk**) in south London has a reputation for being especially family friendly.

Hints for going to the match:

* Professional football matches take place on weekends and on weekday evenings. The traditional kick-off times are 15:00 on Saturday and 19:45 during the week. Always be sure to check the day before the match since the time printed on your ticket can change at short notice due to TV schedules and police requests.

* Most football clubs welcome children, but book seats in the designated family areas, which will be non-smoking and specially stewarded.

* Expect opposing supporters to be strictly segregated. If ever offered a match ticket, check where the seats are located. Avoid sitting with the away supporters unless you and your family are diehard fans of the away team. Equally, you may be asked to leave by the stewards if you are seen to be supporting the away team in a home area.

* Take public transport to the game if at all possible. Roads around the ground may be blocked and parking may be virtually impossible.

* Do not try to take food or drink with you, as it will probably be confiscated. Not only do clubs prefer you to buy food from the concession stands, cans and bottles are regarded as a safety hazard. Beer is available inside the stadium before the match, but cannot be taken to your seat. The bar will close as soon as the match is underway. This applies to corporate boxes as well.

* Dress warmly. Unless in a corporate box, there will be no heating and seats may not be under cover. Matches are usually played rain or shine.

### Rugby
There are two types of rugby played in England – rugby union (15-a-side) and rugby league (13-a-side). There are various national and international

leagues and competitions for both sports. Visit **www.rfu.com** (rugby union) or **www.superleague.co.uk** (rugby league) for more details.

In London and the south, rugby union is far more popular than rugby league. The English national team plays at Twickenham in West London, where Test Matches are played. There is also a Premiership league in which the top 12 professional teams compete. In general, rugby matches have a more relaxed and friendly atmosphere than football matches and opposing supporters are not separated. Tailgate parties in the car park before and after matches are a long-standing Twickenham tradition.

The Six Nations tournament, held in January/February, is the premier northern hemisphere rugby union competition among the national teams of England, Wales, Scotland, Ireland, France and Italy. Twickenham hosts the three home matches in this tournament for the England team.

Tickets for Twickenham are notoriously hard to obtain for matches against Australia, New Zealand, South Africa and the Six Nations competition. For those contests, unless you are a playing or coaching member of a rugby club, your best bet is to book a hospitality package, which will include a ticket, lunch, tea and drinks. These are not cheap, and most are bought for corporate entertainment. Try ticket agency Keith Prowse (✆ 0845 125 4880, **www.keithprowse.co.uk**). For other matches, tickets may be obtained through the team's website or via Ticketmaster.

If you would like to see a domestic rugby union match, there are several professional clubs based in and around London: the Wasps (**www.wasps.co.uk**) in Ealing and the Harlequins (**www.quins.co.uk**), just down the road from Twickenham. Tickets are relatively easy to obtain, except for certain Premiership matches.

### Tennis

Tennis is a very old sport in the UK and there are hundreds of clubs, but its popularity is seasonal due to the inconsistency of weather on outside courts. The Lawn Tennis Association (**LTA**) was founded at Wimbledon and tennis is only played for two weeks of the year at the All England Lawn Tennis and Croquet Club (**AELTC**) on Centre Court and No. 1 Court. The All England Club is home to the Wimbledon Tennis Championship, which is played in June when the whole nation seems to go tennis-mad, particularly if a British player manages to survive the first week. Visit **www.wimbeldon.org** for more information regarding tickets.

Catering at Wimbledon is excellent, yet expensive. Strawberries, champagne, lobster and Pimms are all available within the grounds, but you can also take your own picnic. There is a large, atmospheric grassy picnic area known as the Hill with a large screen relaying live action from the show courts.

There are four main ways to obtain tournament tickets:

- Submit an application into the public ballot for a pair of show court tickets. To obtain an application form, you will need to send a self-addressed, stamped envelope to AELTC, PO Box 98, London SW19 5AE, between 1 August and 15 December the year before you wish to attend. Tickets are awarded randomly to applicants, submitting an application does not guarantee tickets. Days and courts are randomly assigned, so it is not possible to specify a choice in this method.

- If your family or club is a member of the Lawn Tennis Association, you may enter the LTA Advantage ballot for tickets. For more details, phone 0845 873 7202 or visit **www.lta.org.uk**.

- Some tickets go on sale on the day of play. Queues can be very long. Expect to queue overnight for show court tickets or several hours before the grounds open for Ground Tickets. There are approximately 6,000 Ground Tickets available each day, which entitle access to the No. 2 Court unreserved seating and the standing enclosure on Courts 2 through 19.

- Alternatively, many Londoners choose to visit Wimbledon in the late afternoon/early evening, when show court tickets are resold for charity once their original holders (often corporate hospitality guests) have left for the day.

If all else fails, there is always corporate hospitality. Expect to pay at least £500 per person for the day. Try ticket agencies: Keith Prowse (©0845 125 4880, **www.keithprowse.co.uk**) or Sportsworld Group (©0123 555 5844, **www.sportsworld.co.uk**).

Two weeks before Wimbledon, the AEGON Tennis Tournament, a men's tennis tournament, is held at the Queen's Club in west London. Another nice excuse for strawberries and champagne in summer. Visit **www.aegon championships.com** for more information.

## Horse racing

### Cheltenham National Hunt Festival

The most important jump racing meeting on the calendar occurs at

Cheltenham Racecourse each March. The National Hunt Festival, a combination of steeplechase and hurdle racing, features four major Championship races (in addition to Grade 1 contests and Handicap races) over the course of four days, culminating with the Cheltenham Gold Cup race. Apply for tickets and book accommodation from 30 September. A discount scheme is offered for early purchases. Contact ✆0124 251 3014 or visit **www.cheltenham.co.uk**.

### Grand National

The Grand National, held at Aintree Racecourse in Liverpool each April, is perhaps the most famous steeplechase in the world: a four and a half mile race over 30 challenging fences. Tickets are relatively inexpensive and plentiful. Contact ✆0151 522 2929 or visit **www.aintree.co.uk**.

### Royal Ascot

Race meetings are held at Ascot Racecourse in Berkshire year-round: jump racing in the winter and flat racing in the summer. Royal Ascot, held in June, is perhaps the most famous meeting. The Queen, who is an avid owner, always attends. Foreign nationals may obtain tickets for the Royal Enclosure at Royal Ascot by application to their embassy or high commission. Morning dress, smart dress or national dress for men, and hats and skirts for ladies must be worn. Alternatively, you can buy tickets for other enclosures from Ascot Racecourse (✆0870 727 1234, **www.ascot.co.uk**).

### The Derby

The Derby, a classic flat race for three-year-old horses, is run every June at Epsom Downs Racecourse in Surrey. This race is a tradition that dates back to 1779. Go to **www.epsomderby.co.uk** for ticket information.

## Cricket

Cricket is the English summer national game and is famously said to be incomprehensible to foreigners. In fact, it is easy to follow once the basic terms are understood. Many believe that there is nothing more peaceful than spending an afternoon beside a village cricket green lounging on a picnic rug, reading the weekend papers and sipping a cup of tea or glass of wine. You can experience the excitement and atmosphere of a one-day international or a five-day Test Match at either Lord's Cricket Ground, St. John's Wood (✆020 7432 1000, **www.lords.org**) or the Oval Cricket Ground, Kennington (✆020 7582 6660, **www.britoval.com**). Alternatively, contact the English

Cricket Board (© 0870 533 8833, **www.ecb.co.uk**) for additional information, fixtures and tickets.

### Motor racing

The Formula One British Grand Prix is held in July at the Silverstone Circuit in Northamptonshire, located 115km north of London. Tickets are available on © 0844 3750 740 or the venue's website at **www.silverstone.co.uk**. Purchasing early is recommended to ensure availability. The track website provides the full calendar of British motor races for the year.

### Golf

There are more than 2,500 golf courses in the UK and its popularity has increased dramatically with worldwide TV coverage. Many old, established member-only clubs now allow pay and play on weekdays and some weekends. Strict club rules and etiquette must be observed. The biggest annual golf event is the Open Championship, which is rotated around links (seaside) courses in England and Scotland. You will need to book in early spring for general admission tickets. Admission tickets and hospitality may be booked by phone on © 0845 625 8000 or online at **www.british opengolf.co.uk**.

# Fitness and sports facilities

Sport England (**www.sportengland.org.uk**) is an organisation that delivers the government's sporting objectives in the UK. Its mission is to work with others to create opportunities for persons to get involved in sport, and to stay and succeed in sport. Sport England works through nine regional offices that can provide a vast array of information on sporting activities throughout England. Visit the website to research sport opportunities in a specific area.

Most boroughs have a variety of public recreational facilities, such as pools, tennis courts, aerobics classes and parks. Some councils run a residents' discount scheme, such as Westminster's ResCard (**www.westminster.gov.uk**) and Camden's Wellness Card (**www.camden.gov.uk**), which entitles members to reductions on certain gym memberships and other activities. Contact your local council for location, activities, costs and availability. A full listing of councils can be found at **www.direct.gov.uk**. Each council has it's own public sports and leisure centres, which can be found on the council's website.

The UK Fitness Network (**www.ukfitnessnetwork.org**) has formed a partnership between the UK's not for profit leisure centres and clubs. Visit their website for information on joining and leisure centres in your area. In addition, the Jubilee Hall Trust owns some of the best value (there's no joining fee) sports facilities in London (**www.jubileehallclubs.co.uk**), including Jubilee Hall in Covent Garden and The Armoury in Hampstead. The YMCA Sport & Fitness Centres (**www.ymcaclub.co.uk**) also offer good value for money and you can pay for a one-off visit.

### Private health clubs and gyms

There are many private health clubs and gyms located throughout London. Membership rates and services provided vary according to the quality and location of the club. Many clubs have off-peak memberships that cost less than a full membership and, in general, allow you to use the club on weekdays from 09:00-17:00. Additionally, many have flexible payment schedules to accommodate instalments on a monthly basis. Telephone the specific club for membership rate information.

> **DID YOU KNOW?**
>
> London health clubs and gyms are generally expensive to join and often demand a guarantee of at least one year's commitment. When thinking about joining a gym, always ask for at least a fortnight's trial, and if necessary shop around to find the right one for you.

Listed below are some of the more well-known private health clubs with multiple locations that are frequented by Junior League of London members and their families. Check your local residents' magazine or newspaper for the most up-to-date information on new club openings in your area.

Cannons Health Clubs
© 0208 336 2288, www.cannons.co.uk
Many locations across the City, making it handy for after-work visits. Some have pools, some do not. Good value.

David Lloyd
© 0844 543 9783, www.davidlloydleisure.co.uk
Offers full gym: machines, pool, exercise classes and children's facilities. Many locations across London.

### Esporta Health Clubs

✆0118 912 3576, www.esporta.com

Fitness centre chain with more-spacious facilities than most. Some locations (e.g., the Riverside Club in Chiswick) are more like country clubs with tennis courts, outdoor swimming pools and plenty of children's facilities. London branches include Wandsworth, Chiswick, Kingston, Islington, Swiss Cottage and Wimbledon.

### Fitness First

✆01202 845 000, www.fitnessfirst.co.uk

Largest health club operator in Europe. Offers full gym facilities and classes. Many locations across London.

### LA Fitness

✆0844 770 7700, www.lafitness.co.uk

Offers full gym facilities and classes. Many locations across London.

### Virgin Active Health Clubs

✆020 7717 9000, www.virginactive.co.uk

A chain with many branches throughout greater London. Be warned that facilities can vary enormously between branches. Most have pools, a few have indoor running tracks, separate men's and women's gyms, crèches and restaurants. Varied studio programme includes aerobics, spinning, Pilates and yoga.

# Cycling

Cycling on the streets of London is legal but can be dangerous. Cycle routes and lanes are marked throughout the city for safer riding. Map of cycle routes are available at your local council office, libraries, cycle shops and through the Transport for London website at **www.tfl.org.uk**. Please note that lights on your cycle should be used after dark if you are cycling on the street, and that cycling on pavements (sidewalks) is illegal.

You can cycle in parks on marked bicycle paths. For road cycling, South Carriage Drive and Constitution Hill and the Mall near Buckingham Palace are closed to cars on Sunday. Parts of Hampstead Heath, Wimbledon Common and Richmond Park are open for off-road cycling.

London Cycling Campaign (✆020 7234 9310, **www.lcc.org.uk**) seeks to increase cycling in greater London. They publish an interesting guide called *On Your Bike*. Many of the activities happen at the local borough level. To contact your local group, choose your London borough from the website. For more information about cycling in London see *Chapter 6: Transportation – Cycling*.

# Dance and fitness classes

### British Military Fitness
©020 7751 9742, www.britmilfit.com
For something different, try military-style training in London's parks! Classes are conducted by army or marine instructors most days in Hyde Park, Battersea Park, Clapham Common and Hampstead Heath, among others, for varied-ability ranges.

### Danceworks
16 Balderton Street, W1
©020 7629 6183, www.danceworks.net
A variety of dance, aerobic and Pilates classes.

### English National Ballet
Markova House, 39 Jay Mews, SW7
©020 7581 1245, www.ballet.org
Adult ballet class one evening a week. Ten-week courses are available for beginners and those at intermediate levels.

### Pineapple Dance Studio
7 Langley Street, WC2
©020 7836 4004, www.pineapple.uk.com
A variety of dance classes for beginners to professionals.

# Golf

There are very few golf courses in central London, although there are some hidden driving ranges. The courses and ranges below are all open to the public (and you do not need a handicap to play) but offer preferential rates and booking times if you become a member. Do not expect golf carts as they are rare in the UK. For more information on courses in the London area and information about clubs visit The English Golf Union website at **www. englishgolfunion.org**.

Note that at smarter and more traditional golf clubs, shirts with collars are obligatory for both sexes, and ladies' shorts should be at knee length. Some clubs also require men to wear knee-high socks with shorts. Ask your host beforehand if in doubt.

## Driving ranges and golf lessons

### Knightsbridge Golf School

47 Lowndes Square, SW1

✆ 020 7235 2468, www.knightsbridgegolfschool.com

An underground driving range in a converted squash court! Good reputation for tuition. KGS members receive a discount on greens fees at Stoke Park Golf Club in Buckinghamshire.

### Top Golf

Bushey Mill Lane, Watford, WD24

✆ 0192 322 2045, www.topgolf.co.uk

Outside of London, but worth it for the heated bays, food delivery service and the microchips inside each ball, which tell you exactly how far and where each ball is hit. Tuition, putting course, shop, café and children's parties.

## Golf courses

All courses listed below welcome non-members on a casual basis.

### Central London Golf Centre

Burntwood Lane, Wandsworth, SW17

✆ 020 8871 2468, www.clgc.co.uk

Young, informal club with a nine-hole course and driving range. Club hire available and tuition offered, including a recommended group beginner's course.

### Dukes Meadow Golf Course

Dan Mason Drive, Chiswick, W4

✆ 020 8995 0537, www.dukesmeadows.com

Driving range and an all-par-3, nine-hole golf course. Instruction available, but no club hire.

### Richmond Park Golf Course

Roehampton Gate, Priory Lane, SW15

✆ 020 8876 3205, www.richmondparkgolfclub.co.uk
Two 18-hole golf courses.

## Horse riding

Equipment usually can be hired from the stables for a small fee. Hard hats are compulsory in the UK. Most stables require children to be at least four or five years of age to ride.

Hyde Park Riding School
63 Bathurst Mews, W2
✆ 020 7723 2813, www.hydeparkstables.com
Riding by the hour offered for beginner through advanced levels.
Tuition offered for adults and children. Pony camp for children during weekday afternoons.

Kingston Riding Centre
38 Crescent Road, Kingston-Upon-Thames, KT2
✆ 020 8546 6361, www.kingstonridingcentre.com
Lessons available. Famous for their 'Pimm's Hacks' through Richmond Park on summer evenings.

Wimbledon Village Stables
24A/B High Street, Wimbledon, SW19
✆ 020 8946 8579, www.wvstables.com
Offers short courses, lessons and hacks (rides across Wimbledon Common).

## Ice hockey

If you are interested in non-professional UK ice hockey leagues (e.g., women's teams, juniors or recreational play), take a look at the Ice Hockey UK website at **www.icehockeyuk.co.uk**, the internationally recognised governing body for the game within the UK.

## Ice skating

For the winter holiday period (late November – early January), a number of venues throughout London will set up ice rinks. Some of the most notable are

Somerset House, Broadgate Ice Rink (near Liverpool Street station), the Natural History Museum, Hampstead Heath, the Tower of London, Hampton Court Palace and Kew Gardens. Check various websites or *Time Out: London* for the annual locations and openings.

The ice skating rinks below are open year-round:

Alexandra Palace Ice Rink
Alexandra Palace Way, Wood Green, N22
✆ 020 8365 4386, www.alexandrapalace.com
The palace offers a wide range of activities suitable for all ages; including skate training and tuition. They offer children's parties (which even include 15 minutes of tuition time) and private hire. Booking is essential.

Queen's Ice and Bowl
17 Queensway, W2
✆ 020 7229 0172, www.queensiceandbowl.co.uk
Open year-round. Skate hire on premises.

## Martial arts

The Budokwai
GK House, 4 Gilston Road, SW10
✆ 020 7370 1000, www.thebudokwai.com
Offers a range of instruction in judo, karate, aikido and jiu-jitsu; judo classes for children; toddler gym classes and paint groups.

Bujinkan Martial Arts in Central London
17 Duke's Road, WC1
✆ 0870 740 6888, www.bujinkanlondon.org
Japanese budo/ninjutsu classes. Multiple locations.

## Personal training

Personal fitness trainers are an increasingly popular alternative/addition to the use of health club facilities. They can provide a programme to meet your individual fitness needs within your time schedule. Many health clubs offer personal trainers to members for an additional fee.

British Military Fitness

© 020 7751 9742, www.britmilfit.com

See *Dance and fitness* classes above.

Matt Roberts

© 020 7626 0888, www.mattroberts.co.uk

Four personal training centres in Chelsea, Hampstead, Mayfair and the City.

Return to Glory

© 0845 337 4933, www.returntoglory.co.uk

Offers a directory of registered local fitness instructors that will come to your house or gym for sessions. Also includes specialists in yoga and Pilates.

# Rowing

There are many boat clubs along the Thames that train and compete in crews for regattas and head races, the most famous of which are the Henley Royal Regatta in Oxfordshire held in July, and the Head of the River Race on the Thames in March (see *Chapter 17: Annual events* for more details). Most also have active social programmes and are an excellent way to meet people.

Thames Rowing Club

Putney Embankment, SW15

© 020 8788 0798, www.thamesrc.co.uk

A large, successful club with men's, women's and juniors' sections. Beginners welcome.

# Rugby

Men's, women's and mixed touch rugby leagues of various levels competing at many venues in and around London. Emphasis is on the social aspects of the game. Individuals may sign up to be placed on a team. Visit **www. in2touch.com/uk** to learn more about the various leagues and venues.

# Running

Local council gyms and leisure centres often organise running clubs for members.

NikeTown Runners

www.niketownrunners.com

A twice weekly running club covering 3, 4 or 7 miles leaving from
NikeTown in Oxford Circus and up through Regent's park. Runs are either
for women only or mixed. Must pre-register through the website.

Serpentine Running Club

www.serpentine.org.uk

The club covers all aspects of running from a beginner's running guide to
triathlon training. Check the website for information on joining the club,
club events, where to run in London and much more.

# Sailing

Docklands Sailing and Watersports Centre

Millwall Dock, Isle of Dogs, E14

© 020 7537 2626, www.dswc.org

Sailing club offers Royal Yachting Association (**RYA**) courses, evening races
and events. Membership allows full use of sailing boats, canoes, and other
water sport equipment.

Little Ship Club

Upper Thames Street, EC4

© 020 7236 7729, www.littleshipclub.co.uk

Unique sailing club based in the City of London with restaurant, bar
and guest rooms. Holds sailing trips and rallies at clubs across southern
England, plus RYA training and lots of social events. New members
welcome to visit.

Ranelagh Sailing Club

The Embankment, Putney, SW15

© 020 8788 4986, www.ranelagh-sc.co.uk

Friendly club offering year-round sailing on the Thames.

Royal Thames Yacht Club

60 Knightsbridge, SW1

© 020 7235 2121, www.royalthames.com

The oldest sailing club in the UK. Members participate in yachting events
in the UK and abroad and have access to the London clubhouse.

# Swimming

Your local council provides a list of local public pools and/or leisure centres. Some councils offer free pool access to those under 16 and over 60. A list of all swimming pools and their facilities in greater London may be obtained from **www.londonswimming.org**. One of the nicest facilities to visit without a membership is the Oasis Sports Centre (**www.camden.gov/oasis**) in Covent Garden, which has both an indoor and outdoor pool. During the warmer summer months, London has several lidos (outdoor swimming pools), including the Serpentine Lido in Hyde Park and the Parliament Hill Lido in Hampstead Heath.

# Tennis

There is a range of options for the tennis enthusiast in London. You can either enjoy the luxurious facilities of a private club or take advantage of the public courts in the parks, such as Battersea Park (℃ 020 8871 7542), Hampstead Heath (℃ 020 7284 3648), Hyde Park (℃ 020 7262 3474) and Regent's Park (℃ 020 7486 4216), which can be booked by the hour and are good value. Visit **www.willtowin.co.uk** for more information.

Private Tennis Clubs

The Campden Hill Lawn Tennis Club

9 Aubrey Walk, W8

℃ 020 7727 4050, www.chltc.co.uk

Six hard indoor courts and six artificial grass courts outside.

Globe Lawn Tennis Club

190A Haverstock Hill, NW3

℃ 020 7435 0248, www.globetennis.co.uk

Boasts several tennis courts and also provides coaching.

Magdalen Park Tennis Club

38 Magdalen Road, Wandsworth Common, SW18

℃ 020 8874 8313, www.mpltc.org.uk

Very friendly and social with a nice clubhouse. Eight hard courts; six are floodlit. Juniors welcome.

Paddington Sports Club
Castellain Road, W9
✆ 020 7286 8448, www.psclondon.com
Ten all weather courts: seven surfaced in acrylic and three are artificial grass.

# Walking and hiking

## London

In addition to the parks listed in the *Parks* section below, there are a number of established routes and guided tours to try.

The Inner London Ramblers Association (**ILRA**) runs regular free, guided walks at the weekends in the London area. The walks are five to six miles long and start and finish at public transport points within Travelcard zones. No booking required – just show up at the designated station entrance. Call the ILRA on ✆ 020 7370 6180 or visit their website at **www.inner londonramblers.org.uk** for a list of upcoming walks. There is also a comprehensive listing of interesting walks throughout London on the website for individual use.

The Thames Path is a 290 kilometre-long (180 miles) National Trail that follows the course of the Thames River, from Thames Head near Kemble in the Cotswolds, to the Thames Barrier in east London. As well as passing through central London, it also takes in historic places such as Oxford, Henley, Windsor and Greenwich. Various guides are available for this trail online or in bookstores.

## Outside London

Within as little as one hour from central London by train or car, you can walk in beautiful countryside on many public footpaths and trails. Two easily accessible trails by train are the North Downs Way National Trail in Kent (**www.nationaltrail.co.uk**) and the 1066 Country Walk in Sussex (**www.visit1066country.com**).

Try the following for more ideas and information on hiking and walking in the UK:

## Ramblers

✆ 020 7339 8500, www.ramblers.org.uk
The largest charity in the UK working for walkers. Their website contains general information and advice on walking, routes and accommodation.

The Ramblers bookshop on their website is a great resource for literature on the subject of walking. The Ramblers have various local groups meeting in and around London. Visit their website for details.

**The Long Distance Walkers Association**
www.ldwa.org.uk
An association of people with a common interest in walking long distances in rural, mountainous or moorland areas. The website has information on all of the UK's long distance paths.

# Yoga and Pilates

**Alan Herdman Pilates**
63-79 Seymour Street, W2
℗ 020 7402 7001, www.alanherdmanpilates.co.uk
Practices the Pilates technique, including body conditioning and corrective exercise. Other locations.

**Bikram Yoga**
www.bikramyoga.co.uk
Known as 'hot yoga', as it is practiced in a 37°C (104°F) room.
Three centres located in north London (Chalk Farm/Kentish Town), central London (Old Street) and west London (Queen's Park).

**The Life Centre**
15 Edge Street, W8
℗ 020 7221 4602, www.thelifecentre.com
Classes include yoga, Pilates and tai chi; children's classes, workshops and therapies.

**Light Centre**
9 Eccleston Street, SW1
℗ 020 7881 0728, www.lightcentrebelgravia.co.uk
Offers range of classes: yoga, Pilates, tai chi, meditation and capoieira. Also provides therapies.

**Triyoga**
6 Erskine Road, Primrose Hill, NW3
℗ 020 7483 3344, www.triyoga.co.uk

Excellent instructors. Vast array of yoga and Pilates classes for all standards and ages. Also offers post-natal yoga and baby massage classes, workshops and therapies. Other locations in Soho and Covent Garden.

Yogabase
255-257 Liverpool Road, N1
www.yogabase.org.uk
Iyengar, Hatha, Pregnancy and Kirtan yoga. Pilates. All classes are held on a drop-in basis and the fee is paid directly to the teacher.

# Parks

### Royal parks

The Royal Parks (**www.royalparks.gov.uk**) look after eight parks throughout London owned by the Crown.

Bushy Park
450 hectares/1,099 acres lying north of Hampton Court Palace.
Contains the famous Chestnut Avenue with its Arethusa 'Diana' Fountain.

Green Park
16 hectares/350 acres; a peaceful refuge, popular for sunbathing and picnics in good weather; paths used by runners.

Greenwich Park
73 hectares/183 acres with views of the Thames, Docklands and the City of London from its hilltop; contains the Old Royal Observatory, the Royal Naval College, the National Maritime Museum and the Queen's House; sanctuary for deer, foxes and birds.

Hyde Park
140 hectares/350 acres that provide facilities for many different leisure activities and sports as well as being a focal point for public events of all sizes. Contains the Diana, Princess of Wales Memorial Fountain.

Kensington Gardens
111 hectares/275 acres adjacent to Hyde Park; contains Kensington Palace and the Diana, Princess of Wales Memorial Playground; popular with sunbathers and runners; cycling is permitted on designated paths.

### Regent's Park

197 hectares/487 acres that provide the largest outdoor sports area in London; also contains the Open Air Theatre (home of the New Shakespeare Company in the summer), London Zoo and many cafés and restaurants.

### Richmond Park

Largest open space in London (1,000 hectares/2,500 acres); home to a huge array of wildlife; varied landscape of hills, woodland gardens and grasslands. Popular for cycling on unpaved terrain.

### St. James's Park

144 hectares/360 acres of parkland located in the heart of London, (bordered by three royal palaces); live concerts twice a day in the summer; children's playground; cafe.

## Community parks

There are numerous other parks in and outside of London, a selection of which are listed below. Most parks are open from dawn until dusk.

### Alexandra Park and Palace

Musgrove Hill, Wood Green, N22

An 80 hectare/200 acre public park surrounding a palace. Has sporting facilities (including an ice rink) and plenty of attractions for children including a playground, boating lake and small animal enclosure. Children's shows and workshops in the summer. Nature reserve with woodlands, dense scrub, meadow and pond. The Parkland Walk is a shady walk that follows an old rail bed.

### Battersea Park

Albert Bridge Road, SW11

Bordered on one side by the Thames River, the 83 hectare/200 acre park contains a boating lake, children's zoo, deer park, playground, Old English Garden, tree and nature trails, the Peace Pagoda and an herb garden.

### Crystal Palace Park

Thicket Road, Penge, SE19

A 140 hectare/350 acre park with boating and bands during the summer. The maze, farmyard, lake and play area are all popular with children.

### Golders Hill Park
North End Road, Golders Green, NW11

A 63 hectare/159 acre area within Hampstead Heath. Playground and small zoo (deer, goats, ducks, etc), putting green, good café and beautiful gardens.

### Hampstead Heath
Parliament Hill, NW3

316 hectares/791 acres of ponds, woodlands, trails and museums. Famous for kite flying on Parliament Hill with a beautiful view of central London. Swimming ponds, swimming pool, wading pool, tennis courts, concerts in summer at Kenwood House, cafes, playgrounds, animal enclosures, horseback riding, cycling, walking paths and more.

### Highgate Woods
Muswell Hill Road, N6

28 hectares/70 acres of shady woodland, including an adventure playground, nature hut and trails, and a vegetarian café.

### Holland Park
Holland Park, W14

21 hectares/52 acres containing the Kyoto Japanese Garden, rose gardens, abundant wildlife, an ecology centre, a wildlife pond, tennis courts, golf driving range and an adventure playground. There is an open air theatre and opera in the summer against the backdrop of Holland House.

### Primrose Hill
Primrose Hill Road, NW3

24 hectares/61acres of grassy hill; includes a children's playground and outdoor gymnasium. Fantastic views of London.

### Royal Botanic Gardens, Kew
Richmond, Surrey, TW9

120 hectares/300 acres that include a lake, an aquatic garden, a pagoda, Kew Palace and Palm House, among many other things. A World Heritage Site.

## Theme parks

### Alton Towers
Stoke-on-Trent, Staffordshire, ST10

ⓒ 0870 520 4060, www.alton-towers.co.uk

Britain's biggest theme park with rides for all ages. Located three hours outside central London. Open 365 days a year.

### Chessington World of Adventures
Surrey, KT9

✆ 0871 663 4477, www.chessington.co.uk

Rides and roller coasters, zoo, sea life centre and hotel. Geared toward families with children under 12. Open March through October.

### Diggerland
Medway Valley Leisure Park, Strood, ME2

0871 227 7007, www.diggerland.com

A must for Bob the Builder fans. Allows children to ride in and drive dumper trucks and diggers. Additional parks in Durham, Devon and West Yorkshire.

### Legoland Windsor
Berkshire, SL4

✆ 0870 504 0404, www.legoland.co.uk

Set in 60 hectares/150 acres of parkland, contains over 50 interactive rides, attractions and shows geared toward children aged two to 12 and their families. Open March through October.

### Snakes and Ladders
Syon Park, Brentford, TW8

020 8847 0946, www.snakes-and-ladders.co.uk

Vast building housing three separate play areas for toddlers, intermediate and older children under 12. Also has a café and garden, and can host children's parties. Other locations in Abingdon, Dunstable, Ipswich and Slough.

### Thorpe Park
Surrey, KT16

✆ 0870 444 4466, www.thorpepark.co.uk

Amusement park offering attractions, shows, rides and exhibits for all ages. Open March to November.

# British sporting glossary

| | |
|---|---|
| Athletics | Track and field. |
| Cricket | A very popular summer sport. The basic concept of cricket is similar to that of baseball, however the game play and rules are very different. |
| The Derby | Pronounced "dar-bee". A very famous and prestigious flat horse race held in June every year at the Epsom Downs Racecourse in Surrey, England. |
| FA Cup | The main football knock-out competition, open to all clubs in England and Wales (amateur and professional). |
| Fixture | Game, match, contest. |
| Football | Association football (i.e., soccer) or rugby football, but usually refers to the former. NFL football is known as American football. |
| Grand National | The world's best-known horse race over fences, run at Aintree, Liverpool in early April. |
| Hockey | Field hockey. Ice hockey is known as ice hockey. |
| Netball | Women's sport. Foundations come from basketball, although the ball is smaller, the ring is smaller and higher, and there is no backboard. Seven-player teams. |
| The Open | The British Open Championship in golf. |
| Pitch | Field of play. |
| Premiership | An elite league of the best 20 football clubs in England and Wales. There is also a Premiership league in rugby union that consists of the top 12 rugby football clubs in the UK. Generally, this term refers to the football league. |
| Racing/ Race Meeting | Horse racing. |
| Rounders | A version of softball usually played at school. |
| Royal Ascot | The world's most famous horse-race meeting typically held the third week of June. Attended by Her Majesty the Queen. |

| | |
|---|---|
| Rugby | Amateurs play rugby union, which is 15-a-side; professionals play rugby league, which is 13-a-side and a faster game. |
| Six Nations | Premier northern hemisphere rugby competition between England, Wales, Scotland, Ireland, France and Italy. Held in January or February. |
| Test Match | An international rugby or cricket match, lasting either one or four days. |
| Touts | Scalpers. Expensive and dubious sources of hard-to-find tickets. |
| Wimbledon | One of four grand slam tennis tournaments, and the only one played on grass courts, held annually at the All England Club in Wimbledon. |

# Travel

While one could spend a lifetime exploring London and never get bored, a unique advantage of living in London is that it is a great base from which to explore the UK and other countries. The number of travel offerings coupled with London's proximity to continental Europe (affectionately referred to as **the Continent**) and other destinations makes it easy to weekend in the country or visit Paris or Milan for a short break.

The ease of travelling to a wide variety of destinations has spurred an extensive travel industry in London. Numerous resources exist to help plan a getaway locally, within Europe or beyond. Guidebooks to hundreds of destinations are available at bookstores, speciality travel shops and travel agents. Two lovely and comprehensive travel bookstores we'd recommend checking out are Daunt Books and the Travel Bookshop (see *Chapter 12: Shopping – Books* for contact details).

The Internet also provides a myriad of resources for selecting destinations as well as booking transportation and accommodation (see *Online resources* below). Many print resources, including *Time Out London*, the free daily newspapers such as the *Metro* and *London Paper,* and as well as the weekend newspapers, frequently offer travel ideas and advertise special holiday packages. In addition, **www.arrivalguides.com** offers over 400 free travel guides, which are downloadable.

**IN THIS CHAPTER...**

- **Planning your trip**
- **Getting there**
- **Accommodations**
- **Before you travel**

It is advisable to arrange holidays well in advance, especially for peak times such as Christmas, Easter, bank holiday weekends and half term, when large numbers of UK residents travel. Many Europeans holiday in August, so it may be wise to avoid resort destinations during this busy month, although major European business cities are quieter than normal and often offer special rates.

If you book a holiday last minute, you may be able to take advantage of falling prices. Airlines and hotels may reduce fares and/or rates in an effort to fill capacity. Deals can be found on many online booking sites or through travel agents, though your first-choice hotel or flight may not be available.

**DID YOU KNOW?**

A popular getaway for UK residents is the **city break** in which a package deal is offered for a short holiday, mostly in European cities. City break specials are offered through travel agents, online booking sites as well as directly through the transportation provider (airline and train websites) and can also be found in newspapers and travel magazines.

# Planning your trip

In part because of the large number of online resources offered for travel planning, travel agencies and brokers can provide helpful, targeted advice on planning your trip. These agencies and shops frequently offer discounts on package deals and are worthwhile to consider especially when organising a major holiday or a journey to a destination with which you are not familiar.

### Travel agencies and tour operators

Travel agencies and tour operators can provide assistance with selecting a holiday destination as well as booking the arrangements. Package tours, ranging from inexpensive to luxurious, include both transportation to your destination and accommodation, and can include other items of interest such as airport transfers, car hire, sightseeing tours or excursions. Exploring a travel agent's website is a good way to narrow the list of potential destinations.

It is recommended to use International Airline Transport Association (IATA), Association of British Travel Agents (ABTA) or Air Tours Operators Licence (ATOL) approved travel agents, tour operators and ticket brokers, as many travellers have been stranded when some less-reliable companies suddenly go out of business. The following is a selection of approved travel agents and tour operators:

### Abercrombie & Kent
✆ 0845 618 2200, www.abercrombiekent.co.uk
Specialising in luxury holidays worldwide.

### FlightCentre
✆ 0870 499 0040, www.flightcentre.co.uk
Targets the cost-conscious traveller and specialises in flights, holiday packages, domestic travel and ancillary sales.

### Goodacre & Townsend
✆ 020 7434 2255, www.goodtown.co.uk
Luxury bespoke travel consultancy for worldwide destinations.

### Kuoni Travel
✆ 01306 747 002, www.kuoni.co.uk
Known as a quality tour operator offering long haul and short breaks with a wide range of travel partners.

### Newmont Travel
✆ 020 890 1155, www.newmont.co.uk
Specialises in travel to the Caribbean.

### Original Travel
✆ 020 7978 7333, www.originaltravel.co.uk
Offers tailor-made holiday packages to unique destinations.

### Powder Byrne
✆ 020 8246 5300, www.powderbyrne.com
Specialises in luxury family holidays, including family ski programmes.

### ScottDunn
✆ 020 8682 5400, wwwscottdunn.com
Luxury tailor-made holidays (e.g., families, ski, villas, honeymoons).

### Trailfinders
✆ 0845 058 5858, www.trailfinders.com
Offers discounted airfares, hotels, tours, cruises and vehicle rental.

**15**

**TRAVEL**

### Ticket brokers/consolidators

Ticket brokers/consolidators offer flights at a discount. Most charter flights are linked to package tours, but ticket brokers/consolidators will sell tickets on a seat-only basis. Some also offer discounted seats on scheduled (non-charter) airlines.

You will find ticket broker and consolidator advertisements in the travel sections of the Sunday and daily newspapers and in the back of the weekly magazine *Time Out London*.

### Online resources

#### Planning/booking

Booking your own travel arrangements is relatively easy when using the vast number of available online resources. A selection of the most popular is listed below. Please note that it is often less expensive to book airfare and accommodation together using these resources rather than booking the items separately.

Online travel agencies include:
**www.dialaflight.com**
**www.ebookers.com**
**www.expedia.co.uk**
**www.lastminute.com**
**www.opodo.co.uk**

If purchasing your trip components separately (i.e., air, hotel, car), it is also useful to check the growing number of price comparison travel websites. These sites pull information from many of the online travel agencies as well as directly from the travel operator/supplier.

Travel comparison websites include:
**www.flightsdirect.com**
**www.kayak.co.uk**
**www.skyscanner.net**

#### Destination Feedback

A website that offers travellers the opportunity to review or post opinions about destinations, hotels and resorts, museums, etc. is **www.tripadvisor. com** and is often a good starting point for considering a destination.

# Getting there

There are five major international airports, an international rail station and many national railway stations in Greater London. A detailed listing of the airports, railway stations and other transportation links is available in *Chapter 6: Transportation*.

## By air

The British Airport Authority (**BAA**) operates two of the three largest London airports: Heathrow and Stansted. BAA has an informative website (**www.baa.co.uk**) detailing real-time arrival and departure information, directions, methods of public transport available and more.

Below is a list of the five international airports in and around London. Consult *Chapter 6: Transportation – London airports* for a detailed listing of the airports and how to get to and/or from them.

Gatwick Airport
West Sussex, RH6
℗ 0844 335 1802, www.gatwickairport.com
UK's second busiest airport. Accessible by rail, bus, coach, taxi or car.

Heathrow Airport
Hounslow, Middlesex, TW6
℗ 0870 000 0123, www.heathrowairport.com
London's primary airport. Accessible by rail, bus, coach, tube, taxi or car.

London City Airport
Royal Docks, E16
℗ 020 7646 0088, www.londoncityairport.com
Accessible by DLR, bus, taxi or car. The DLR provides connections to the tube and train network.

Luton Airport
Bedfordshire, LU2
℗ 0158 240 5100, www.london-luton.co.uk
Accessible by rail, bus, coach, and taxi or car.

Stansted Airport
Essex, CM24
℗ 0870 000 0303, www.stanstedairport.com
Accessible by rail, bus, coach, and taxi or car.

Often the best airfares are found on the individual airline's website. Many airlines will charge you a fee if you book a flight on the telephone, so be sure to enquire about surcharges if you choose to book over the telephone. Always confirm the terms and conditions of any discount fares, which may include a required length of stay, change penalties and cancellation charges.

Aside from the airlines' websites, the online resources listed above will list a variety of fares to get you to your destination. These general-use websites may not include the discount airlines (such as, easyJet, Monarch and Ryanair) so be sure to consult those airlines' websites directly, particularly for intra-Europe travel. There are some excellent fares to destinations in and around Europe on these low-cost airlines if you are prepared to forego some of the conveniences associated with traditional airlines. Be aware that many of these airlines may use alternative airports, so attention should be paid to the destination airport and consideration given to the onward journey after landing. Each discount airline is different and should be consulted for its specific services.

## By rail

There are numerous railway stations and operators in and around London. Consult *Chapter 6: Transportation – Trains* for a more thorough listing.

### Domestic

When researching or booking rail tickets, you can visit the National Rail website (**www.nationalrail.co.uk**) or the individual train operator websites. Bookings can be made online, over the phone, or at the train station. For a good online retailer for reduced train fares visit **www.thetrainline.com**. Many trains offer both reserved and unreserved seating. It is recommended that if you want an assigned seat (where available), book the tickets in advance.

### International

The Channel Tunnel, commonly referred to as **the Chunnel**, links England and France and has greatly reduced travel time to the Continent. Using the Chunnel, Paris is now only 2 and a quarter hours from London. The Chunnel is rail-only and cannot be driven through in a car, though there is a 'drive-on' service. Two rail operators use the Chunnel for passenger travel:

*Eurostar* (passengers only) ℂ 08432 186 186, **www.eurostar.com**. Trains depart London's St. Pancras International (with stops at Ebbsfleet and Ashford in Kent) directly to Calais, Paris (Gare du Nord and Disneyland Resort Paris), Lille (Europa) and Avignon in France and to Brussels (Gare du Midi) in Belgium. Eurostar also run a ski train to the French Alps and a summer service to Avignon. Tickets are priced in a similar way to flights and vary according to class, so to obtain the best deals you will probably need to buy a non-flexible ticket with a Saturday night stay well in advance of your trip. Book online to avoid a telephone-booking surcharge. You can add on connecting train journeys throughout France, Belgium and select other countries to your Eurostar ticket. If you are travelling to Brussels, your Eurostar ticket is valid to any station in Belgium within 24 hours.

*Eurotunnel* (passengers and cars) ©0844 335 3535, **www.eurotunnel. com**. Eurotunnel offers a 35 minute drive-on service from Folkestone in Kent to Calais, France leaving every 20 minutes. Fares vary and tickets may be purchased online or by phone. During peak travel times you may have to wait, as booking does not guarantee you a particular time.

## DID YOU KNOW?

The Orient Express operates day and weekend trips around the UK, as well as rail trips and river cruises in Europe, Asia and South America (**www.orient-express.com**).

# Accommodations

Whether you are seeking to rent a cottage in Wales or a suite in a European city hotel, your first stop should be the travel supplements of the weekend papers. *The Observer* (Sunday), *The Telegraph* (Saturday and Sunday) and *The Times* (Saturday and Sunday) are particularly good, and frequently feature special offers and discounts available exclusively to their readers. Late spring is a particularly good time to look for reduced fares and rates for the summer holidays as operators seek to sell off any unsold capacity. In major business cities, such as Milan, Paris and even London, August is a good month to find excellent room rates within cities because the local population has fled to seaside resorts for *la vacance*.

Resources for locating accommodations within Britain include:

Bed and Breakfast Nationwide
©0125 583 1235, www.bedandbreakfastnationwide.com
Features B&B homes, farms, and guesthouses throughout the UK.

15

TRAVEL

### Cottages4you

✆ 0845 268 0760, www.cottages4you.co.uk

Offers a wide range of quality cottages throughout the British Isles.

### English Country Cottages

✆ 0870 268 0785, www.english-country-cottages.co.uk

Links on their site to their sister companies' Scottish, Irish, and French Country Cottages. Their database contains over 3,000 properties from which to choose your ideal cottage holiday home. Properties for rent vary from converted farmhouses to medieval castles.

### Farm Stay UK

✆ 0247 669 6909, www.farmstayuk.co.uk

Opportunities to stay with farming families in rural settings throughout Britain.

### Hoseasons

✆ 0844 847 1356, www.hoseasons.co.uk

Self-catering holidays in coastal and countryside settings throughout Britain, Ireland and Europe.

### Lakeland Cottage Company

Cumbria/Lake District

✆ 0153 953 8180, www.lakeland-cottage-company.co.uk

Self-catering holiday cottages in the Lake District.

### The London Bed and Breakfast Agency

✆ 020 7586 2768, www.londonbb.com

Offers both rooms in family homes and self-catered flats for stays of two or more nights.

### The National Trust

✆ 0844 800 1895, www.nationaltrust.org.uk

A non-profit organisation and special interest group which purchases or is bequeathed historic properties or places of great natural beauty that are preserved for the nation. Many of these properties are available for holiday or weekend stays.

### Northern Ireland Tourist Board

✆ 0289 024 6609, www.discovernorthernireland.com

Assistance with locating accommodations in Northern Ireland and other general tourism advice.

Visit London

℗ 08701 566 366, www.visitlondon.com

Provides information, travel and destination advice, including accommodation assistance for those interested in travel in and around London.

Visit Britain

www.visitbritain.com

Offers a search that will locate various types of accommodation in Britain including hotels, B&Bs, self-catered apartments, campus locations and hostels.

In addition to the more specialist resources listed above, and the general flight and accommodations websites listed earlier in this chapter, the following websites provide information on and make reservations for hotels and other accommodations around the world:

www.itwg.com

Offers Italian hotels reservations at discounted negotiated rates, travel packages dedicated to activities such as art, wellness, sport, and relaxation, special rates on car rentals, air tickets and ferry tickets for major destinations on the Mediterranean Sea.

www.laterooms.com

Late booking database for hotels offering rooms in the UK, Ireland, continental Europe and worldwide.

www.mrandmrssmith.com

Specialises in booking boutique and luxury hotels worldwide.

www.tablethotels.com

Offers selection of luxury and boutique hotels around the world.

www.venere.com

Find and book hotels, B&Bs and apartments worldwide.

# Before you travel

### Paying for your holiday

Be aware that some ticket brokers, travel agents, and airlines will charge you extra to pay by credit card for holidays and flights. It may be worth doing so, however, because most credit card companies provide refunds if you pay with their card and your travel broker, travel agent, or flight operator subsequently goes out of business. Travel insurance may also reduce this risk, consult *Travel insurance* below.

## Travel insurance

Package tour operators will often try to sell you holiday insurance. Be sure to review the terms and conditions of the insurance offered to see if it will cover the risks you are concerned about. Inquire about what coverage will exist if the tour operator goes out of business, or should you find yourself with a sudden injury or illness abroad.

A good option to consider if you travel abroad more than twice a year is annual multi-trip coverage. The Post Office, major banks and credit card companies, and companies specialising in travel or insurance offer this product. Visit the Foreign & Commonwealth Office website (**www.fco.gov. uk**) to view its tips on what to look for in a policy.

## Health and safety

The UK Foreign & Commonwealth Office (✆ 020 7008 1500, **www.fco.gov. uk**) can provide you with up-to-date, country-specific travel advice regarding health and safety issues. The Department of Health (**www.dh.gov.uk**) and the National Health Service (**NHS**) (**www.nhs.uk**) also offer advice on health issues associated with travel.

## Immunisations and vaccinations

In order to enter certain countries, immunisations may be necessary, so review your itinerary-specific immunisation and other health requirements at least six weeks before you travel. There are several ways to determine which immunisations and vaccinations, if any, you need to before you can travel:

### Contact your GP

Under the NHS, some immunisations and vaccinations may be carried out by your GP. Some immunisations, such as for polio and tetanus (and sometimes hepatitis and meningitis) are free of charge on the NHS. Other immunisations may require you to pay a fee or may not be easily available to your doctor, and would require a visit to a clinic.

### Contact Medical Advisory Services for Travellers Abroad (MASTA)

✆ 0845 600 2236, www.masta-travel-health.com

MASTA is a travel health provider with a network of travel clinics offering advice and treatment including a comprehensive immunisation service. For a small fee, MASTA can also provide you with a 'Health Brief' containing medical advice specifically tailored to your journey, which can then be taken to one of their local travel clinics. Visit the website to find the clinic nearest you or call to make an appointment at MASTA's central London travel clinic located near Oxford Circus.

### Go directly to an immunisation clinic

Appointments can be made easily and the clinics are familiar with the necessary immunisations. A few large travel agents have immunisation clinics. Keep in mind that if you need several immunisations, it may be worth shopping around as prices vary considerably.

### Trailfinders Travel Clinic

194 Kensington High Street, W8
© 020 7938 3999, www.trailfinders.com
No appointment necessary.

For information regarding immunisations for children, please see *Chapter 7: Healthcare – Paediatric care.*

## Health care abroad

The UK has reciprocal healthcare agreements with all European Economic Area (**EEA**) countries, and certain non-EEA countries, which enable travellers to receive free or low-cost emergency care. Persons carrying a European Health Insurance Card (**EHIC**) are eligible to receive healthcare that becomes necessary during visits to any of these countries. The EHIC is available to persons who ordinarily reside in the UK, with some restrictions. You can apply for an EHIC by telephone (© 0845 606 2030), by filling in and posting the application at your local post office or at **www.ehic.org.uk**.

Outside the EEA, barring certain exceptions (including Australia, New Zealand and Russia) you will have to pay for treatment. Package tour operators will try to sell you travel insurance (which usually has a health-related benefit). If you travel abroad several times a year, a better option to consider is annual multi-trip travel insurance, offered by a variety of sources (see *Travel insurance* above). Be sure to examine the coverage provision in any insurance policy you consider in order to determine its coverage of health care issues.

15

TRAVEL

# 16

# Culture

There is something to entertain or culturally stimulate just about everyone in London. Whether you prefer art exhibits, musical or dance performances or just a few laughs, you'll be able to find something to suit your tastes. The best place to start looking and planning is London's weekly entertainment guide, *Time Out*. It's the essential guide to what is on offer each week and published every Tuesday and available at news agents or can be viewed online at **www.timeout.com/london**. London's *Time Out* magazine lists current and upcoming events, locations, dates, times, ticket prices and publishes reviews and previews.

London benefits from a wide range of venues for the performing arts. Each venue will have its own schemes relating to membership benefits and discount tickets. Some venues offer concessions for certain groups such as students, pensioners, union members or residents of certain neighbourhoods (e.g., Westminster, Barbican). Other venues reserve a set number of tickets for same-day sales, often at a discount. Still others offer membership schemes with benefits that include early booking information and ticket discounts. Check with the specific venue to determine what discount schemes they offer either in advance or for same-day performances.

## IN THIS CHAPTER...

- Museums and galleries
- Historic houses
- Classical music
- Contemporary music
- Jazz
- Opera
- Dance
- Theatre
- Comedy

# Museums and galleries

London's museums are varied and range from broad, mass appeal to those with a more specific, defined focus. There is free admission to all national museums and galleries in London, although they do charge for special exhibitions. Many of these special exhibitions can be very popular, so it is a good idea to check the website and book tickets ahead of time online. As with most museums, donations from visitors and supporters are a large part of the operational budget. Accordingly, most museums offer membership or 'friend' programs. Becoming a supporter gives you special privileges such as easier accessibility to major exhibitions, which are often free of charge, discounts on entrance fees, restaurants and gift shops and invitations to special functions. Privileges vary, so contact the institution directly for information.

A leader among the many worthwhile charities for the arts in London is the National Art Collections Fund (℃ 020 7225 4800, **www.artfund.org**). This charity is committed to saving art for everyone to enjoy by aiding in the purchase of art for galleries and museums. Membership provides free entry to many museum, galleries and historic properties, as well as substantial discounts on many exhibitions, talks and travel offers.

The following lists some of the museums and galleries popularly visited. Before your visit, check the website for opening hours. Where it is stated that admission is free, all of these venues encourage and welcome donations from their visitors. The ☺ symbol indicates that the museum or gallery is child-friendly (for more information about places in London to visit with children see *Chapter 8: Children – Entertaining your children*).

Bankside Gallery
48 Hopton Street, SE1
℃ 020 7928 7521, www.banksidegallery.com
Home of two historic art societies: the Royal Watercolour Society and the Royal Society of Painter-Printmakers. Admission free.

Banqueting House
Whitehall, SW1
℃ 0844 482 7777, www.hrp.org.uk
The Banqueting House, designed by Inigo Jones, is all that remains of Whitehall Palace, the sovereign's principal residence from 1530 until 1698

when it was destroyed by fire. Renowned for its architecture and painting, the building is also famous as the site of King Charles I's execution. Admission charge.

## Barbican Art Gallery
Barbican Centre, Silk Street, EC2
☎020 7638 4141, www.barbican.org.uk/artgallery
Located in the Barbican arts complex, this gallery curates and develops internationally renowned exhibitions, offering a varied programme of work from 20th century art and photography to modern design and architecture. Admission charge.

## The British Library
96 Euston Road, NW1
☎0843 208 1144, www.bl.uk
The UK's national library and the world's largest library in terms of total number of items. Admission free.

## British Museum
Great Russell Street, WC1
☎020 7323 8000, www.britishmuseum.org
The British Museum houses a vast collection of human cultural history, including the Rosetta Stone. Free general admission; charge for special exhibitions.

## Buckingham Palace
The Mall, SW1
☎020 7766 7300, www.royalcollection.org.uk
Built in the early 1700s by the Duke of Buckingham, it has served as the British monarch's London residence since the reign of Queen Victoria. Its State Rooms, which house the Royal Collection, are open to visitors for two months every year (late July – early September). Admission charge.

## Cabinet War Rooms and Churchill Museum
Clive Steps, King Charles Street, SW1
☎020 7930 6961, www.iwm.org.uk
The hidden underground rooms where Churchill and his government lived and worked during World War II. A very in-depth chronology of Winston Churchill's life. Admission charge.

## Courtauld Institute of Art Gallery
Somerset House, Strand, WC2
© 020 7848 2526, www.courtauld.ac.uk
The Courtauld collection consists of Old Masters, Impressionist and Post-Impressionist paintings as well as other notable painting and drawing collections. Admission charge.

## ☺ The Dickens House Museum
48 Doughty Street, WC1
© 020 7405 2127, www.dickensmuseum.com
The only surviving London house in which Dickens lived and wrote some of his best-known works. Original manuscripts exhibited. Admission charge.

## Dulwich Picture Gallery
Gallery Road, Dulwich Village, SE21
© 020 8693 5254, www.dulwichpicturegallery.org.uk
Important collection of old masters paintings, including works by Van Dyck, Rembrandt, Gainsborough and Poussin. Visiting exhibitions. The gallery was designed by Sir John Soane as England's first public art gallery. Admission charge.

## The Fan Museum
12 Crooms Hill, Greenwich, SE10
© 020 8305 1441, www.fan-museum.org
Delightful private collection of 2,000 fans from different countries displayed in an 18th century townhouse. Admission charge.

## Garden Museum
Lambeth Palace Road, SE1
© 020 7401 8865, www.gardenmuseum.org.uk
The collection covers gardening in its broadest sense. Objects on display range from specialist equipment to improvised tools. The museum gardens contain an interesting collection of plants and flowers. Admission charge.

## ☺ Geffrye Museum
Kingsland Road, E2
© 020 7739 9893, www.geffrye-museum.org.uk
English domestic-period (17th century to the present) rooms especially arranged for children's enjoyment and participation. Free admission.

**Goldsmith's Hall**

Foster Lane, EC2

✆ 020 7606 7010, www.thegoldsmiths.co.uk/hall

Important antique silver and gold plate collection. Largest collection of modern silver and jewellery in Britain. Not open to the public except during exhibitions and on Open Days when free guided tours may be booked.

**Guildhall Art Gallery**

Guildhall Yard, EC2

✆ 020 7332 3700, www.guildhall-art-gallery.org.uk

Centre of the City of London's government since medieval times. The gallery exhibits the permanent collection of paintings, such as Pre-Raphaelites, belonging to the Corporation of London and contains the Guildhall Library and Clock Museum. The remains of a Roman amphitheatre and large medieval crypts lie beneath the ancient site. Free admission.

**☺ Hampton Court Palace**

East Molesey, Surrey, KT8

✆ 0844 482 7777, www.hrp.org.uk

500-year-old Hampton Court Palace has something to offer everyone. Set in 60 acres of world-famous gardens including its own Maze, the palace showcases its history from the days of Henry VIII to George II. Many special events throughout the year, including an important flower show and summer music festival. Admission charge.

**Hayward Gallery**

South Bank Centre, Belvedere Road, SE1

✆ 0871 663 2500, www.hayward.org.uk

Temporary exhibitions and lectures on historical and contemporary fine and decorative arts of major importance. Admission charge.

**☺ HMS Belfast**

Morgan's Lane, Tooley Street, SE1

✆ 020 7940 6300, www.hmsbelfast.iwm.org.uk

This former WWII battle cruiser serves as a floating museum of 20th century British naval power. Admission charge.

**16**

**CULTURE**

Hogarth's House
Great West Road, Hogarth Lane, W4
✆020 8994 6757
A charming early 18th century house which was once the country home of
William Hogarth, the artist, critic and satirist. It is now a gallery where most
of his well-known engravings are on display. Free admission.

☺Horniman Museum
100 London Road, Forest Hill, SE23
✆020 8699 1872, www.horniman.ac.uk
Impressive collection of ethnography, musical instruments, decorative arts,
natural history and gardens collected from the world travels of Victorian
tea-trader Frederick J. Horniman. Free admission.

☺Imperial War Museum
Lambeth Road, SE1
✆020 7416 5000, www.iwm.org.uk
Permanent exhibitions of all aspects of wars in which Britain and the
Commonwealth have been involved since 1914. Includes weaponry,
vehicles, photographs, war paintings and posters. Archival films
shown on weekends and holidays. Free general admission; charge for
special exhibitions.

Institute of Contemporary Arts
The Mall, SW1
✆020 7930 3647, www.ica.org.uk
Changing exhibitions of avant garde art covering visual arts, music and
cinema. Known for introducing emerging contemporary artists to the
international community. Admission charge.

The Jewish Museum
Raymond Burton House, 129-131 Albert Street, NW1
✆020 7284 7384, www.jewishmuseum.org.uk
Extensive collection of Jewish religious antiquities. Admission charge.

Dr Johnson's House
17 Gough Square, EC4
✆020 7353 3745, www.drjohnsonshouse.org
Small library with relics located in a furnished house in which Samuel

Johnson lived and worked on England's first definitive dictionary from 1748 to 1759. Admission charge.

Keats' House Museum
Keats Grove, Hampstead NW3
✆ 020 7332 3863, www.cityoflondon.gov.uk/keats
House where John Keats lived from 1818 to 1820, which inspired some of Keats's most memorable poetry. The house and gardens are open to the public year-round. Admission charge.

Kensington Palace
Kensington Gardens, W8
✆ 0844 482 7777, www.hrp.org.uk
Acquired by William and Mary in 1689 when it was called Nottingham House, Kensington Palace has been a royal home for over 300 years. Birthplace of Queen Victoria and home to Princess Diana between 1981 and 1997. Admission charge.

Kenwood House – see *Historic houses* under *English Heritage* below.

☺ Kew Bridge Steam Museum
Green Dragon Lane, Brentford, Middlesex, TW8
✆ 020 8568 4757, www.kbsm.org
Housed in a magnificent 19th century water pumping station, the museum displays major developments in steam engine technology and centres around the station's famous Cornish engines in their original engine houses and its rotative engines, some of which can be seen in action each weekend. Admission charge.

Leighton House Museum
2 Holland Park Road, W14
✆ 020 7602 3316, www.rbkc.gov.uk/leightonhousemuseum
Late 19th century home of the artist Lord Leighton, who designed its notable Arab Hall. Contains works by Leighton and other major Victorian artists. Admission charge.

☺ London Dungeon
28 Tooley Street, SE1
✆ 020 7403 7221, www.thedungeons.com
Located on the site of a medieval prison, a 'horror experience' of some of

16

CULTURE

the city's grimmest history. Definitely not for the squeamish or those under 10 years old; interesting otherwise. Admission charge.

☺London Transport Museum

Covent Garden Piazza, WC2

✆020 7379 6344, www.ltmuseum.co.uk

Features items that reflect all aspects of the history of public transport in London from 1800 to present. Admission charge; children under 16 free.

☺Madame Tussaud's

Marylebone Road, NW1

✆0871 894 3000, www.madame-tussauds.co.uk

The famous collection of wax figures of historic and contemporary celebrities. The former London Planetarium now houses a Star Dome show. Admission charge.

☺Museum of London

150 London Wall, EC2

✆020 7001 9844, www.museumoflondon.org.uk

The world's largest urban museum. Leads the visitor through the chronological development of London's history from prehistory until today. Exhibits include the Lord Mayor's coach and a wealth of archaeological objects and historical reconstructions. Free admission.

National Archives Museum

Kew, Richmond, Surrey TW9

✆020 8876 3444, www.nationalarchives.gov.uk

The National Archives of England, Wales and the United Kingdom has one of the largest archival collections in the world, spanning 1,000 years of British history, from the Domesday Book of 1086 to government papers recently released to the public. There is also a rolling programme of exhibitions. Free admission.

☺National Army Museum

Royal Hospital Road, SW3

✆020 7730 0717, www.national-army-museum.ac.uk

Extensive display of army mementoes, equipment and colours from various British and colonial regiments from 1485. Free admission.

☺National Gallery

Trafalgar Square, WC2

✆020 7747 2885; www.nationalgallery.org.uk

World-renowned collection of masterpieces from all schools and movements in art. Free general admission; charge for special exhibitions.

☺National Maritime Museum

Romney Road, Greenwich, SE10

✆020 8858 4422, www.nmm.ac.uk

Exhibitions relating to all aspects of Britain's maritime power. The Queen's House and the Royal Observatory, which houses the Peter Harrison Planetarium, in Greenwich Park are also part of the complex. Greenwich Park stretches up the hill behind the museum. Free admission.

☺National Portrait Gallery

St. Martin's Place, WC2

✆020 7306 0055, www.npg.org.uk

Beautiful galleries, arranged by period, with portraits of notable personalities from each era in British history from the Tudors to the present. Free general admission; charge for special exhibitions.

☺Natural History Museum

Cromwell Road, SW7

✆020 7942 5000, www.nhm.ac.uk

Innovative exhibitions of zoology, entomology, palaeontology, mineralogy and botany. Children love the dinosaur exhibit as well as the life-sized blue whale, creepy crawlies and the earthquake simulator. Free general admission; charge for special exhibitions.

Old Royal Naval College

King William Walk, Greenwich, SE10

✆020 8269 4747, www.oldroyalnavalcollege.org

Housed in a late-17th century hospital on the Thames, partially designed by Christopher Wren, this is considered to be the great baroque masterpiece of English architecture. The site of Greenwich palace was reputedly Henry VIII's favourite palace and the birthplace of Elizabeth I. The chapel and the Great Hall, together with the grounds of the Old Royal Naval College, are open to the public. Free admission.

**Queen's Gallery**

Buckingham Palace Road, SW1

✆ 020 7766 7301, www.royalcollection.org.uk

Changing exhibitions of art and objects from the Royal Collection. Admission charge.

**Royal Academy of Arts**

Burlington House, Piccadilly, W1

✆ 020 7300 8000, www.royalacademy.org.uk

An independent fine arts institution which supports contemporary artists and promotes interest in the arts through a comprehensive and ambitious exhibition programme. The Summer Exhibition is a hugely popular show of contemporary art held every year since 1769. Also renowned for many major loan exhibitions. Admission charge.

☺ **Royal Air Force Museum**

Grahame Park Way, Hendon NW9

✆ 020 8205 2266, www.rafmuseum.org.uk

National museum devoted to aviation and the comprehensive history of the RAF. The Battle of Britain wing houses a unique collection of memorabilia and machinery dedicated to the people involved in the battle. Donations suggested.

☺ **Royal Hospital Chelsea**

Royal Hospital Road, SW3

✆ 020 7881 5200, www.chelsea-pensioners.co.uk

A small museum containing artefacts left by deceased In-Pensioners is located within the impressive Christopher Wren-designed structure. The entrance hall is dedicated to the memory of the Duke of Wellington and displays objects associated with him. Visitors may also see the famous Chapel (open for services and concerts), the pensioners' dining room and walk in the park. Free admission.

☺ **Royal Mews**

Buckingham Palace Road, SW1

✆ 020 7766 7302, www.royalcollection.org.uk

Splendid collection of state coaches, carriages and the royal horses. Limited opening hours. Admission charge.

☺Science Museum

Exhibition Road, SW7

✆0870 870 4868, www.sciencemuseum.org.uk

Comprehensive displays of the history of mathematics, chemistry, physics, engineering, transport and industry. There are several children's play areas throughout. The Garden area allows those less than six years old to experiment with water, sound and construction. The Launch Pad is a popular hands-on exhibit for children of all ages. Free general admission; charge for special exhibitions.

Sir John Soane's Museum

13 Lincoln's Inn Fields, WC2

✆020 7405 2107, www.soane.org

Built in the early 19th century by the architect as his private residence. Contains his collection of art, furniture and antiquities. Excellent tour for limited numbers for a fee on Saturday afternoons. Donations encouraged.

☺Syon House

Brentford, Middlesex, TW8

✆020 8560 0882, www.syonpark.co.uk

Syon Park is home to Syon House, the last surviving ducal residence complete with its country estate in Greater London. Tour the Duke of Northumberland's London home, view the magnificent state and private apartments and enjoy the spectacular great conservatory and 40 acres of gardens. Syon Park is also home to various attractions for children: the London Butterfly House, the Tropical Forest and Snakes and Ladders (an indoor/outdoor adventure playground). Admission charge.

Tate Britain

Millbank, SW1

✆020 7887 8888, www.tate.org.uk/britain

The national collection of British art (from 1500 to present day), including works by William Hogarth, Thomas Gainsborough and Francis Bacon. Free general admission; charge for special exhibitions.

☺Tate Modern

Bankside, SE1

✆020 7887 8888, www.tate.org.uk/modern

A national gallery, comprised of the national collection of international modern art from 1900 to the present. It includes important works by Picasso, Matisse, Dali, Pollock and Warhol. Entrance is free, but donations are encouraged. Free general admission; charge for special exhibitions.

## ☺ Tower of London

Tower Hill, EC3

✆ 0844 482 7777, www.hrp.org.uk

Impressive fortification, parts of which date to Norman times; includes the White Tower, the Crown Jewels and an extensive armoury collection. It is the execution site of three queens and home to many legends and myths. Admission charge.

## ☺ V&A Museum of Childhood

Cambridge Heath Road, E2

✆ 020 8983 5200, www.vam.ac.uk/moc

Houses the Victoria and Albert Museum's collection of childhood-related objects and artefacts dating back to the 16th century. Re-opened in late 2006 after a redevelopment. The collection features toys, games, childcare, clothing, furniture, art and photography. Free admission.

## ☺ Victoria and Albert Museum

Cromwell Road, SW7

✆ 020 7942 2000, www.vam.ac.uk

One of the truly great collections of art and design in the world. Fine and decorative arts covering most periods of history from many of the world's richest cultures. Free general admission; charge for special exhibitions.

## Wallace Collection

Hertford House, Manchester Square, W1

✆ 020 7563 9500, www.wallacecollection.org

Private collection assembled during the 19th century with an emphasis on French 18th century fine and decorative arts. Fine collection of arms and armour. Free admission.

## Wesley's House and Chapel

49 City Road, EC1

✆ 020 7253 2262, www.wesleyschapel.org.uk

Home of the founder of Methodism; the complex of Georgian and Victorian buildings contain a large collection of his personal possessions. Free admission.

### William Morris Gallery

Water House, Lloyd Park, Forest Road, Walthamstow E17

℅ 020 8496 4390, www.walthamforest.gov.uk/wmg

Childhood home of the English Arts & Crafts designer, William Morris. The collection includes furniture, pictures, stained glass, wallpapers and textiles designed by Morris and his contemporaries. Free admission.

### Wimbledon Lawn Tennis Museum

Church Road, SW19

℅ 020 8946 6131, www.wimbledon.org

Offers a glimpse of how tennis has become a multimillion dollar professional sport, played all over the world. The museum includes memorabilia from many famous players, views of Centre Court and a state-of-the-art audiovisual theatre showing highlights of great players in action. Admission charge.

# Historic houses

### The National Trust

The National Trust (℅ 0844 800 1895, **www.nationaltrust.org.uk**) is a charity that protects and opens to the public over 300 historic houses and gardens and 49 industrial monuments and mills throughout the UK. The National Trust produces a handbook to stately properties and membership entitles you to discounts on many admissions. The properties under the National Trust's management often serve as museums. A sampling of some of the properties found in Greater London is listed below.

### Carlyle's House

24 Cheyne Row, SW3

℅ 020 7352 7087

Queen Anne period home of writer John Carlyle and his wife Jane. Paintings, decorative arts, personal effects, manuscripts and Carlyle's library. Admission charge.

### Fenton House

Windmill Hill, NW3

℅ 020 7435 3471

Late-17th century house with walled gardens and an outstanding collection of porcelain and early keyboard instruments. Admission charge.

16

CULTURE

### Ham House
Ham Street, Richmond-upon-Thames, TW10
℡020 8940 1950
Superb 17th century house along the Thames with an important collection
of Stuart and early Georgian furnishings. Restored formal gardens.
Admission charge.

### Sutton House
2 and 4 Homerton High Street, E9
℡020 8986 2264
Late-16th century Tudor home built by a prominent courtier of Henry VIII.
Admission charge.

## English Heritage
English Heritage (℡0870 333 1181, **www.english-heritage.org.uk**) is a
not-for-profit organisation, partly funded by the government, that seeks to
conserve and enhance the historic environment and broaden public access to
and understanding of England's heritage. It cares for over 400 historic
properties, which may also serve as museums, and opens them to visitors.
Membership benefits include free or reduced admission to its properties and
events. More information on each of its properties, including those highlighted
below, may be found on the website.

### Apsley House
149 Piccadilly, W1
℡020 7499 5676
Home of Arthur Wellesley, the first Duke of Wellington; contains his art
collection and military memorabilia. Admission charge.

### Chiswick House
Burlington Lane, Chiswick, W4
℡020 8995 0508
18th century villa set in extensive grounds; built by Lord Burlington,
influenced by Palladio and Indigo Jones. Gardens by William Kent.
Admission charge.

### Kenwood House
Hampstead Lane, NW3
℡020 8348 1286

Set in splendid grounds beside Hampstead Heath, this outstanding neoclassical house holds one of the most important collections of paintings ever given to the nation, including works by Rembrandt, Vermeer, Turner, Reynolds and Gainsborough. The house was remodelled by Robert Adam from 1764 to 1779, when he transformed the original brick building into a majestic villa for Lord Mansfield. Free admission.

Ranger's House (The Wernher Collection)
Chesterfield Walk, Blackheath, SE10
© 020 8853 0035
Stunning collection of medieval and Renaissance art purchased by the diamond magnate and philanthropist Sir Julius Wernher (1850-1912). Nearly 700 works of art are displayed within the elegant mansion's early Georgian panelled interiors. Among them are rare, early religious paintings and Dutch old masters, Gothic ivories, bronzes and silver treasures, and a fine jewellery collection of more than 100 Renaissance pieces.

# Classical music

World-famous classical musicians as well as up-and-comers perform regularly at venues large and small in London. There are five major orchestras: the BBC Symphony Orchestra (**www.bbc.co.uk/symphonyorchestra**), the London Philharmonic Orchestra (**www.lpo.co.uk**), the London Symphony Orchestra (**www.lso.co.uk**), the Philharmonia Orchestra (**www.philharmonia. co.uk**) and the Royal Philharmonic Orchestra (**www.rpo.co.uk**). Below is a list of some of the major classical venues.

Barbican Centre
Silk Street, EC2
© 020 7638 8891, www.barbican.org.uk
Its Resident Orchestra is the London Symphony Orchestra and its Associate Orchestra is the BBC Orchestra. The Barbican presents a diverse programme of performing and visual arts, encompassing all forms of classical and contemporary music, international theatre and dance, visual arts and design, and a cinema programme which blends first-run films with special themed seasons.

Cadogan Hall

5 Sloane Terrace, SW1

✆ 020 7730 4500, www.cadoganhall.com

Intimate 900-seat concert hall offering classical, as well as other types
of music performances, including opera and choral, jazz, rock and pop.
The Royal Philharmonic Orchestra is the resident orchestra.

Royal Albert Hall

Kensington Gore, SW7

✆ 0845 401 5045, www.royalalberthall.com

A great variety of musical events in various genres are staged here, including
Christmas concerts, The Proms (a popular series of performances held
throughout the summer) and performances by popular contemporary artists.

Royal College of Music

Prince Consort Road, SW7

✆ 020 7591 4314, www.rcm.ac.uk

Events offered include large-scale orchestral concerts, opera and chamber
concerts, as well as jazz and contemporary music features. Many events are
free of charge.

South Bank Centre

Belvedere Road, SE1

✆ 020 7960 4200, www.southbankcentre.co.uk

London's premier classical venue (including the Royal Festival Hall, Queen
Elizabeth's Hall and the Purcell Room), Southbank Centre's diverse musical
programme includes classical and world music, rock and pop, jazz and dance.
The venue offers theatrical events and dance performances and serves as
the home of the London Philharmonic Orchestra and the Opera Factory.

St. John's Smith Square

Smith Square, SW1

✆ 020 7222 1061, www.sjss.org.uk

This concert hall is situated in a restored Queen Anne church and presents
a varied programme of classical music.

St. Martin-in-the Fields

Trafalgar Square, WC2

✆ 020 7766 1100, www.stmartins-in-the-fields.org

Anglican church in Trafalgar Square. Offers evening concerts and free lunchtime concerts.

## Wigmore Hall
36 Wigmore Street, W1
℗020 7935 2141, www.wigmore-hall.org.uk
A small recital hall, known for its acoustics, offers a variety of performances which are often particularly attractive to music connoisseurs. Attracts leading classical musicians famed for its presentation of chamber music and song.

# Contemporary music

There is also a wealth of smaller venues that attract big-name artists, as well as newcomers who are up-and-coming on the London music scene. A small selection follows. Check websites and ticketmaster (℗0844 856 0202, **www. ticketmaster.co.uk**) for event information.

## HMV Forum
9-17 Highgate Road, NW5
℗020 7428 4099, www.meanfiddler.com

## HMV Hammersmith Apollo
Queen Caroline Street, W6
℗020 8563 3800, www.meanfiddler.com

## Jazz Café – see below under *Jazz* music.

## O2 Academy Brixton
211 Stockwell Road, SW9
℗020 7771 3000, www.o2academybrixton.co.uk

## O2 Arena
Peninsula Square, The Isle of Dogs, SE10
℗020 8463 2000, www.theo2.co.uk

## O2 Shepherds Bush Empire
Shepherds Bush Green, W12
℗020 8354 3300, www.o2shepardsbushempire.co.uk

Royal Albert Hall — see above under *Classical music*.

Wembley Arena
Empire Way, Wembley, HA9
✆0844 815 0815, www.whatsonwembley.com
A major concert venue in London that attracts major artists seeking a stadium audience.

# Jazz

100 Club
100 Oxford Street, W1
✆020 7636 0933, www.the100club.co.uk
Various musical styles offered, including jazz, blues, rock, punk and R&B.

606 Club
90 Lots Road, SW10
✆020 7352 5953, www.606club.co.uk
Jazz club restaurant.

Jazz Café
5 Parkway, NW1
✆020 7485 6834, www.jazzcafe.co.uk
Popular with locals and gig-goers.

Ronnie Scott's
47 Frith Street, W1
✆020 7439 0747, www.ronniescotts.co.uk
World-famous nightclub presenting jazz music of an international standard.

# Opera

English National Opera
London Coliseum, St. Martin's Lane, WC2
✆0871 911 0200, www.eno.org
The resident opera company sings its performances in English.

### Glyndebourne Festival Opera
Glyndebourne, Lewes, BN8
✆ 0127 381 2321, www.glyndebourne.com
Opera performed in the summer in the grounds of an Elizabethan house. Famous for black-tie picnics on the lawn. The company tours the UK in the fall.

### Opera Holland Park
Stable Yard, Holland Park, W8
✆ 0845 230 9769, www.operahollandpark.com
Opera is presented during the summer in a covered outdoor setting.

### Royal College of Music – see above under *Classical music.*

### Royal Opera
The Royal Opera House, Bow Street, WC2
✆ 020 7304 4000, www.roh.org.uk
Based in the beautiful and glamorous Royal Opera House in Covent Garden, this opera company conducts a regular program of performances in London.

# Dance

For a current list of news and events related to ballet and dance in the UK visit **www.ballet.co.uk**.

### English National Ballet
39 Jay Mews, SW7
✆ 020 7581 1245, www.ballet.org.uk
Internationally acclaimed classical ballet company, employing British and international talent. Tours extensively throughout the UK, and presents two high-profile seasons in London, at the London Coliseum at Christmas and at Royal Albert Hall in the summer.

### The Peacock Theatre
Portugal Street, WC2
✆ 0844 412 4300, www.peacocktheatre.com
Sister theatre to Sadler's Wells (see below), it hosts a variety of contemporary dance shows.

### Rambert Dance Company

94 Chiswick High Road, W4

℃ 020 8630 0600; www.rambert.org.uk

The oldest dance company in Britain, committed to presenting a broad range on modern repertoire, tours annually through Britain as well as internationally. Many performances in London occur at Sadler's Wells.

### Royal Ballet

The Royal Opera House, Bow Street, WC2

℃ 020 7304 4000, www.royalballet.org

Based at the Royal Opera House, the Royal Ballet is the UK's most prestigious ballet company. The Royal Ballet's repertory showcases the great classical ballets alongside new works both by international choreographers and choreographers from within the Company. Extensive international touring.

### Sadler's Wells Theatre

Rosebery Avenue, EC1

℃ 0844 412 4300, www.sadlerswells.com

The UK's leading dance house, dedicated to contemporary dance, ranging from cutting-edge performances to mainstream dance, both international and UK.

## Theatre

16

The concentration of London theatre venues, particularly the large, commercial ones, is in London's West End. The **www.londontheatre.co.uk** website provides comprehensive coverage of all London theatre productions.

Tickets to most West End shows are available from theatre box offices, ticket agencies (e.g., Ticketmaster), major department stores, hotels and online. Useful reference websites are **www.londontheatre.co.uk, www.official londontheatre.co.uk** and **www.expressevents.com**.

Theatre box offices frequently offer same-day price reductions on standby tickets (either on a limited number of tickets released that morning or for concessions) and returned tickets can often be bought for full price one hour before the show. As a rule, these tickets can be bought from the box office in person only.

Half-price tickets for same-day performances are more readily available at tkts (in the clock tower building on the south side of the garden in Leicester Square), which is open Monday to Saturday 10:00 to 19:00 and Sunday 12:00 to 15:00. There is also a tkts booth in the Brent Cross Shopping Centre. Most tickets are sold at half price plus a service charge per ticket. Visit **www.tkts.co.uk** for more details.

While London is well known for its West End theatres, the smaller-scale productions in the fringe theatres and venues should not be overlooked. Some of the smaller theatres of note are:

### Donmar Warehouse
39 Earlham Street, WC2
℗0844 871 7624, www.donmarwarehouse.com
One of London's leading independent producing theatres offers an intimate studio theatre seating 250.

### Old Vic
The Cut, SE1
℗0844 871 7628, www.oldvictheatre.com
Iconic theatre building. Kevin Spacey is the artistic director of the Old Vic Theatre Company.

### Royal National Theatre
South Bank, SE1
℗020 7452 3000, www.nationaltheatre.org.uk
Three theatres (the Olivier, the Lyttelton and the Cottesloe) all under one roof, offering an eclectic mix of new plays and classics.

### Shakespeare's Globe
21 New Globe Walk, SE1
℗020 7902 1400, www.shakespeares-globe.org
Dedicated to the experience and international understanding of Shakespeare in performance, this reproduction of the original Globe theatre offers performances in its open-air theatre from May through October, as well as tours and educational events year-round.

# Comedy

For a thorough list of pubs and clubs that provide stand-up comedy events visit **www.comedyonline.co.uk**. Comedy clubs and venues include:

The Bedford
77 Bedford Hill, SW12
☎020 8682 8940, www.thebedford.co.uk
Hosts the Banana Cabaret Comedy on Friday and Saturday nights. Also serves as live music venue and offers dancing classes.

The Chuckle Club
Houghton Street (London School of Economics), WC2
☎020 7476 1672, www.chuckleclub.com
Open Saturdays only.

Comedy Café
66 Rivington Street, EC2
☎020 7739 5706, www.comedycafe.co.uk
Open Wednesday through Saturday.

The Comedy Store
1a Oxendon Street, SW1
☎0844 847 1728, www.thecomedystore.co.uk
First opened in 1979.

Jongleurs
Multiple locations
☎0870 011 1960, www.jongleurs.com

Newsrevue
Canal Café Theatre, Delamere Terrace, W2
☎020 7289 6054, www.newsrevue.com
A fast-paced show of hilarious sketches and songs based on absolutely anything in the news – politics, sport or celebrities. Performances are Thursday through Sunday.

Up The Creek
302 Creek Road, Greenwich, SE10
☎020 8858 4581, www.up-the-creek.com
Friday and Saturday night comedy shows; disco thereafter.

# 17

# Annual events

London is an exciting city and the summer months are particularly busy! To assist you in planning a pleasurable year, we have provided a month-by-month schedule of events, along with advice on when and where to obtain tickets. For those events requiring advance planning and/or ticket purchase, we have added reminders at the time of year when you must send away for tickets.

**DID YOU KNOW?**

If you live in Westminster you may qualify for a **My Westminster ResCard**. Residents of the City of Westminster are eligible for a whole range of special offers and discounted tickets to sights and cultural venues and activities in the area. For information contact ✆020 7641 6000 or visit **www.rescard.com**

Please note that the following information is accurate at the time of publication. It is strongly suggested that you verify details before making your plans. You should either call the venue directly or contact the following information services for assistance: Visit London at © 08701 566 366 or **www.visitlondon. com** or Visit Britain at **www.visitbritain.com**. The social diary sold by Aspinal of London (**www.aspinaloflondon.com**), which is updated yearly with the complete listings of UK sporting, social and cultural events, can also be very helpful when planning for annual events.

Here are a few other helpful hints:

- Dress codes are often in effect. Ask your host/hostess or someone who has attended the event before for advice.

- When booking an event, always enquire if it is possible or necessary to book the car park.

- For more popular events, such as Wimbledon, the Queen's Garden Party, Trooping the Colour and Ascot, tickets must be obtained through a lottery or ballot. Entry forms, referred to as ballots, must be submitted by a certain deadline.

- Individual castles, stately homes and numerous other venues offer their own calendar of events. Visit the venue's website, telephone, write or email to request a detailed schedule of events.

See *Chapter 14: Sports and leisure* for more information on applying for tickets for certain of the sporting events listed below.

## January

Reminders:

- Submit your application for Ballots to Trooping the Colour. See *May* and *June* below.

- Bookings open for the Chelsea Flower Show (see *May* below), the Derby Festival (see *June* below), Beating the Retreat (see *June* below) and the Goodwood Festival (see *July* below).

- Application forms available for submitting work (amateur or professional) to the Royal Academy Summer Exhibition. See *June* below.

## January Store Sales

Most stores have major sales beginning in late December (Boxing Day for department stores) and ending in late January.

## New Year's Day

1 January – Bank Holiday

## New Year's Day Parade

1 January

www.londonparade.co.uk

This is the official birthday for all race horses. Lord Mayor of Westminster's parade begins as Big Ben strikes 12 noon at Whitehall and ends at Piccadilly. Entertainment continues in Hyde Park throughout the day and concludes with a fireworks display, marching bands and colourful floats. Tickets through the website from October.

## Royal Epiphany Gifts Service

6 January

Chapel Royals, St. James's Palace, Pall Mall, SW1

℗ 020 7930 4832, www.royal.gov.uk

Officers of the royal household give gold, frankincense and myrrh in the Chapel Royal at St James Palace. The gold is changed for coin which is given to charity.

## London International Boat Show

Early January

ExCeL Exhibition Centre, Royal Victoria Dock, E16

www.londonboatshow.com

The largest boat show in Europe and among the most prestigious boat shows in the world. The latest designs in pleasure crafts, yachts and equipment are displayed. Tours of the largest luxury yachts are on a first come first served appointment basis – get there early!

## Opening of the Old Bailey

Early January

An ancient ceremony to open the new court session where the Queen's Justices are in full-bottomed wigs and the Mayor of London is in his 19th century robes and ostrich plumed hat. The Lord Mayor leads a procession from Mansion House to Central Criminal Court to open a new session.

Charles I Commemoration
Las Sunday in January
Whitehall, SW1
Procession from St. James Palace to the Banqueting House commemorates the anniversary of the execution of Charles I. Wreaths are laid on the statue of Charles I near Trafalgar Square. There is a special service in Whitehall outside the former palace to commemorate the 'royal martyr'.

## February
Reminders:

- Tickets go on sale for Daily Mail Ideal Home Show. See *March* below.
- Apply for an entry form for London Triathlon. See *August* below.
- Phone for tickets to Hampton Court Palace Flower Show. See *June* below.
- Ticket ballot for Trooping the Colour must be submitted. See *June* below.

Chinese New Year Celebrations
Early February
www.londonchinatown.org
London's celebration for the Chinese New Year includes traditional and contemporary Chinese entertainment, fireworks in Leicester Square, cultural stalls, food, decorations and lion dance displays in Chinatown and performance stage with local Chinese artists. This is usually on the Sunday nearest the date of the New Year.

Accession of H.M. the Queen
6 February
Hyde Park and Tower of London
Anniversary salute of 41 guns in Hyde Park by the King's Troop of the Royal Horse Artillery and a 62-gun salute at the Tower of London by the Honourable Artillery Company. No tickets required.

Clown Service
First Sunday in February
Holy Trinity Church, Beechwood Road, E8
In memory of the famous clown Joseph Grimaldi (1778-1837), clowns gather for a church service at Holy Trinity Church. The service is attended by many clowns in full costume. No tickets required.

London Fashion Week
Mid February
www.londonfashionweek.co.uk
Europe's largest selling exhibition for designer fashion. The event is
held biannually (the second show is usually in September, see below).
Check website for details.

Great Spitalfields Pancake Day Race
Late February Or Early March (Shrove Tuesday)
The Old Truman Brewery, 91 Brick Lane, E1
www.alternativearts.co.uk
The tradition dates back to the time when people emptied their pantries
of all ingredients and made pancakes before fasting for Lent. Now races
are held where teams run for the finish line while flipping pancakes in
frying pans.

## March
Reminders:

- Obtain application and sponsorship to the Royal Enclosure at Royal Ascot.
  See *June* below.

- Send for admission badges to Henley Royal Regatta. See *June* below.

Cakes and Ale Ceremony
Ash Wednesday
Members of the Worshipful Company of Stationers (founded in 1403)
proceed from Stationers Hall to St Paul's Cathedral to hear a sermon.
Cakes and ale are then dispensed to all.

Oranges and Lemons Children's Service
Third Thursday of March
St. Clement Danes, The Strand, WC2
A church service of thanks for the restoration of the bells of St. Clement
Dane (of nursery rhyme fame). Children of the St. Clement's Dane
Primary School receive an orange and a lemon each.

Head of the River Race
End of March (usually the Saturday before University Boat Race)
www.horr.co.uk

A rowing journey from Mortlake to Putney, it is considered to be the largest continuous rowing event in the world. There is a continuous procession of boats throughout the race; the best view is from the north side of Hammersmith Bridge.

Oxford and Cambridge University Boat Race
Saturday in March or April
www.theboatrace.org
Held annually since 1829, the race course is from Putney to Mortlake on the Thames. Starting time varies according to the tides. The race can be viewed from many vantage points: bridges, banks, and riverside pubs. Visit the website for more information, timing and maps.

Daily Mail Ideal Home Show
Several weeks in March
Earl's Court Exhibition Centre, Warwick Road, SW5
www.idealhomeshow.co.uk
The largest annual consumer home show in the world.

BADA Antiques and Fine Art Fair
End of March
The Duke of York Square, SW3
www.bada-antiques-fair.co.uk
An annual showcase of furniture, paintings, silver, glass, ceramics, jewellery and more. Very high quality and authentic.

RHS London Flower Show
Second week of March
www.rhs.org.uk
The Royal Horticultural Society's flower show celebrating spring and the early daffodil competition.

The Affordable Art Fair
Second week of March
Battersea Park
www.affordableartfair.co.uk
Numerous galleries throughout London and other parts of the UK display their various collections of art. A great place to browse, buy and learn about

art all under one roof. The event is held bi-annually (the second show is usually in *October*, see below).

### Yonex All England Badminton Championships

Second weekend of March

National Indoor Arena, Birmingham, B40

www.allenglandbadminton.com

Normally held in the National Indoor Arena in Birmingham. Book directly online or write to: Badminton Association of England, National Indoor Arena, PO Box 334, Birmingham, B40 1NS.

### Cheltenham National Hunt Festival, Gloucestershire

Second/third week of March

www.cheltenham-festival.co.uk

One of the most important jump racing events of the year; top British and Irish horses competing. Visit website or *Chapter 14: Sports and leisure* for more details.

### Mothering Sunday or British Mother's Day

The fourth Sunday of Lent

### British Summer Time Begins (BST)

Last Sunday in March

Clocks move forward one hour. UK Spring daylight savings begins a few weeks after North America adjusts their clocks.

## April

Reminders:

- Deadline for submitting paintings to the Royal Academy Summer Exhibition. See *May* below.

- Submit entry for The London Triatholon. See *August* below.

### John Stow's Quill Pen Memorial Service

5 April

St. Andrew's Undershaft Church, EC3

© 020 7932 1100

John Stow wrote The Survey of London in 1598 at the age of 73. This memorial service is attended by the Lord Mayor. As part of the service, the Lord Mayor places a quill in the hand of Stow's statue.

### FA Cup Final
April or May
Climax of the English football season. See *Chapter 14: Sports and leisure* for more details.

### The Grand National Steeplechase
www.aintree.co.uk
Many consider this to be the most famous steeplechase in the world, run at Aintree racecourse, near Liverpool. Visit the website or see *Chapter 14: Sports and leisure* for more details.

### Maundy Thursday
Thursday before Good Friday
Held at Westminster Abbey every tenth year and at different cathedrals around the country during the other nine. The Queen distributes purses of specially minted coins to as many poor men and women as the years of her age.

### Good Friday
Friday before Easter Sunday – Bank Holiday

### Hot Cross Buns Service
Good Friday
St Bartholomew-the-Great, 6 Kinghorn Street, EC1
In a ceremony that dates back hundreds of years, 21 widows are given money and hot-cross buns after a church service at St Bartholomew-the-Great in Smithfield.

### Easter Sunday Service
Easter Sunday
St. George's Chapel, Windsor Castle, Windsor, Berkshire, SL4
Seating at 10:00. The Queen and the Royal Family worship together in St. George's Chapel. Visitors can attend. If you are seated toward the front of the Nave, you may be sitting with the Royal Family in the choir stalls. The queue is long, so arrive early. Many people do not enter the chapel; so do not be discouraged by the size of the queue.

### Easter Sunday Parade
Easter Sunday
Battersea Park, Albert Bridge Road, SW11
A carnival parade with colourful floats and bands.

### Easter Monday
Monday following Easter Sunday – Bank Holiday

### London Harness Horse Parade
Easter Monday
South of England showground, Ardingly, West Sussex RH17
www.lhhp.co.uk
Since 2006, the annual London Harness Horse Parade moved outside of London and takes place Sussex. Steeped in tradition, the parade offers onlookers a glimpse into a world gone by and for those participating, a chance to show off their best turnouts as well as meet up with friends and fellow enthusiasts. The Parade in its present form is actually an amalgam of two traditional parades – the London Cart Horse Parade, which was founded in 1885, and the London Van Horse Parade, which was founded in 1904. Tickets not required.

### The London Marathon
Late April
www.london-marathon.co.uk
The famous London marathon is made up of competitors from around the world: international marathon runners, serious runners, celebrities, disabled runners and those just out for fun. The race starts in Greenwich Park and winds throughout many areas of London and finishes outside of Buckingham Palace.

### H.M. The Queen's Birthday
21 April
Hyde Park and Tower of London
A 41-gun salute to mark the actual (not the official) birthday of The Queen, fired by the King's Troop Royal Horse Artillery in Hyde Park (opposite the Dorchester Hotel), and a 62-gun royal salute fired by the Honourable Artillery Company at the Tower of London (on London Wharf). Her official birthday is celebrated at Trooping the Colour, see *June* below.

### St. George's Day
23 April
St. George has been the patron saint of England since the 14th century. On this day, Englishmen wear an English red rose in their lapels (St. George's

symbol) and the flag of St. George (a red cross on white background) is flown from many buildings throughout England.

### Shakespeare's Birthday
23 April
www.shakespeare-country.co.uk
Shakespeare's birthday is celebrated in his hometown of Stratford-upon-Avon every year on the weekend closest to 23rd April. The highlight is the floral procession of dignitaries from all over the world between his birthplace and Holy Trinity Church.

### Scottish Military Tattoo
Dates May Vary
www.thescottishtattoo.com
Celebrated in London's Royal Albert Hall. The story of some of Scotland's heroes is interwoven with the best of Scottish (and Irish) music, song and dance. The massed pipes and drums are led by the pipes and drums of the London Regiment.

## May

Reminders:
- Apply for Steward's Enclosure at Henley Regatta. See *June* below.

### May Day
First Monday in May – Bank Holiday

### The Badminton Horse Trials
Early May
www.badminton-horse.co.uk
At Badminton, Avon, Gloucestershire. International equestrian competition.

### Polo Season Begins
Early May to September
The Guards Polo Club, Windsor Great Park, TW20
© 01784 434 212, www.guardspoloclub.com
At Windsor Great Park, matches are held most Saturdays and Sundays.

### Glyndebourne Festival
May to August
Glyndebourne, Lewes, East Sussex, BN8

✆01273 813 813, www.glyndebourne.com

International festival of opera. Attendees dress formally, take a picnic and dine on the grass with wine or champagne in hand. The festival is popular so book early for tickets. Special train services run from Victoria Station to Glyndebourne and return from Lewes.

## Royal Windsor Horse Show
Mid May

Royal Mews, Windsor Castle, Windsor, Berkshire SL4

✆01753 860 633, www.royal-windsor-horse-show.co.uk

At Windsor Castle, an international show with jumping and driving, various displays and trade exhibits. It is possible to become a member for a fee that allows one access to the Members' Enclosure for the week of the show.

## Bath Festival
Mid/late May

www.bathmusicfest.org.uk

Festival of music and arts with concerts, exhibitions, tours and lectures in Bath.

## Lilies And Roses
21 May

Tower of London

Henry VI founded both Eton College and King's College Cambridge. Every year on the anniversary of Henry's murder in the Tower of London, delegates from the schools place flowers on the spot of the king's death – lilies from Eton and roses from King's.

## Oak Apple Day
29 May

The Chelsea Pensioners honour Charles II, founder of the Royal Hospital in Chelsea, on the anniversary of Charles II's escape after the Battle of Worcester. The king's statue is decorated with oak leaves in memory of the fact that Charles hid in an oak tree to escape his pursuers.

## RHS Chelsea Flower Show
Late May

www.rhs.org.uk/chelsea

Held at the Chelsea Royal Hospital Grounds, this is the world's leading horticultural event; often visited by the Royal Family. Tuesday and Wednesday are reserved for RHS members with admittance to the general public on Thursday, Friday and Saturday. Tickets are limited and all sold in advance. Apply to RHS after 1 January. No children under five are admitted.

### Trooping The Colour
First Rehearsal – Last Saturday in May
www.trooping-the-colour.co.uk
From Buckingham Palace along the Mall to Horse Guards Parade, Whitehall and back again. The first of two rehearsals (the second held in June) to prepare for the actual Trooping the Colour, which occurs the second Saturday in June, in the presence of H.M. the Queen. A magnificent parade of colourful military units celebrates the Queen's official birthday. Tickets required. See *June* for ticket information.

### Hay Festival Wales
Late May/early June
Hay-on-Wye, Wales
www.hayfestival.com
For 10 days, this tiny town in Wales (1,300 people and 39 bookshops) is overwhelmed with visitors coming to enjoy a carnival of literature. The program is full of guest speakers, discussion panels, renowned authors and a full program for children.

### Regent's Park Open Air Theatre Season
May to September
Open Air Theatre, Inner Circle, Regent's Park, NW1
℃ 0844 826 4242, www.openairtheatre.org.uk
A full programme of plays, both Shakespearean and more modern works.

### Scotland's Highland Games
May to September
www.albagames.co.uk
Traditional Scottish games and lots of local colour.

### Chichester Festival Theatre Season
May to October
Chichester Festival Theatre, Oaklands Park, PO19
℃ 01243 781 312, www.cft.org.uk

A rich history of theatre making with an expanded programme of classic plays, musicals and premieres.

## Shakespeare's Globe Theatre

May to October

Shakespeare's Globe, 21 New Globe Walk, Bankside, SE1

℃020 7902 1400, www.shakespeares-globe.org

Enjoy outdoor theatre in the reconstructed Globe Theatre in the heart of London on the bank of the Thames River.

## Spring Bank Holiday

Last Monday in May – Bank Holiday

## June

Reminders:

• Frieze Art Fair Tickets go on sale. See *October* below.

## Beating the Bounds

Early June

The Tower of London

℃020 7626 4184

This ceremony takes place every three years at many churches throughout the UK; one of the most famous is at the Tower of London. The event harkens back to the days when the majority of parishioners were illiterate, and 'beating on the boundary marks of the parishes' taught them where the boundaries lay. This event is held on Ascension Day (the 40th day after Easter) every three years. The last was held in 2008.

## London Open Garden Squares Weekend

Early June

www.opensquares.org

This is the one weekend per year where gardens that require key entry are open to the general public. A great opportunity to discover beautiful gardens and enjoy special activities. The purchase of one ticket allows entry to all participating gardens over the entire weekend.

## Royal Academy Summer Exhibition

June to August

Royal Academy of Arts, Piccadilly, W1

©0207 300 8000, www.royalacademy.org.uk

The Summer Exhibition is the largest open contemporary art exhibition in the world, drawing together a wide range of new work by both established and unknown living artists. You may purchase tickets on the day or pre-book tickets. If you are an amateur or professional artist you can also submit work to the Summer Exhibition.

### Medieval Jousting Tournaments
June to August

www.knightsroyal.co.uk

Jousting tournaments take place at various castles throughout the UK during the summer months. They make for a fun day out; visit the castle, picnic on the grounds and enjoy the jousting tournament in period costume. Check the website for more information and the schedule of events/venues.

### H.R.H. The Duke of Edinburgh's Birthday
10 June

A 41-gun salute fired by the King's Troop, Royal Horse Artillery at noon in Hyde Park (opposite the Dorchester Hotel), and a 62-gun royal salute fired by the Honourable Artillery Company at one o'clock at the Tower of London (on London Wharf). No tickets required.

### Trooping the Colour (The Queen's Birthday Parade)
Second Saturday in June

www.trooping-the-colour.co.uk

Two rehearsals are held before the official event (on the last Saturday in May and the first Saturday in June). The official event is held on the second Saturday in June. Tickets are allocated by lottery. Send a letter requesting tickets along with a self-addressed envelope (s.a.e.) between 1 January and 28 February to: Brigade Major, HQ Household Division, Horse Guards, Whitehall, SW1A 2AX to receive an application. Only two tickets are allocated per successful entry. Even though tickets are required for the event, anyone can go to St James's Park or in front of Buckingham Palace to get a glimpse of the Queen. The event is broadcast live on BBC1, and highlights are shown later on the same day on BBC2.

### Beating Retreat
Early June

www.royalmarinesregimental.co.uk

This is a musical spectacle of sound and colour held on two successive evenings in the Horse Guards Parade, Whitehall. It has origins to the years of organised warfare when the beating of drums and the parading of Post Guards heralded the closing of camp gates and the lowering of flags at the end of a day of battle. Today, it is a ceremony reserved for special occasions. The event begins at 21.00 hours with the salute being taken by Her Majesty the Queen or another member of the royal family.

### The Derby (pronounced 'dar-be')
First weekend in June
✆ 0137 247 0047, www.epsomderby.co.uk
On Epsom Downs, this is the most famous and prestigious horse race in the world. It covers one and a half miles. Created at a noble dinner party in 1779 and named after one of the diners – Lord Derby. Bookings open 1 January.

### Biggin Hill International Air Fair
Early June
Biggin Hill Airport, Biggin Hill, Kent
www.militaryairshows.co.uk
Jet formation aerobatics, historic aircraft rally, modern military jets and extensive ground exhibition.

### H.M. the Queen's Official Birthday Gun Salute
Mid-June; Variable Each Year
A 41-gun salute is fired by the King's Troop, Royal Horse Artillery at noon in Hyde Park and a 62-gun royal salute fired by the Honourable Artillery Company at one o'clock at the Tower of London (on London Wharf). No tickets required.

### AEGON Tennis Tournament
Mid-June
The Queen's Club, Palliser Road, W14
www.aegonchampionships.com
Men's tennis tournament on grass held at the Queen's Club two weeks before Wimbledon. Tickets are allocated by ballot, but to have access to the ballot, you must be registered for their mailing list. Visit the website for more details.

### Order of the Garter Ceremony
Late June
www.trooping-the-colour.co.uk

In June, a special service marks the oldest order of chivalry in England. The Knights of the Garter gather at St. George's Chapel in Windsor Castle, where new knights take the oath and are invested with the insignia. It is attended by the Queen and is preceded by a colourful procession of knights wearing their blue velvet robes and black velvet hats with white plumes. A limited number of tickets are available for members of the public. Applications must be sent between 1 January and 1 March each year to The Superintendent, Windsor Castle, Windsor, Berkshire SL4 1NJ. Visit the website for more information.

### Knollys Red Rose Ceremony

24 June

© 020 7283 2383

In the 14th century, Sir Robert Knollys was fined for building an unauthorised footbridge across Seething Lane. The fine imposed was one red rose from his garden to be given to the Lord Mayor every year. Today, his descendants along with the churchwardens of All-Hallows-by-the-Tower continue the tradition. Contact: The Clerk to the Company of Watermen and Lighterman of the River Thames at Watermen's Hall, 16 St. Mary at Hill, EC3R 8EE.

### Henley Royal Regatta

Late June or early July

Henley-on-Thames, Oxfordshire, RG9

© 01491 572 153, www.hrr.co.uk

This international rowing event is also a popular social occasion. For those with access to the Steward's Enclosure (reserved for members and their guests), women may only wear dresses or suits with a hemline below the knee (trousers, culottes, and divided skirts are not permitted), and men must wear a jacket and tie. The more informal Regatta Enclosure is for the general public and tickets may be purchased in advance after 1 May, or upon arrival. Alternatively, take a picnic and sit alongside the tow path for free.

### Wimbledon Tennis Championships (Wimbledon)

Last Week In June Or First Week In July

www.wimbledon.org

For the public ballot, you must fill out and return the application form postmarked no later than 15 December the year before you want to attend. See *Chapter 14: Sports and leisure* for more details on applying for tickets. Note that the tube stop is Southfields, not Wimbledon.

### Royal Ascot
Usually held third week In June
www.ascot.co.uk

The world's most famous race meeting dating back to 1711. Tuesday through Friday is attended by the Royal Family. Formal attire, hats and gloves required for ladies and full morning suit for men if you have tickets for certain enclosures. To obtain passes for the Royal Enclosure, contact your embassy or high commission for information regarding allocated tickets. For general tickets and information, visit the website.

### The Queen's Cup Final International Polo Tournament
Usually held third week In June
www.guardspoloclub.com

Polo is the fastest growing premium sport in the UK. The Queen's Cup is held at The Guards Polo Club; Royal Windsor Great Park, Windsor. Visit the website for more information and details.

### Holland Park Opera Season
June to August
www.operahollandpark.com

Featuring the Royal Philharmonic Orchestra, these outdoor concerts offer beautiful music in a fantastic setting. Holland House, one of the oldest houses in Kensington, acts as a backdrop and many people picnic beforehand in the gardens – you can even collect a picnic hamper from the bar.

### City of London Festival Programme
Late June/early July
www.colf.org

Each summer the City of London Festival brings the City's unique buildings and outdoor spaces to life with an extensive artistic programme of music, visual arts, film, walks and talks, much of it free to the public. Check the website for more information.

### English Heritage Picnic Concerts
Late June to August
www.picnicconcerts.com

Summer evening musical concerts are held in late June, July and August on the grounds of several historic houses around London, including 18th century Kenwood House in Hampstead Heath. Arrive early and bring a picnic, a blanket, and plenty to drink. Advance booking is advised as most concerts sell out. Visit the website (**www.picnicconcerts.com**) for details.

Many other manor houses hold outdoor concerts during the summer. Dates vary each year so contact the individual locations. Some of the most popular are:

Audley End House, Essex; **www.english-heritage.org.uk**

Leeds Castle, Maidstone, Kent; **www.leeds-castle.com**

Hampton Court Palace, Surrey; **www.hrp.org.uk/hamptoncourtpalace**

Hever Castle, Edenbridge, Kent; **www.hevercastle.co.uk**

Marble Hill, Twickenham; **www.english-heritage.org.uk**

Pevensey Castle, East Sussex; **www.english-heritage.org.uk**

Portchester Castle, Hampshire; **www.english-heritage.org.uk**

Somerset House, London; **www.somersethouse.org.uk**

Warwick Castle, Warwickshire; **www.warwick-castle.co.uk**

Wrest Park House, Bedfordshire; **www.english-heritage.org.uk**

## July

Reminders:
- Book tickets for Buckingham Palace. See August below.

### Royal Garden Parties at Buckingham Palace
Mid July
www.royal.gov.uk
Three parties are held during the summer at Buckingham Palace, as well as one at the Palace of Holyroodhouse in Edinburgh. Over 30,000 people attend. A cross-section of people is chosen to attend to ensure that all areas of the community are represented. The Queen and the Duke of Edinburgh along with several other members of the royal family circulate among the crowd. Traditional high tea is served. For more information, visit the website.

### Promenade Concerts (The BBC Proms)
Mid July to early September

www.bbc.co.uk/proms

The world's greatest classical music festival held at the Royal Albert Hall throughout the summer. Visit the website for details and ticket information. Guidebooks are available in April including a booking form.

## British F1 Grand Prix
Early July
www.formula1.com

Few sporting occasions match the intensity, glamour and drama of the British Grand Prix. Whether a wide-eyed first timer or seasoned veteran, the experience is not to be missed. Check the website for race location and ticket prices.

## Hampton Court Flower Show
Early July
www.rhs.org.uk/hamptoncourt

The world's largest flower show presented by the Royal Horticultural Society. Displays from more than 700 exhibitors featuring flowers, plants, accessories, landscape design ideas, the world's largest annual gathering of roses in full bloom and much, much more.

## Swan Upping
Last Monday in July
✆020 7414 2271, www.royal.gov.uk

Swan Upping is the annual census of the swan population on parts of the River Thames. The Dyers and Vintner's Companies have the right, established in medieval times, to keep swans on the Thames River. So, too, does the Crown. Every year the Queen's Swan Keeper and Swan Markers from the two livery companies row in skiffs along the river to mark the cygnets (baby swans). You can enjoy a view of the proceedings from several pubs along the river. For information on where the boats will be at specific times telephone or check the website for further details.

## Doggett's Coat and Badge Race
Late July or early August

Possibly the oldest rowing race in the world, this event was begun by Irish actor Thomas Dogett in 1715 to mark the crowning of George I. Six water boatmen race against the tide from London Bridge to Albert Bridge. The prize is a scarlet livery with a large silver badge.

Glorious Goodwood Horseracing
Last Tuesday to Saturday in July
www.goodwood.co.uk
Horseracing at one of the most beautiful courses in the world, on top of the Sussex Downs. It is one of the highlights of the social summer season – famously described by King Edward VII as 'a garden party with racing tacked on'.

British Open Golf Championship
Mid July
www.randa.org
Known for its challenging and always interesting finishes, the British Open is one of the world's favourite and oldest sporting events.

Women's British Open
Late July
www.lgu.org
A leading event in women's professional golf and the only tournament that is classified as a major by both the Ladies European Tour and the LPGA Tour.

## August

Reminders:

• Request ballot forms for Wimbledon tickets for next year. See June above.

Cowes Week
Late July or early August
www.cowesweek.co.uk
Cowes Week, on the Isle of Wight, is one of the UK's longest running and most successful sporting events. It stages up to 40 daily races for over 1,000 boats and is the largest sailing regatta of its kind in the world.

Buckingham Palace opens to visitors
Early August to end of September
www.the-royal-collection.com/royaltickets
Buckingham Palace is the official London residence of Her Majesty the Queen. The Palace's state rooms and garden are open to visitors while the Queen is on her summer holidays in Scotland. Advance tickets (which will

**17**

ANNUAL EVENTS

allow you to avoid some of the long queues) go on sale on line. You can also purchase tickets on the day of your visit from the Ticket Office at Canada Gate in Green Park between 09:00 and 16:00.

### The London Triatholon
Early August
www.thelondontriatholon.co.uk
Participate in or be a spectator of the world's largest triatholon on the closed roads of London. See website for more details.

### Jersey Battle of Flowers
Mid August
www.battleofflowers.com
On the island of Jersey in the Channel Islands. A three-hour parade of floats displaying thousands of flowers, bands, etc. held on Thursday afternoon and Friday evening by moonlight. Crowds gather along the route. Tickets required for the arena.

### Edinburgh International Festival
Mid August
www.eif.co.uk
The Edinburgh International Festival presents a rich programme of classical music, theatre, opera and dance in six major theatres and concert halls and a number of smaller venues, over a three-week period in late summer each year. It is said to be the largest festival of the arts.

### Edinburgh Military Tattoo
Three weeks in August
www.edinburgh-tattoo.co.uk
One of the most spectacular shows in the world. A military pageant held on flood lit grounds of Edinburgh Castle. Tickets sell quickly. Bookings can be accepted as early as December of the prior year.

### Summer Bank Holiday
Last Monday in August – Bank Holiday

### Notting Hill Carnival
August Bank Holiday Sunday and Monday
www.nottinghillcarnival.org.uk
This is the largest street festival in Europe involving over one million

visitors. An explosion of fun, food, culture and music that began in 1965 when Trinidian immigrants and individuals of Notting Hill brought the people together after the race riots of the 1950s.

## September

Reminders:

• Apply for Chelsea Flower Show Gala Preview tickets. See *May* above.

### Great River Race
Early September
℡ 020 8398 9057, www.greatriverrace.co.uk
A 22-mile boat race from Richmond, Surrey to Island Gardens, Greenwich involving various types of boats including: Chinese dragon boats, Viking Longboats, whalers, canoes and more.

### Horseman's Sunday
Mid September
www.stjohns-hydepark.com/horsemans
Church of St. John and St. Michael, Hyde Park Crescent, W2. A morning service dedicated to the horse with mounted vicar and congregation followed by a procession of 100 horses through Hyde Park.

### London Open House
Mid September
www.londonopenhouse.org
Provides the public free access to over 700 buildings (of historical, architectural and/or community interest) throughout London that are normally closed to the public. Takes place over a two-day weekend. An Open House directory is for sale which lists all sites and details.

### Mayor's Thames Festival
Mid September
www.thamesfestival.org
Along the banks of the River Thames between Westminster Bridge and Tower Bridge. A spectacular, free, outdoor festival including art exhibitions, shows, street theatre, children's activities and music. Tens of thousands dance in the streets at the festival's climactic event, a spectacular Night Carnival that's a vivid mixture of fireworks, masquerade, dance, music and fantastic costumes.

London Fashion Week
Mid September
www.londonfashionweek.co.uk
Biannual event in February and September. Europe's largest selling
exhibition for designer fashion.

Admission of Sheriffs
28 September or the Friday preceding
℗020 7606 3030
The livery companies of the city elect two sheriffs on Midsummer Day.
Today, the new sheriffs march in a colourful procession from Mansion
House to the Guildhall to be installed in office.

Election of the Lord Mayor
29 September
℗020 7606 3030
In a ceremony that dates from 1546, the Lord Mayor is selected at the
Guildhall, then rides in state to Mansion House while the city bells ring out.

## October

Reminders:

• Send for Royal Epiphany Tickets. See *January* above.

• Send for Cheltenham Hunt Meeting Tickets. See *March* above.

• Apply for a place in the London Marathon. See *April* above.

Pearly Kings and Queens Festival
First Sunday in October
www.pearlysociety.co.uk
Pearlies are dedicated charity workers who continually assist with
fundraising activities for a multitude of organizations. They attend a
Harvest Festival Service in traditional full dress of sequined costumes
and distinguished pearl-buttoned shirts. This is held at St Paul's Church,
Covent Garden. The produce is donated to St Martin's-in-the-Fields
Homeless Centre.

Horse of the Year Show
Early October
℗08700 101 052, www.hoys.co.uk

At the NEC in Birmingham. The climax of national show jumping and showing seasons. Tickets usually sell out quickly.

### Frieze Art Fair
Mid October
www.friezeartfair.com
Held at Regent's Park, the Frieze Art Fair features over 150 of the most exciting contemporary art galleries in the world. The fair also includes specially commissioned artists' projects, a prestigious talks programme and an artist-led education schedule.

### London Film Festival
Mid October
www.lff.org.uk
The London Film Festival is the UK's largest public film event, screening more than 300 features, documentaries and shorts from almost 50 countries. It also provides an extensive programme of industry events, public forums, education events, lectures, masterclasses and Q&A's with film-makers and film talent.

### Trafalgar Parade and Service
21 October or nearest Sunday
Trafalgar Square, WC2
A march through Trafalgar Square remembers the triumph of Lord Nelson at Trafalgar in 1805. Wreaths are laid at the foot of Nelson's Column in the Square.

### Quit-Rents Ceremony
Late October
© 020 7947 6131
Dating back more than 800 years, the Ceremony is the oldest legal act that is still performed other than the Coronation. It is held to mark the occasion when the City Solicitor pays one of the Queen's officials (the Remembrancer) a token for the rent of properties and land leased long ago. For Shropshire he pays two knives (one blunt and one sharp) and for the Forge in the Strand he pays sixty-one nails and six horseshoes. For more information, contact: The Chief Clerk to the Queen's Remembrancer, The Queen's Remembrancers' Office, Room E113, Royal Courts of Justice, Strand, WC2A 2LL.

The Affordable Art Fair
Late October
Battersea Park
www.affordableartfair.co.uk

Over 20 galleries offer a stunning array of contemporary art from just £50 up to £3,000. From the hottest young talent to firmly established household names, with so much choice you are bound to find something you love whether you're an experience collector or simply looking for a masterpiece for the mantel.

State Opening of Parliament
October or November
www.parliament.uk

English pageantry at its finest. Her Majesty the Queen rides in the Irish state coach from Buckingham Palace to the House of Lords, where she addresses both houses of Parliament from the Throne in the House of Lords. Viewing along the route. The House of Lords is not open to the public. Check current dates and information on the website.

Opening of the Law Courts
Late October or early November
℡ 020 7219 3000, www.parliament.uk

At Westminster Abbey. A closed service is held at Westminster Abbey attended by Her Majesty's Judges and Queen's Counsel dressed in state robes and wigs. Afterwards, the Lord Chancellor leads the procession from the East end of the Abbey to the House of Lords. The first motion of the year constitutes the official opening of the Courts.

British Summer Time Ends (GMT)
Last Sunday of October

Clocks are set back one hour to Greenwich Mean Time.

## November

Reminders:

- Send for New Year's Day Parade Tickets. See *January* above.

- Book Gala Preview Tickets for Hampton Court Palace Flower Show. See *July* above.

### Guy Fawkes Day (Bonfire Night)
5 November

Bonfires, fireworks and burning effigies of Guy Fawkes throughout the UK on the nearest weekend to this date, celebrate his failure to blow up the King and the Houses of Parliament in the Gunpowder Plot of 1605. There is a particularly spectacular event at Leeds Castle in Kent. The Evening Standard and Metro newspapers publish lists of bonfires and fireworks displays in the London area in the week leading up to Guy Fawkes Day.

### H.R.H. Prince of Wales' Birthday
14 November

### London To Brighton Rally (RAC Veteran Car Run)
First Sunday in November
✆ 017 5368 1736

This event is only open to cars built between 1895 and 1904, commemorating the repeal of the 'Red Flag Laws' in 1905. With over 500 cars taking part in the 60-mile run to Brighton, it is the largest gathering of old cars in the world. Departures start from 08:00 at Hyde Park Corner with pre-departure festivities and along the route. No tickets required. Contact: The RAC Motor Sports Association Ltd.; Motor Sports House, Riverside Park, Colnbrook, Slough SL3 OHG.

### Junior League of London Boutique de Noel
Early November
✆ 020 7499 7159, www.jll.org.uk

The Junior League of London's annual Christmas shopping fair features unique gifts from selected exhibitors as well as live and silent auctions. The event is held over two days, starting with an evening event and then a full day event. Funds generated by Boutique de Noel support the community projects of the Junior League of London. To be an exhibitor or to buy tickets contact the Junior League office or visit the website.

### Lord Mayor's Procession and Show
Second Saturday in November
www.lordmayorsshow.org

The new Lord Mayor takes up his post in a colourful procession from Guildhall to the Royal Courts of Justice in his 18th Century Gold State Carriage, escorted by medieval-costumed bodyguards, elaborate floats, acrobats, trumpeters and livery companies. The route is three miles long and features over 6,500 people. No tickets required for viewing along the route.

The Sunday closest to 11 November
The main national commemoration is held around the Cenotaph at Whitehall. A service is held in memory of those killed in battle since 1914. It is attended by the Queen, members of the Royal Family, the Prime Minister, members of the Cabinet and members of the Opposition. Two minutes silence is observed as Big Ben strikes 11:00. During the week that precedes this event, volunteers sell poppies in the streets to raise money for ex-servicemen. Poppy wreaths are placed at many war memorials in village high streets and gravesites.

## December

Reminders:

- Last day to send in Ballots for Wimbledon is 15 December. See *June* above.

- Apply for a place in the London Marathon. See *April* above.

- In mid-December outdoor skating rinks open for the holiday season around the city: Somerset House, Marble Arch, Natural History Museum, Hampstead Heath and others. Skates are for hire. Tickets are to be booked in advance.

Christmas Tree Lighting Ceremony
Mid December
Trafalgar Square, WC2
Each year an enormous Christmas tree is donated by the people of Oslo, Norway in remembrance and thanks for British assistance during World War II. Carol services are sung every evening beneath the tree until Christmas.

Handel's Messiah
Early December
St Paul's Cathedral, EC4
© 020 7236 4128
Performances of Handel's Messiah during the Christmas season are annual events around the UK. One outstanding production is held at St. Paul's

**17**

**ANNUAL EVENTS**

Cathedral. It is ticketed but free, by post from The Chapter House, St. Paul's Churchyard, EC4M 8AD. Arrive early for good seats.

### Christmas Concerts and Carols
Throughout December
Royal Albert Hall, Kensington Gore, SW7
www.royalalberthall.com
Various concerts to cover all tastes and ages including carols by candlelight on Christmas Eve. Visit website for details.

### Children's Pantomimes
Mid December to mid January
Held throughout Britain in local theatres and Town Halls. Traditional pantomimes with male/female roles reversed, audience participation, sing-along and candy thrown into the audience. Especially popular in London and the seaside resort towns (e.g., Bournemouth). Check theatre listings or local newspapers for information.

### Christmas
25 December – Bank Holiday
The Queen's Christmas message is broadcast.

### Christmas Day Swim Race
25 December
Serpentine Lake, Hyde Park
www.serpentineswimmingclub.com
The Peter Pan Cup has taken place every Christmas Day since 1864. While most of us are still tucked up in bed or tearing into a bulging stocking, members of the Serpentine Swimming Club are competing in their annual race across the icy waters of the Serpentine in Hyde Park.

### Boxing Day
26 December – Bank Holiday

### New Year's Eve
31 December
Big Ben tolls at midnight. Enormous crowds gather at Trafalgar Square creating a huge party atmosphere to ring in the New Year.

# 18

# Organisations

The primary concern of building your new life in London is becoming part of a community here. You may initially build your community with your work or student colleagues or you may have arrived here without a job or on your own. To really get the most out of the city, it is great to meet people who share your common interests and who may be able to share some insider knowledge. The writers of this book are all expats who joined the Junior League of London (see the section *Charitable, social and service organisations* below) and found some sense of common purpose and fun. We encourage you to get involved and engage with London and other Londoners!!

As an expat, you may find that the first community you are a part of is based on your nationality and the first section below lists selected embassies and high commissions. If you are working or looking for work, it may be useful to join one of the professional organisations. In addition, many universities and university consortiums have clubs in London or the UK, which we have not attempted to list in this chapter, so check with your alumni group if that is something that might interest you.

## IN THIS CHAPTER...

- **Embassies and high commissions**
- **Professional organisations**
- **Charitable, social and service organisations**
- **Places of worship**

# Embassies and high commissions

In general, your embassy or high commission represents your government and the consular office within each embassy or high commission concerns itself with individual citizens. Therefore, communication with your embassy or high commission will be primarily through the consular office. Consular offices are also located in other cities where there is a high concentration of citizens of a specific nationality.

Consular offices will help you with:

## Emergencies

* Death of a citizen abroad
* Arrests (the embassy will provide you with the names of lawyers)
* Financial assistance

## Non-emergencies

* Passports – help with stolen or lost passports, applications and renewals
* Registering births and deaths
* Tax obligations (see *Chapter 3: Money, banking and taxation*)
* Voting – assistance with absentee balloting
* Notary public

Most foreign states and Commonwealth countries maintain representatives in London. The British Foreign and Commonwealth Office compile an alphabetical listing of such foreign representatives, which can be found at **www.fco.gov.uk**. It is also available in hard copy from The Stationary Office, PO Box 29, Norwich, NR3 1GN. The website provides: the name of the Ambassador or High Commissioner; the address, telephone and fax numbers of the embassy or high commission in London; and, where available, the website and email address for each mission.

The following is a partial list of embassies in London:

Australian High Commission
Australia House, Strand, WC2
℗ 020 7379 4334, www.uk.embassy.gov.au

Austrian Embassy

18 Belgrave Mews West, SW1

✆020 7344 3250, www.bmeia.gv.at/london

Belgian Embassy

17 Grosvenor Crescent, SW1

✆020 7470 3700, www.diplobel.org/uk

Brazilian Embassy

32 Green Street, W1

✆020 7399 9000, www.brazil.org.uk

Canadian High Commission

Macdonald House, 1 Grosvenor Square, W1

✆020 7258 6600, www.london.gc.ca

French Embassy

58 Knightsbridge, SW1

✆020 7073 1000, www.ambafrance-uk.org

Embassy of the Federal Republic of Germany

23 Belgrave Square, SW1

✆020 7824 1300, www.london.diplo.de

Greek Embassy

1A Holland Park, W11

✆020 7229 3850, www.greekembassy.org.uk

High Commission of India

India House, Aldwych, WC2

✆020 7836 8484, www.hcilondon.in

Embassy of Ireland

17 Grosvenor Place, SW1

✆020 7235 2171, www.embassyofireland.co.uk

Italian Embassy

14 Three Kings Yard, Davies Street, W1

✆020 7312 2200, www.amblondra.esteri.it

Japanese Embassy

101-104 Piccadilly, W1

✆020 7465 6500, www.uk.emb-japan.go.jp

Embassy of Luxembourg

27 Wilton Crescent, SW1

✆020 7235 6961, www.luxembourgembassy.co.uk

Royal Netherlands Embassy

38 Hyde Park Gate, SW7

✆020 7590 3200, www.netherlands-embassy.org.uk

New Zealand High Commission

New Zealand House, 80 Haymarket, SW1

✆020 7930 8422, www.nzembassy.com/uk

Russian Embassy

6/7 Kensington Palace Gardens, W8

✆020 7229 3628, www.rusemb.org.uk

South African High Commission

South Africa House, Trafalgar Square, WC2

✆020 7451 7299, www.southafricahouse.com

Spanish Embassy

39 Chesham Place, SW1

✆020 7235 5555, www.mae.es/embajadas/londres/en

Embassy of Sweden

11 Montagu Place, W1

✆020 7917 6400, www.swedish-embassy.org.uk

Embassy of Switzerland

16-18 Montagu Place, W1

✆020 7616 6000, www.swissembassy.org.uk

Embassy of the United Arab Emirates

30 Prince's Gate, SW7

✆020 7581 1281, www.uaeembassyuk.net

Embassy of the United States of America

24 Grosvenor Square, W1

✆ 020 7499 9000, www.usembassy.org.uk

# Professional organisations

Association of MBAs

25 Hosier Lane, EC1

✆ 020 7246 2686, www.mbaworld.com

Professional membership association for MBA students and graduates.

British American Business

75 Brook Street, W1

✆ 020 7290 9888, www.babinc.org

Independent, non-profit organisation that provides assistance to member companies in the expansion of their activities on both sides of the Atlantic. Services to members include publications, luncheons, lectures and seminars relating to Anglo-American affairs and business.

Institute of Directors

116 Pall Mall, SW1

✆ 020 7766 8866, www.iod.co.uk

Business leader network that provides business resources and support to senior level professionals.

Chartered Management Institute

2 Savoy Court, The Strand, WC2

✆ 020 7497 0580, www.managers.org.uk

An independent chartered professional body dedicated to management and leadership that supports and advises individuals and organisations and engages policy makers and key influencers in government and the management profession.

The Law Society

The Law Society's Hall, 113 Chancery Lane, WC2

✆ 020 7242 1222, www.lawsociety.org.uk

The Law Society represents solicitors in England and Wales. The services it provides range from negotiating with and lobbying the profession's regulators, government and others, to offering training and advice.

# Charitable, social and service organisations

### The American Society in London
The English Speaking Union, Dartmouth House, 37 Charles Street, W1
Ⓒ 020 7539 3400, www.americansocietyuk.com
The oldest American expatriate club in the UK, it promotes America and its
friendship with Great Britain. American citizens living in the UK are eligible
for membership as are British subjects or others who have either resided in
the US or have close US connections.

### The American Women of Surrey
PO Box 185, Cobham, Surrey KT11
Ⓒ 079 1026 7962, www.awsurrey.org
A social club and support group for American women living in Surrey.

### American Women's Club of London
68 Old Brompton Road, SW7
Ⓒ 020 7589 8292, www.awclondon.org
Social, recreational and charitable club with facilities for American women
living in London.

### Canadian Women's Club
1 Grosvenor Square, W1
Ⓒ 020 7258 6344, www.canadianwomenlondon.org
A diverse group of women brought together by their common ties to
Canada. Organises various activities, social events, and enables members
to undertake projects of interest.

### CARE International
10-13 Rushworth Street, SE1
Ⓒ 020 7934 9334, www.careinternational.org.uk
Charitable organisation founded in America after World War II. Today it
is a confederation of humanitarian organisations that act together to provide
emergency responses and assist long-term development to the world's
poorest people.

Chilterns American Women's Club

PO Box 445, Gerrards Cross, Buckinghamshire, SL9

✆ 07523 699 460, www.cawc.co.uk

Operates in the Gerrards Cross and Beaconsfield area.

CTC – The National Cyclists Organisation

CTC Parklands, Railton Road, Guildford, Surrey, GU2

✆ 0844 736 8450, www.ctc.org.uk

Britain's national cycling organisation.

Contemporary Art Society

11-15 Emerald Street, WC1

✆ 020 7831 1243, www.contemporaryartsociety.org

A national membership organisation, including contemporary art enthusiasts and collectors, curators and artists among others. CAS organises events to develop insight into contemporary art and collecting, including gallery and museum visits, artists' talks and trips to international art shows.

Democrats Abroad (UK)

DAUK Suite 340, 56 Gloucester Road, London, SW7

✆ 020 7724 9796, www.democratsabroad.org.uk

The official organisation of the US Democratic Party in the United Kingdom with the power to organise and elect delegates to the Democratic National Convention.

English Heritage

1 Waterhouse Square, 138-142 Holborn, EC1

✆ 020 7973 3000, www.english-heritage.org.uk

Offers exhibitions, museums and guided tours as well as historical re-enactments, displays, concerts and other special events. Funds from the membership help protect and preserve England's historical legacy.

English Speaking Union

Dartmouth House, 37 Charles Street, W1

✆ 020 7529 1550, www.esu.org

A worldwide registered charity with facilities supported by membership and donations, it aims to promote international understanding through a variety of social and educational activities, including scholarships, lectures, outings and receptions.

18

ORGANISATIONS

## FOCUS
13 Prince of Wales Terrace, W8
℄020 7937 7799, www.focus-info.org
A membership-based organisation that assists professionals and their families
to successfully settle in the UK. Functions as a clearinghouse for information
regarding community services, schools, childcare, organisations, etc. Offers
a telephone information line, personal advice, career and educational services,
and seminars and workshops for the international community in the UK.

## Hampstead Women's Club (HWC)
www.hwcinlondon.co.uk
Multinational, social organisation for women and their families living in
London. HWC offers a full calendar of social, educational and charitable
activities to enable members to meet people and experience London and
encourage a sense of community.

## The Junior League of London (JLL)
9 Fitzmaurice Place, W1
℄020 7499 8159, www.jll.org.uk
An international organisation of women committed to promoting voluntary
service, developing the potential of women and improving communities
through effective action and the leadership of trained volunteers. A registered
UK charity, it provides volunteers and resources to support projects that
help to eliminate poverty and its effects in London.

## The Kensington Chelsea Women's Club (KCWC)
Box 567, 28 Old Brompton Road, SW7
℄020 7863 7562, www.kcwc.org.uk
Since 1983, KCWC has provided social contact and cultural exchange
for women in London, both expatriates and British nationals. It is one of
the largest women's clubs in London. There are monthly meetings with
prominent guest speakers.

## The Lansdowne Club
9 Fitzmaurice Place, W1
℄020 7629 7200, www.lansdowneclub.com
A private club that offers a swimming pool, squash courts and fencing as
well as a ballroom, a restaurant and regular activities such as Scottish
country dancing, chess and bridge.

London Ladies Club
PO Box 3870, SW1
✆ 020 7730 4640, www.londonladies.co.uk
A social club which offers access to the city's top institutions such as museums, colleges, social clubs and societies.

The National Trust
36 Queen Anne's Gate, SW1
✆ 0844 800 1895, www.nationaltrust.org.uk
A non-profit organisation and special interest group that purchases or is bequeathed historic properties or places of great natural beauty which are preserved for the nation. Membership entitles you with free entry to properties, various publications, etc. There are also local branches that sponsor activities and trips.

Republicans Abroad (UK)
www.republicansabroad-uk.org
Political interest group supporting the US Republican Party with the power to organise and elect delegates to the Republican National Convention.

Rotary Club of London
6 York Gate, NW1
✆ 020 7847 5429, www.londonrotaryclub.org.uk
One of four Rotary Clubs in the UK and Ireland, it encourages and fosters the ideal of service as a basis of worthy enterprise and is involved with community projects.

Sport England
3rd Floor, Victoria House, Bloomsbury Square, WC1
✆ 0207 273 1551, www.sportengland.org.uk
Sport organisation works through nine regional offices to provide a vast array of information on sporting activities throughout England. Visit the website to research sport opportunities in a specific area.

St. John's Wood Women's Club (SJWWC)
Box 185, 176 Finchley Road, NW3
www.sjwwc.org.uk
Predominantly civic and social expatriate club with most members living in the northern sector of London and with many of its members being permanent residents of the UK. SJWWC sponsors over 20 activities a

ORGANISATIONS

month, ranging from golf and tennis, to culinary, country hikes, local travel, stitchery and more.

University Women's Club

2 Audley Square, W1

℘ 020 7499 2268, www.universitywomensclub.com

Social club with facilities for women university graduates or women who are not graduates but are professionally qualified.

Victorian Society

1 Priory Gardens, W4

℘ 020 8994 1019, www.victorian-society.org.uk

Special interest group concerned with the preservation and education of Victorian England through trips, seminars and lectures.

Women's Resource Centre (WRC)

Ground Floor East, 33-41 Dallington Street, EC1

℘ 020 7324 3030, www.wrc.org.uk

Coordinating and support organisation for voluntary and community projects that work for and with women. WRC is a national organisation with a London focus, providing information, training, developmental support, networking opportunities and policy consultation within the non-profit sector.

# Places of worship

## Baptist

Bethesda Baptist Church

Kensington Place, W8

℘ 020 7221 7039, www.bethesdabaptist.org.uk

## Buddhist

The Buddhist Society

58 Eccleston Square, SW1

℘ 020 7834 5858, thebuddhistsociety.org

West London Buddhist Centre

94 Westbourne Park Villas, W2

℘ 020 7727 9382, www.westlondonbuddhistcentre.com

## Catholic

Archdiocese of Westminster
Vaughan House, 46 Francis Street, London, SW1
www.rcdow.org.uk
The website contains a list of local parishes.

Brompton Oratory
Brompton Road, SW7
✆020 7808 0900, www.bromptonoratory.com
The largest Catholic Church in London.

Holy Cross Roman Catholic Church
22 Cortayne Road, SW6
✆020 7736 1068

St. James's Roman Catholic Church
Spanish Place, 22 George Street, W1
✆020 7935 0943, www.spanishplace.hemscott.net

St. Mary's Catholic Church
4 Holly Place, NW3
✆020 7435 6678

## Church of England

Diocese of London
36 Causton Street, SW1
✆020 7932 1100, www.london.anglican.org
The Diocese website contains a list of churches and a church finder.

Holy Trinity Brompton
Brompton Road, SW7
✆0845 644 7533, www.htb.org.uk
Evangelical church with contemporary worship style and Sunday school for
children. Located behind Brompton Oratory.

St. Lukes and Christ Church
Sydney Street, SW3
✆020 7351 7365, www.chelseaparish.org
Traditional-style worship but not High Anglican. Children's Sunday school.

St. Michael's Church

Chester Square, SW1

✆ 020 7730 8889, www.stmichaelschurch.org.uk

Family oriented with children's Sunday school.

## Hindu

Shree Swaminarayan Mandir

105-119 Brentfield Road, Neasden, NW10

✆ 020 8965 2651, www.mandir.org

Popularly known as the Neasden Temple, the Mandir (pictured at the front of this chapter) is Europe's first traditional Hindu temple.

## Interdenominational

American Church in London

79a Tottenham Court Road, W1

✆ 020 7580 2791, www.amchurch.co.uk

An international and interdenominational, Christ-centred community of faith located in the heart of London.

## Islam

Islamic Universal Association

20 Penzance Place, Holland Park Avenue, W11

✆ 020 7602 5273, www.majma.org

London Central Mosque and Islamic Cultural Centre

146 Park Road, NW8

✆ 020 7725 2213, www.iccuk.org

The largest mosque in London, located in Regent's Park.

## Jewish

For a list of London synagogues, go to www.kosherdelight.com.

Belsize Square Synagogue

51 Belsize Square, NW3

✆ 020 7794 3949, www.synagogue.org.uk

Independent synagogue (neither reform nor orthodox).

The Movement for Reform Judaism
The Sternberg Centre, 80 East End Road, N3
✆ 020 8349 5640, www.reformjudaism.org.uk
Contact for information about reform synagogues in London.

United Synagogue, London Beth Din
305 Ballards Lane, N12
✆ 020 8343 6270, www.theus.org.uk
Orthodox synagogue.

West London Synagogue
34 Upper Berkeley Street, W1
✆ 020 7723 4404, www.wsl.org.uk
The first reform synagogue in the UK.

## Methodist

Methodist Central Hall Westminster
Storeys Gate, SW1
✆ 020 7222 8010, www.methodist-central-hall.org.uk

## Mormon

Church of Jesus Christ of Latter Day Saints
64-68 Exhibition Road, SW7
✆ 020 7584 8685, www.lds.org.uk

## Unitarian-Universalists

Essex Church Congregation
Essex Hall, 1-6 Essex Street, WC2
✆ 020 7221 6514, www.unitarian.org.uk

Rosslyn Hill Unitarian Chapel
Pilgrim's Place, NW3
✆ 020 7433 3267, www.rosslynhillchapel.com

transition *n.* [F. (TRANSITION)] ... passage or change from one state or action or subject or set of circumstances to another; period during which one style of art develops into another, esp. (Archit.) between Norman and Early English; transitional *a.*, transitionally *adv.* [F or L (prec.)]

transitive /'trænsitiv, 'trɑː-/ *a.* (of verb) taking direct object expressed or understood. [L (TRANSIT)]

transitory /'trænsitəri, 'trɑː-/ *a.* not long-lasting, merely temporary; transitorily *adv.*; transitoriness [AF *transitorie* f. L (TRANSIT)]

translate /træns'leit, trɑː-/ ... the sense of (word or text etc.) ... language, in plainer words; ... another form of representation (... lates emotion into music, ...; ... language); infer or declare ... of, interpret; remove (bishop ...); move from one person ... condition to another; translator *n.* [L (TR...

transliterate /træns... represent (word etc...

# 19

# Glossary

This chapter is meant to be a resource for Americans who, although they speak fluent English, may need some help translating and understanding certain British terms. The Junior League of London's American members have found this chapter both extremely useful and fun and we hope you will too.

If you're interested in a more comprehensive list of words, expressions and further explanations, check out the humorous Best of British website at **www.effingpot.com**. See *Chapter 2: Housing – British terminology* for more property and real estate terminology. For some common British words related to babies and children, see *Chapter 8: Children – Mummy speak*. For more food related words, see *Chapter 10: Cooking, food and drink – Food glossary*. And if it's sports words you're interested in translating, see *Chapter 14: Sports and leisure – British sporting glossary*.

Finally, we want to quickly highlight two commonly misunderstood British words (sometimes with ill effects): fanny and pants. Read below to see how these are interpreted and more. Before you know it you'll be asking for the bill in restaurants, throwing your rubbish in the bin and will have it all sussed!

| British | American |
|---|---|
| **A** | |
| A&E | emergency room |
| adjustable spanner | monkey wrench |
| aerial | antenna |
| afternoon tea | tea |
| agony aunt | advice columnist |
| airing cupboard | linen closet |
| American football | football |
| anorak | parka (lined) |
| aubergine | eggplant |
| Aussie | Australian |
| | |
| **B** | |
| bank holiday | legal holiday |
| banknote, note | bill (money) |
| barnet | haircut |
| barrister | lawyer (trial) |
| basin | sink |
| baths | swimming pool |
| beaker | sippy cup |
| bespoke | custom |
| bill | check (restaurant) |
| bin | garbage |
| biro | ballpoint pen |
| biscuit | cookie |
| blind/roller blind | shade (window) |
| boiler | furnace/hot water heater |
| boiler suit | coverall (workmen's) |
| bonnet | hood (car) |
| book | make reservations |
| boot | trunk (car) |
| Boxing Day | December 26th |
| braces | suspenders |
| break, holiday | recess (school break) |
| brackets | parentheses |

| British | American |
|---|---|
| brolly | umbrella |
| builder | contractor |
| bumper | fender (car) |
| business suit | lounge suit |

## C

| British | American |
|---|---|
| car boot sale | garage sale |
| car park | parking lot |
| caravan | trailer/camper/mobile home |
| carrier bag | shopping bag |
| cheeky | flippant |
| cheers | thanks |
| chemist | drugstore/pharmacy |
| chewing gum | gum |
| childminder | babysitter |
| chips | french fries |
| chuffed | pleased |
| cinema | movie house/theatre |
| the City | financial district |
| class/form | grade (school) |
| cleaner/domestic | maid or janitor |
| cling film | saran wrap |
| cloakroom | checkrooms/half-bath/powder room |
| clothes peg | clothes pin |
| coach | tour bus |
| cockney | accent or person from east end of London |
| confectioners/sweet shop | candy store |
| conservatory | porch (enclosed) |
| continental Europe/the continent | Europe |
| cooker | oven/range |
| cot | crib/baby bed |
| cotton | thread |
| cotton bud | Q tip |
| cotton reel | spool (thread) |
| cotton wool | cotton balls |

| British | American |
|---------|----------|
| courgette | zucchini |
| court shoe | pump (shoe) |
| cow gum/studio gum | rubber cement |
| cowboy builders | swindler (home repair) |
| crèche | daycare centre/nursery |
| crib | cradle |
| crisps | potato chips |
| cuppa | cup of tea |
| curling tongs | curling iron |
| curtains | drapes/draperies |
| cutlery | silverware |
| CV | résumé |
| cycle | bicycle |

**D**

| British | American |
|---------|----------|
| decorator | painter |
| delivery lorry/van | delivery truck |
| diary | calendar (personal) |
| directory enquiries | directory assistance |
| district | precinct |
| diversion | detour |
| DIY | do-it-yourself |
| dodgy | not to be trusted |
| domestic help | cleaning lady |
| double number (e.g., double 5) | number used twice (e.g., 55) |
| drain | sewer pipe (soil pipe) |
| draper (materials) | dry goods store |
| draughts | checkers (game) |
| drawing pin | thumb tack |
| dress circle | mezzanine |
| dressing gown | bathrobe |
| drinks party | cocktail party |
| dual carriageway | divided highway |
| dummy | pacifier (for baby) |
| dustbin/bin | garbage/trash can |
| duvet | comforter |

| British | American |
|---|---|
| **E** | |
| earth wire | ground wire |
| elastic bands | rubber bands |
| electrical points | outlets |
| emulsion | paint (interior house) |
| engineer | repairman |
| enquiry | information (phone) |
| estate agent | real estate agent |
| estate car | station wagon |
| extension lead | extension cord |
| | |
| **F** | |
| fancy (v) | desire |
| fancy dress | costume |
| fanny (slang) | a woman's genitals |
| Father Christmas | Santa Claus |
| filch | steal |
| film | movie |
| first floor | second floor |
| fitted carpet | wall-to-wall carpet |
| fiver | five pound note |
| flannel/face cloth | washcloth |
| flyover | overpass (highway) |
| football | soccer |
| fortnight | two weeks |
| fringe | bangs |
| fruit machine | slot machine |
| full stop | period (punctuation) |
| | |
| **G** | |
| garden | backyard |
| gear lever | gear shift (car) |
| geyser | water heater (gas) |
| gin or vodka martini | martini |
| golf buggy | electric golf cart |

| British | American |
|---|---|
| grease proof paper | wax paper |
| grill | broil/broiler |
| ground floor | first floor |

**H**

| British | American |
|---|---|
| haberdashery | notions |
| half term | school vacation |
| hallmarked | solid sterling (silver) |
| handbag | purse/pocketbook |
| hand brake | parking brake |
| hard shoulder | shoulder (highway) |
| hardware | housewares/hardware |
| hard grip/kirby grip | bobbie pin |
| headmaster/headmistress | principal (school) |
| high street | main street |
| hire | rent (goods, car) |
| hire purchase | time payment |
| hire purchase plan | instalment payment plan |
| hiya | hi there (friendly hello) |
| hob | stove/cooktop |
| holiday | vacation |
| Hoover | vacuum |
| hose pipe | garden hose |

**I**

| British | American |
|---|---|
| immersion heater | water heater (electric) |
| interflora | f.t.d. (florist) |
| interval | intermission |
| invoice | bill (account) |
| ironmonger | hardware store |

**J**

| British | American |
|---|---|
| jab | shot/injection |
| jacket potato | baked potato |
| jam | jelly |

| British | American |
|---|---|
| jelly | jello/gelatin |
| joint | roast (piece of meat) |
| jug | pitcher |
| juggernaut | truck (semi) |
| jumper | sweater/pullover |
| jump leads | jumper cables (car) |
| junior school | elementary school |

## K

| British | American |
|---|---|
| kagoule | parka (unlined) |
| kerb | curb (sidewalk) |
| kip | nap |
| kit | sports clothes/equipment |
| kitchen roll | paper towels |
| kiwi | new zealander |
| knackered | tired |
| knickers/pants | underpants/panties |
| knickerbockers/plus fours | knickers |
| knock about (tennis) | warm up (tennis) |

## L

| British | American |
|---|---|
| label | tag |
| ladder (in tights) | run (in nylons) |
| ladybird | ladybug |
| larder | pantry |
| lavatory/toilet/loo | bathroom |
| lay-by | pull-off (driving) |
| lead (dog) | leash (dog) |
| lead | electric cord/wire |
| lemon squash | lemonade |
| lemonade | Seven-up/Sprite |
| let | rent (real estate) |
| lift | elevator |
| limited/ltd | incorporated/inc. |
| liquidiser | blender |

| British | American |
|---|---|
| lodger | roomer/boarder |
| loft | attic |
| loo | restroom/toilet |
| lorry | truck |
| lost property | lost and found |

## M

| | |
|---|---|
| macintosh | raincoat |
| maisonette | duplex/triplex |
| manual transmission | stick shift |
| mate | buddy |
| methylated spirits | denatured alcohol |
| milk float | milk truck |
| mince | hamburger meat/ground beef or other meat |
| mobile | cell phone |
| Moses basket | bassinet |
| m.o.t. | motor vehicle inspection test |
| motorbike | motorcycle |
| motorway | freeway/super highway |

## N

| | |
|---|---|
| nappy | diaper |
| neat | straight (cocktail) |
| net curtains | sheers (under drapes) |
| newsagent | news dealer/newsstand |
| nil/nought | zero |
| noughts and crosses | tic-tac-toe |
| number/registration plate | licence plate |

## O

| | |
|---|---|
| off-licence | liquor store |
| on the pull | on the prowl |
| oven gloves/mitt | pot holder/gloves |
| overtake | pass (vehicle) |

| British | American |
|---|---|
| **P** | |
| packed lunch | sack or bag lunch |
| paddle | wade |
| pants | underwear |
| paraffin | kerosene |
| parcel | package |
| parcel tape | packing tape |
| pavement | sidewalk |
| pay rise | raise |
| pelmet | valance (drapes) |
| petrol | gasoline |
| phone box | pay telephone booth |
| pillar box (antiquated) post box | mailbox |
| pinafore dress | jumper |
| pissed | drunk |
| plaster (elastoplast) | adhesive bandage (band aid) |
| point/power point/plug socket | outlet/socket (electrical) |
| porter | doorman |
| post/postman | mail/mailman |
| postal order | money order |
| postcode | zip code |
| pram | buggy |
| prep (or homework) | homework |
| press studs/poppers | snaps (sewing) |
| public/fee paying school/private | private school |
| pudding/sweet | dessert |
| purse | change purse/wallet |
| pushchair | stroller |
| **Q** | |
| quay (pron. 'key') | wharf/pier |
| queue | line (stand in) |
| **R** | |
| removal van | moving van |

| British | American |
|---|---|
| removal company | moving company |
| return ticket | round trip ticket |
| reverse charges | call collect |
| ring up | call (telephone) |
| roundabout | traffic circle |
| rubber | eraser |
| rubbish/refuse | garbage (trash) |

## S

| British | American |
|---|---|
| s.a.e. | stamped addressed envelope |
| saloon | sedan (car) |
| scribbling pad/book/jotter | scratch pad |
| secondary school | high school |
| sellotape or sticky tape | scotch tape |
| serviette | napkin |
| shop assistant | sales clerk |
| sideboards | sideburns |
| silencer | muffler (car) |
| single ticket | one way ticket |
| sitting/reception room/lounge | living room |
| skip | dumpster (construction) |
| skipping rope | jump rope |
| skirting board | baseboard |
| snog | make out (kiss) |
| solicitor | lawyer/attorney |
| spanner | wrench |
| spectacles/specs | eyeglasses |
| spirits | liquor |
| squaddie | young person in the military |
| stabilisers | training wheels |
| stand | run (for public office) |
| stalls | orchestra seats (theatre) |
| starter | appetiser |
| state school/grammar school | public school |
| stone | pit (of fruit)/weight (1 stone = 14 pounds) |

| British | American |
|---|---|
| stroke/oblique | slash (/) |
| subway | underground/pedestrian passage |
| surgery | doctor's/dentist's office |
| surgical spirit | rubbing alcohol |
| suspenders | garter belt |
| suss | figure out |
| sweets/chocolate bar | candy/candy bar |
| swimming costume | bathing suit |

## T

| British | American |
|---|---|
| ta | thanks |
| table tennis bat | ping pong paddle |
| take-away | take out (food) |
| tap | faucet |
| tarmac | pavement |
| tea | children's supper/dinner |
| tea trolley | tea cart |
| teat | nipple (baby bottle) |
| telly | television |
| tenner | ten pound note |
| term (school) | semester |
| theatre/operating theatre | surgery (medical) |
| tights | panty hose |
| till | cash register |
| timetable | schedule |
| tin | can |
| tip (rubbish) | dump (garbage) |
| toilet | bathroom |
| torch | flashlight |
| tracksuit bottoms | sweatpants |
| trainers/plimsolls | sneakers/tennis shoes |
| travelling rug | blanket (travelling) |
| treble number (e.g., treble 5) | number used three times (e.g., 555) |
| trolley | grocery cart |
| trousers | pants |

| British | American |
|---------|----------|
| tube/underground | subway |
| turn-ups (trousers) | cuffs (pants) |
| turf | sod (new grass) |

**U**

| | |
|---------|----------|
| university | college/university |

**V**

| | |
|---------|----------|
| valance | dust ruffle |
| verge/hard shoulder | soft shoulder (road) |
| vest | t-shirt/undershirt |

**W**

| | |
|---------|----------|
| waistcoat | vest |
| wardrobe | closet (hanging clothes) |
| washing up | doing the dishes |
| washing up liquid | dishwashing liquid (hand) |
| wash your hands | wash up |
| wellies (Wellington boots) | boots (waterproof) |
| whinging | whining |
| white or black (as in coffee) | with or without milk/cream |
| windcheater | windbreaker |
| windscreen | windshield |
| wing mirror | review view mirror (outside) |

**Z**

| | |
|---------|----------|
| zebra crossing | crosswalk |
| 'zed' (pron.) | z |

# Index

INDEX

INDEX

i
INDEX

INDEX

i

INDEX

SATs (Statutory Assessment Tests)   168
schools
    A levels   168-9, 170, 174
    age/grade equivalents   173-4
    American schools   28, 193, 194, 196, 200-1
    applying to American universities   200
    boarding schools   170, 182-3, 188-9
    boys' schools   170, 179-83
    British school system   168-70, 173-5, 201-2
    co-educational schools   189-93, 194-7
    Common Entrance Exam   170
    educational consultants   172-3, 198
    French schools   26, 196
    GCSE   168, 169
    German schools   196
    girls' schools   170, 183-8
    IB (International Baccalaureate)   193-4
    independent schools   168, 169, 170-1, 173-93, 194-7, 199-200
    Independent Schools Inspectorate (ISI)   170
    International GCSE   169
    international schools   170, 193-6
    Japanese schools   197
    junior schools   179-81, 183-6
    League Tables   169
    learning difficulties   197-200
    Norwegian schools   197
    nursery schools   173, 175-9
    Ofsted   169
    preparatory schools   170, 179-81, 183-6
    pre-school   173, 174
    primary schools   168, 174
    private schools   168, 169, 170-1, 173-93, 194-7, 199-200
    public schools see independent schools
    publications   171-2
    SATs   168
    secondary schools   173, 174
    senior schools   173, 174, 182-3, 186-8
    special needs   197-200

INDEX

# Measurement conversions

## Liquid measures

| Description | UK imperial/metric | US imperial |
|---|---|---|
| Teaspoon | 5 ml | 1/6 oz |
| Dessertspoon | 10 ml | 1/3 oz |
| Tablespoon | 15 ml | 1/2 oz |
| Gill | 150 ml | 5 oz |
| Cup | 10 oz/290 ml | 8 oz/250 ml |
| Pint | 20 oz/585 ml | 16 oz/470 ml |

## Dry measures

| Ingredient | UK imperial | UK metric | US imperial |
|---|---|---|---|
| Flour | 5 oz | 140 g | 1 cup |
| Sugar | 1 oz | 25 g | 2 tbsp |
| | 8 oz | 225 g | 1 cup |
| Brown sugar | 6 oz | 170 g | 1 cup |
| Breadcrumbs or nuts | 4 oz | 115 g | 1 cup |
| Yeast | 1/4 oz | 7 g | 2½ tsp |
| Butter | 1 oz | 30 g | 2 tbsp |
| | 8 oz | 230 g | 1 cup |
| | 4 oz | 113 g | 1 stick (8 tbsp) |

When measuring dry ingredients such as flour or sugar for a British recipe, remember to weigh the items as the ingredients will be listed in ounces or grams. (Remember, eight ounces of two different ingredients may have distinctly different volumes.)

## Further conversions

| | |
|---|---|
| Ounces to grams | Multiply by 28 |
| Quarts to litres | Multiply quarts by 0.95 |
| Pounds to grams | Multiply pounds by 450 |
| Pounds to kilograms | Multiply pounds by 0.450 |
| Kilograms to pounds | Multiply kilograms by 2.2 |
| Stones to pounds | Multiply by 14 |
| Centigrade to fahrenheit | Multiply C by 1.8 and add 32 |
| Fahrenheit to centigrade | Multiply F by 5, subtract 32 and then divide by 9 |

# Cooking temperatures

| Celsius | Fahrenheit | Gas mark | Description |
|---|---|---|---|
| 110 | 225 | $\frac{1}{4}$ | Very slow |
| 125 | 250 | $\frac{1}{2}$ | Very slow |
| 140 | 275 | 1 | Slow |
| 150 | 300 | 2 | Slow |
| 165 | 325 | 3 | Moderate |
| 180 | 350 | 4 | Moderate |
| 190 | 375 | 5 | Moderate/hot |
| 200 | 400 | 6 | Moderate/hot |
| 220 | 425 | 7 | Hot |
| 230 | 450 | 8 | Hot |
| 240 | 475 | 9 | Very hot |

For fan-assisted ovens you should either turn the heat down slightly or decrease the cooking time.

42271786R00250

Made in the USA
San Bernardino, CA
30 November 2016